W9-ASV-457

THE OFFICIAL®
IDENTIFICATION AND
PRICE GUIDE TO

ANTIQUE &
MODERN DOLLS

JULIE COLLIER

Contributing Author
MARTIE COOK

FOURTH EDITION

HOUSE OF COLLECTIBLES

NEW YORK

Important Notice. All of the information, including valuations, in this book has been compiled from the most reliable sources, and every effort has been made to eliminate errors and questionable data. Nevertheless, the possibility of error, in a work of such immense scope, always exists. The publisher will not be held responsible for losses which may occur in the purchase, sale, or other transaction of items because of information contained herein. Readers who feel they have discovered errors are invited to *write* and inform us, so they may be corrected in subsequent editions. Those seeking further information on the topics covered in this book are advised to refer to the complete line of *Official Price Guides* published by the House of Collectibles.

© 1989 Random House, Inc.

All rights reserved under International and
Pan-American Copyright Conventions.

Published by: The House of Collectibles
201 East 50th Street
New York, New York 10022

Distributed by Ballantine Books, a division of Random House, Inc., New York, and simultaneously in Canada by Random House of Canada Limited, Toronto.

Manufactured in the United States of America

ISBN: 0-876-37091-1

10 9 8 7 6 5 4 3 2 1

TO GRANDMOTHER TODD

Two bisque dolls found in her antique
shop started Martie and me collecting
twenty-five years ago

TABLE OF CONTENTS

INTRODUCTION

How to Use This Book 1
Market Trends 2
Tips for Buying 4
Reproductions and Fakes 12
Dating 13
Caring for Dolls 15
Where to Find Dolls 17
Tips for Selling 23

PART 1

DOLLS AND PRICES · BY MATERIAL

All-Bisque 27
American, English, and Japanese Bisque 44
French Bisque 50
German Bisque 95
American Dolls with German Bisque Heads 177
Molded-Hair Bisque 186
Celluloid 190
China 194
Cloth 204
Composition and Papier-Mâché 227
Metal 275
Plastic 278
Wax 335
Wood 339

PART 2

DOLLS AND PRICES · BY TYPE

"Belton Type"   347
Black Dolls   348
Boudoir Dolls   361
Bye-Lo Babies   363
Googly-Eyed Dolls   367
Pincushion Figures   374
Kewpies   376
Mechanical Dolls   380
Multi-Face and Topsy-Turvy Dolls   387
Modern Doll Artists   391
Oriental Dolls   394

PART 3

APPENDIXES

Doll Body Types   403
Glossary   406
Initials Found in Doll Marks   417
Trademark Names   420
Abbreviations Used in Doll Advertisements 427
Doll Museums   430
Auction Galleries   433
Bibliography   434
Pictorial Trademark Index   439
Index By Mold Number   451
Index of Letters Found in Doll Marks   455
General Index   457

ACKNOWLEDGMENTS

Many thanks to contributing author Martie Cook. Martie is a veteran researcher who, in the course of doing work for this book, uncovered such elusive facts as the founders of the American Character and Arranbee doll companies.

Our most grateful thanks to the following:

Barbara Berger at Richard Withington, Inc., Olivia Bristol and Sue Broomhead at Christie's South Kensington, Laurie Green at Marvin Cohen Auctions, Dana Hawkes at Sotheby's, New York, and Janet Homfeld at the Margaret Woodbury Strong Museum for allowing us to use their beautiful photographs.

Paul and Francis Sackett, Douglas Chew, Brian Cook, Pat Alsen, Dorothy Balz, Grace Young, and Nancy Spore for their assistance with additional photography.

Margaret Austin at Kenner Products, Karen Gersham at Coleco, Arlene Cannarozzi at the Plastics Institute of America, Joan Canning at the Brooklyn Public Library, Jacqueline and Lewis Erwin, David Cook, Mrs. Warren Knauer, John Milward, and Pete Hernon for providing special information and advice. We appreciate the assistance of Kenner Products in providing background information on the Star Wars dolls.

Jurgen and Marianne Cieslik for allowing us to use the GM numbers so meticulously researched for their *German Doll Encyclopedia*, Chassie Post for organizing the museums section, and the crack staff of the Winnetka Public Library, Winnetka, Illinois, for locating many out-of-print books and articles after major libraries had given up.

Much appreciation also to our editors, Leslie Booth and Dorothy Harris, at House of Collectibles, and to Barbara Goldstein. Last, Martie and I would like to give a big thank you to our mother, Mildred Todd, for her technical help and constant encouragement in this project.

INTRODUCTION

HOW TO USE THIS BOOK

T his book is divided into two major sections; the first classifies dolls by material and the second by type. If you are not a seasoned collector, the following will save you time and effort in locating your doll. More experienced collectors may want to skip ahead.

The first point of identification is the material of a doll's head. If you can identify the material of your doll's head, look it up in the alphabetical table of contents; then see if you can find a picture of the doll in the pages indicated. If there is a mark on the back of the doll's head or shoulders, you can narrow your search by matching the name, letter, or number or by finding its trademark in one of the indices at the back of the book. If you cannot find your doll in the first section, or if it is of a type that can be made from more than one material, such as "Oriental" or "mechanical," turn to the second section of the book.

Each category begins with a brief introduction to provide a bit of quick-reference background information. You will also find a condition table that lists price adjustments that should be made for each positive or negative factor.

Entries within a category begin with a short synopsis of the manufacturer's history, comments on the types of dolls produced, and illustrations of common examples of the marks found on that company's dolls. Following that is a list of various models produced by the company and price ranges for each. Also included, from time to time, is a special feature called "Crib Notes," which will give you quick tips, value hints, and interesting facts about the dolls listed in that section.

At the back of the book you will find a glossary, a list of common abbreviations used by dealers and collectors, photographs of basic body types for comparison and identification, an index of pictorial trademarks, and indices of alphabetical and numerical marks.

The prices in this guide have been gathered from specialty shops, dealer lists, shows, auctions, and advertisements in doll periodicals. Readers should keep in mind that they reflect retail value—the prices you will have to pay to purchase particular dolls, not the prices you will receive for selling them privately. If you do not have a business of your own and wish to sell a doll you find listed here, you can generally expect to receive half of the quoted price. At first this may strike you as unfair; however, you must consider the time, effort, and money a dealer puts into running his or her business. Then the price difference begins to make sense. If you still find this half-price idea distressing, remember that this system works for every retail business in the world. Besides, a few years from now your dolls *will* be worth the prices in this book!

MARKET TRENDS

Twenty-five years ago you could have walked into an antique doll shop and purchased a pretty 18-inch Simon & Halbig bisque doll for $40, a 22-inch early Jumeau bébé for $250, or a Mme Alexander composition Sonja Henie, crisp and fresh in its original box, for $15. At that same time you would have paid $300 for a parian-type lady with a fancy molded hairdo, $100 for a mid-19th-century china doll, and $200 for a small 1830s papier-mâché with an apollo-knot hairstyle, not much less than they would cost today. Why did some dolls soar in price while others stagnated? Looking back, we can make a fairly good analysis of what happened.

The first antique doll collectors of number, active during the 1920s to 1950s, were attracted to dolls that were truly antiques at the time: the carved-wood, papier-mâché, wax, and china dolls of the late 18th to early 19th centuries. Only late 19th-century dolls of the highest quality were also actively collected. Prized were the exquisite lady dolls of the 1860s to 1880s, either parian-type with elaborate molded hairstyles or French Parisiennes, whose extravagant clothing could cost many times more than the dolls themselves.

The huge influx of new collectors during the late 1960s and early 1970s changed former views of desirability and with them the direction of the market. Unhindered by tradition, and far enough removed in time from the later bisque child dolls to appreciate them anew, the new generation of collectors became enamored of the sweet-faced French and German children of the late 19th to early 20th centuries and passed over the more severelooking (and expensive) lady dolls.

As prices for anything bisque swiftly rose, sometimes indiscriminately, collectors with less money turned to good-quality, but little-collected, dolls of later periods, such as Mme Alexander. As a result, today many Mme Alexander hard-plastic dolls from the 1950s command higher prices than do German bisque dolls of the early 20th century.

It is easy to analyze trends in hindsight, but it would be much more useful to be able to predict them beforehand. We know what happened when the big influx of new collectors arrived, but what caused their arrival at that particular time? Can we learn to predict major changes in the market? Probably not. The whole field of collectibles is like the stock market. Both are somewhat risky because performance is dependent on unpredictable factors. And there are more dedicated minds than ours trying to predict stock market trends. Nevertheless, if you plan to be a serious collector, it would be wise to learn as much as you can about the doll market, and that includes trends in prices, collector numbers, and popularity of various categories. Keep in mind that because there is a strong element of emotion involved in the purchase of a doll, the market is not influenced by fluctuations in the economy as much as other types of investments are. Committed collectors will continue to buy dolls whether they think they can make money on them or not.

TIPS FOR BUYING

The good news is that there are still dolls available in every category and in every price range. If you are just beginning a collection, you have more than likely already purchased two or three dolls and are anxious to acquire more. Before you do, we suggest that you attend several doll shows, or doll auctions, visit a good doll museum, and read as many books on dolls as you can find. You may not decide to change direction, but at least you will have some knowledge and a solid background from which to make future choices. Our advice is that you buy the best you can afford. This means that if you collect Mme Alexanders and have $100 a month to spend, it is wiser to buy one perfect doll every two or three months than a doll in only average condition once a month. After several years you will be more satisfied with your collection, and your investment will be better protected, because fine-quality dolls increase more rapidly in value than do mediocre ones. If you can't save enough to buy a totally mint modern doll, buy an undressed doll in perfect condition. You can look for mint clothes later. By the same token, if you come across mint outfits or accessories at reasonable prices, snap them up even if you don't have the dolls they go with. You can easily sell them later or trade them for the clothes you want.

If your sights are set on antique dolls but you have little money to spend, here are some that can still be found for less than $50: small late-period china dolls and Frozen Charlottes, certain types of all-bisque dolls, most pincushion figures, and some types of composition and peg-wooden dolls.

You may be lucky enough to adore a type of doll that everyone else considers worthless. This works only if you honestly love the dolls, because you will probably have them for the rest of your life (and your heirs for the rest of theirs). If you are one of only ten people on the face of the earth, the others unknown to you, who collects corncob clowns, you will have some difficulty in reselling them should you decide to begin collecting something else.

4

Unpopular dolls should not be confused with "sleepers," dolls that a healthy percentage of educated collectors feel are underpriced and may soon be on the rise. Examples of such dolls at the present time are unusual china dolls, "parian" types, extra-nice German dolly faces, and good wax dolls. But again, do not buy sleepers unless you truly like them; they may never awaken.

If you have a substantial amount of money to spend and are buying mainly for investment, your best bet is to look for classic high-quality dolls in original or excellent condition, such as early Bru and Jumeau bébés, German character dolls, and rare molds from well-respected German and French factories. Even if your motives are frankly pecuniary, buy dolls you like the looks of, because you may end up living with them for a long time.

CONDITION

If you are considering buying dolls as an investment (and with today's prices, nearly every purchase has become an investment), it is crucial that you understand how different flaws effect the value of different types of dolls. A nearly invisible hairline crack in the forehead of a bisque doll can reduce its value by one-half or more, while a small crack in its composition body is all but meaningless. A collector will not hesitate to pay full price for a bisque doll with messy hair, but a hard-plastic Mme Alexander "Lissy" with its hair combed out of the original set is worth only half the price of a doll in pristine condition. Each category has its own very specific condition requirements.

Collectors understand that dolls are made to be played with and certainly don't expect 100-year-old bisque dolls to look as if they were just delivered from the factory. It is acceptable for wigs to be mussed, clothes to be soiled and even slightly torn, and kid or composition bodies to show dirt and scuffs. For the 30-year-old plastic or vinyl doll, the rules are much more strict. To command top price, modern dolls must not be faded or yellowed, must have original, clean, fresh, unwashed clothing, and must retain hairstyles in original sets. The newer the doll, the more it should look as if it just came home from the store.

Composition dolls are extremely susceptible to changes in temperature, and nine out of ten will show some degree of crazing. For this reason, the state of hair and clothing is immensely important, and a desirable doll (such as Deanna Durbin or other personality) with perfect hair and clothing is an important find. If it is also uncrazed, you have made a major discovery.

You will rarely find an early cloth doll in excellent condition. Expect a little fading and discoloration on even the best examples, as well as some softening of the features on stiffened "mask" faces. Large splits and holes or major paint loss mean expensive repairs and reduced value because of the restoration; so if you encounter these flaws, it might be best to wait until a cleaner version of the doll comes along.

Wax dolls are a hardier breed than most collectors imagine. You've probably seen some poured waxes with flattened noses or chins; however, I think we can assume you won't be leaving your doll lying face down summer after summer to bake in an attic trunk as other long-ago owners did. Wax-over-composition dolls frequently have cracked surfaces since the two materials from which they are made expand and contract at different temperatures and degrees of humidity.

See the condition tables at the beginning of each section for a list of factors influencing the value of that type of doll and the approximate amount these factors will raise or lower its selling price.

RESTORATION

Any restoration to the head of a doll (other than replacing its wig or resetting its eyes) is serious business. Once a bisque head has been cracked or broken, even the most expert "invisible" restoration cannot bring back its full value. As a matter of fact—with apologies to professional restorers, many of whom do excellent work—the resale value is only a bit higher than that of the unrestored piece. If bisque doll collectors seem more intolerant than, say, teddy bear collectors, it is simply because they are following in the footsteps of generations of porcelain collectors who consider cracked porcelain like a cracked egg—it's either perfect or it's ruined. If the doll is a family heirloom or one of your favorites that you have no intention of selling, then by all means have it restored.

A composition body may have moderate areas of restoration, including repainting, rebuilding, and even replaced parts, without altering its value significantly.

A 20th-century doll with a head of composition or plastic may have slight restoration or small areas of repainting on the body. Any restoration to the head, however, will cause its value to plummet. The only "restoration" tolerable in a hard-plastic or later doll is the restringing of its rubber bands. This is considered normal maintenance in any doll and will not affect its value unless done poorly or with inappropriate materials.

QUALITY

Variations in quality are most obvious between dolls at the opposite ends of the price spectrum. Almost anyone can tell that a Huret lady doll is of higher quality than a celluloid fairground kewpie. But there are subtle differences in quality between doll heads that emerge from exactly the same mold. An eye that is able to discern this difference will be able to assemble a collection that is not just good but fine.

In bisque, look for a smooth, creamy, fine-grained surface, free from black spots and pitting. Color should be subtle and natural-looking. High color is usually indicative of late or inexpensive dolls. Features should be expertly and surely painted, as though the brush were guided by some sense of design. Extra detail, such as feathered brows instead of one-stroke, shaded lids, and outlined lips, all contribute to a doll's overall quality.

Variations in quality, though perhaps more subjective, are also apparent in the designs of the dolls themselves. Take the Simon & Halbig 1249 "Santa" mold, for example. Though technically a "dolly face," it has an open, lively expression and slightly protruding ears that make it look more like a real little girl. This sets it apart from the more typical dolly faces such as the 550 and 1079. Collectors are aware of this subtle difference, and have made the "Santa" one of their favorites. They will pay up to twice as much for one as for one of its more ordinary counterparts.

Composition and plastic dolls, because of more mechanical production methods, are less subject to variations in quality between dolls of the same model. So focus instead on the aforementioned design factor. For example, compare the exceptional quality of Effanbee composition American Children, with their realistic expressions, beautiful proportions, and expensive clothing, with the uninspired faces and bodies of Arranbee's "Debuteen" (both series were produced during the late 1930s). You'll pay four times as much for the Effanbee, but most collectors feel it's well worth it. Other judgments will not be so easy to make; if you were born with a "good eye," you are fortunate indeed. If not, take heart: a discerning eye can be developed if you will take the time to look, read, and listen.

SIZE

As a general rule of thumb, the value of any particular type of doll increases proportionately with its size. With time, you should be able to calculate the price of any doll of standard size for which you know the price of one or two sizes in the series. I say "standard" size because the exceptions to this rule are sizes produced in minimal quantities, usually very large or very small. Very large dolls are more popular now than ever despite the fact that bisque heads have a tendency to look somewhat grotesque in huge sizes.

ORIGINALITY

Every collector dreams of finding an antique doll in a totally pristine state, a doll that looks as if it has just come out of the factory and into his or her hands. The older a doll, the more unlikely that that will happen. This means that if you are fortunate enough to come across an 1840s wax-over-composition doll with a healthy, pink, uncrazed finish, wearing its original commercial gauze dress, undergarments, straw bonnet, and kid slippers, you should expect to pay (and pay willingly!) at least 100% above the going retail rate. On the other hand, any doll made after 1930 for which you pay full retail price should be completely original. Late composition, hard plastic, and vinyl dolls are not old enough or

8

rare enough to be hard to find with original clothes and wigs. Obviously, this applies to body parts as well.

With bisque and china dolls, a replaced wig, cloth upper arm, or composition body part is not of major importance in itself; however, two or three replacement parts in one doll can ruin its appeal. Replacement eyes can also be a problem unless they are expertly set and are the same age and type as the original ones. A doll's personality is easily altered with the wrong set of eyes. Because in some cases it is difficult (if not impossible) to tell an appropriate old composition or kid body from an original one, this is not always a crucial point with collectors. The same is true for period cloth bodies of china dolls. These bodies were often homemade and likely to be replaced two or three times during a doll's first hundred years. Modern replacement bodies for bisque or china dolls are another matter: because you are essentially buying only the head, the average value of a specimen in such condition is one third below normal price.

At one time it was considered acceptable to "make over" any old doll one could lay one's hands on, whether it needed it or not. Often Saran wigs and brightly colored synethetic fabrics were employed in recostuming 19th- and early 20th-century bisque dolls. This may have added to their value in the 1950s, but it is a definite detraction today. A doll in faded and mended original dress and wispy mohair wig is actually a better investment than one in replacement clothing, no matter how expertly made or correct in style. Replacement antique clothing that fits and is correct in period is preferable to synthetics; however, a note should accompany the doll stating that the clothing is replaced.

In sum, an original doll is worth paying double for, small unobtrusive replacement body parts are acceptable in most antique dolls, and dolls should be left in their original clothing even though you know you could make much prettier outfits.

RARITY

Rarity is not always an indication of value. The doll your great aunt Edna made out of tree bark and walnut shells may be old and may be rare (there is only one, remember), but put that doll up for sale and you will be disappointed. A rare doll must be desired to have value. And in fact many very *good* rare dolls are undervalued because collectors are less familiar with them and therefore feel less confident about purchasing them.

For this reason, rare dolls with the greatest value are normally those that are rare within established categories—for example, unusual sizes of popular dolls or interesting variations of more common models, such as brown-eyed chinas, the Kämmer & Reinhardt character child No. 101 with glass eyes instead of painted, a black version of the popular S&H 1079, or a 24-inch Toni doll.

Other examples of desirable rarity are hard-to-find members of a series, such as Barbie No. 1 or the Kestner 247 character baby from the 200 series.

There are many, many "safe" rarities to hunt for. From time to time you may run into a doll that excites you but carries a hefty price tag and you can't "look it up." If you have kept your eyes open and done your homework, on such occasions why not take the plunge and let your instincts guide you? Some wonderful things have been collected in this way.

MARKS

In advertisements describing bisque dolls, or on shop tags hanging from their wrists, you will sometimes see the term "signed," as though it were the most desirable thing the writer could think to tell you about the doll. In fact, this usually indicates that the seller is unfamiliar with dolls; the whole business of marks is much more complex. A majority of the bisque dolls you will find are impressed on the backs of their heads or shoulderplates with mold numbers (which identify the particular model) and size numbers. At least half are also marked with the name or initials of the maker. An experienced collector can tell you the maker (and often the mold number as well) simply by looking at a doll's face. Although the name of the maker is one of the first things a prospective buyer wants to know, this can usually be determined by the mold number. The additional presence of the maker's initials has surprisingly little effect on the value of the doll. There are obvious exceptions, such as rare sets of initials or early dolls that are marked with only a name or initials; however, an obscure mark by a known factory, or the lack of any mark at all, can be much more intriguing than a run-of-the-mill "signed" specimen, like the A. M. 390.

For those who are unabashedly searching for prices, the mold number (usually a two- or three-digit number found near the maker's initials or in the center of the back of the head), when present, is the real key to finding the value of a doll. You may spot the initials S&H and know that you are holding a doll made by Simon & Halbig, but it is the mold number that will tell you whether you are holding a $700 character baby (mold 1294) or a $2500 one (mold 1488).

Most dolls made by Armand Marseille, an extremely prolific German company known for its inexpensive, uninspired products (sorry, A. M. fans), will be of less value than those made by better German firms like Kestner. However, Marseille also produced some fine early heads (the 1894 mold) and late character molds (the 230 or 231 called "Fany") that are extremely popular with collectors and hence far more expensive than the standard Kestner dolly face molds.

A label or stamp on an early doll's body, especially a 19th-century doll, is always a lucky find and enhances the doll's historical and monetary value significantly. Because so few early to mid-19th-century dolls were marked, a stamp on the body is often the only clue to its maker and is a valuable aid in dating. But be careful: Stamps and labels often bear only the name of the shop from which the doll was sold, or the name of the maker of the body, not the name of the firm that made the head.

All collectors are grateful that most dollmakers marked their products in a permanent way. Marks provide a method of easy reference. In conversation, a mold number gives an immediate picture without the necessity of laborious description. Hunting for the meaning of marks is stimulating and fun, and a known mark is a reassuring guarantee of an accepted value range. However, it is easy to become overly dependent on marks and in so doing impede the development of your own critical eye. Here's some advice that will help you rely on yourself rather than on the listings in this book: Instead of turning the doll over the minute it's in your hands, force yourself to take a long, appraising look at each doll you pick up—at its expression, the quality of the bisque and decoration, the wig, the body, the clothes; see if you can guess its age and maker—and decide for yourself whether this is a "good" doll or not before you look at its mark.

REPRODUCTIONS AND FAKES

Europeans often say that there are more fakes made in America than in any other country. That is not precisely true. There are more *reproductions* made in the United States than in any other country, but there is an important difference between the two. Both are copied from already existing dolls, nearly always from molds taken from the originals; however, the reproductions are marked with the maker's name and date, whereas the fakes are not. Reproductions are meant to duplicate the original dolls as faithfully as possible. Because they are marked, even the most novice collector should not have to worry about inadvertently mistaking one for the real thing.

Many collectors purchase reproductions because they cannot afford or cannot find the originals. Though the quality of reproductions is generally erratic, some are beautifully made and very difficult to tell from the originals. The problem with buying reproductions is that, like all copies of works of art, they have little resale value. Unless you are fortunate enough to find a willing buyer, the Jumeau reproduction you pay $200 for today will be worth about $50 when you try to sell it tomorrow. When you purchase a reproduction, it should be with the idea of keeping it and enjoying it in your collection—forever.

In case you come across a bisque doll you suspect may be an unmarked reproduction, there are some guidelines you can use to help you decide whether it is or not.

The porcelain used by dollmakers today is much finer than the earlier variety and has a silky-feeling surface. It is also free of dark kiln dirt speckles and most of the small imperfections one is likely to find on an antique head. Another important clue is in the decoration: No matter how carefully the artist paints facial details such as eyebrows, eyelashes, nostrils, and mouth, it is nearly impossible to copy the "assembly line" look of the antique doll's features, painted with the deftness and competence of one who paints dozens of heads a day. Indeed,the modern dollmaker wants results as close to perfection as possible and would never dream of trying to reproduce the imperfections resulting from the haste of long-ago factory workers.

Reproductions made with the deliberate intent to deceive are another matter. Fortunately, considering the escalation of doll prices over the past twenty years, fakes have not surfaced on the market in commensurate numbers. And most of them are so bad even a moderately educated buyer would be able to spot one. The bisque looks heavy and opaque and its tint is often grayish, orangish, or far too white. The color and thickness as well as the painting technique of eyebrows, eyelashes, and lips is unlike any you will find on a true doll of the period. Even an expert can occasionally be fooled by an excellent fake (and there *are* a small number of them floating around, mainly in the expensive French categories) but an educated collector will seldom be fooled by a mediocre fake. Therefore, it is important for you to look at a sufficient number of dolls before you begin buying so that you are familiar with the way they should look.

DATING

At present, exact dating is not as important to collectors of late 19th- or early 20th-century dolls as it is to collectors of other antiques. One reason for this is that so many types of antique dolls, such as china, papier-mâché, and many bisques, were produced over long periods of time with little change in design; indeed, often the same molds were used, so trying to pin down an exact date for a given doll is pointless. And because most factories were producing the same types of dolls at the same time, we do not experience the continual emergence of major personalities and innovations of design as we do in other fields, such as painting or sculpture. Perhaps when more original records are uncovered or when recently completed research is sorted out, it will be possible to credit more designers and dating will become the focus of more attention. For the time being, understanding the general time frame during which certain types of dolls appeared and knowing key dates for important artists and factories is enough for most antique doll collectors.

On the other hand, dates are extremely important to collectors of modern dolls. They can track manufacturers and minor design changes through a myriad of company catalogs, string tags, and original labeled boxes. Because a change in the color of dress trimming from one year to another can mean many dollars in the pocketbook, collectors have made a point of learning all of the dates connected to their manufacturers of choice and can reel them off at the drop of a hat.

For those collectors who wish to date the antique dolls that pass through their hands, here are some methods by which this can be done:

1. Any doll marked with the country of origin was probably made after 1891, when such identification became mandatory for U.S. imports. Some dolls were marked this way before 1891, but not many.

2. Many dolls can be dated by their mold numbers; just remember that most molds were used for a decade or more, so an approximate date is the best you can achieve.

3. There are some elements of construction to which you can affix a patent date. For example, the *ne plus ultra* joint on a kid body was not introduced until 1883, so dolls with that joint on their original bodies must be later than that date.

4. A molded hairstyle can give you an approximate date, especially the fancy ones on high-quality chinas and parian types.

5. If hairstyle and clothing are original, they can be excellent clues to dating a doll, especially with modish types such as the French lady dolls, which were beautifully dressed and coiffed in the height of fashion. It would be worthwhile to teach yourself about 19th- and early 20th-century textiles and fashion. You'd be surprised at how often this knowledge will serve you.

6. Learn a general chronology for basic methods of manufacture and materials used, body and facial types, popularity of various

types of dolls, and so forth. When you pick up an unmarked 1920s baby doll, you should not be wondering whether it could date from the Civil War era.

By the way, do not rely on well-meant documentation provided by the previous owner. After three or four well-educated, reliable-looking people show you genealogical evidence proving that the Kewpie bride and groom (or Barbie and Ken, or whatever) sat atop an ancestor's wedding cake in 1741, you will learn to reserve judgment until you have researched the story yourself.

CARING FOR DOLLS

As temporary guardian of all of the dolls in your collection, it should be your goal to pass them on in the same condition in which you acquired them.

Ideally, dolls should be displayed in glass cases, away from direct sunlight or harsh artificial light and at a constant moderate temperature and state of humidity. Most dolls have not been fortunate enough to receive such treatment, as millions of crazed Shirley Temples and jaundiced Ginnys will attest. Common dolls that suffer most from temperature and humidity changes are those of composition, wax over composition, painted wood, and painted bisque. If you live in an area of harsh seasonal changes and have not yet begun to collect these types, you will save worry and maintenance expense if you stick to less fragile categories such as china, hard plastic, or bisque. (The painted composition bodies of most bisque dolls tend to resist cracking and peeling better than the composition used on later all-composition dolls.) Wigs and clothing will still need to be protected from dust and temperature changes and from insect infestations if they are of wool, silk, or mohair. The two types of bugs that will cause you the most annoyance are moths and carpet beetles. If you are unlucky enough to acquire an infested collection, you can treat it by sealing the dolls in closed containers with moth crystals (try not to let the crystals touch the dolls directly) for a couple of weeks.

Dolls not on display should be wrapped carefully and stored under your bed or in a closet—not in the attic, where temperatures are more extreme. Bisque-head dolls with sleep eyes should be stored facedown so that the weighted eye mechanism cannot come loose and fall against the back of the head. A spool tied between china feet will keep them from knocking together and cracking. Dolls should not be stored in tied plastic bags where humidity can collect.

CLEANING

A good book on cleaning and repair will go into much more detail than is possible here, but following are a few general tips:

A bisque or china head can be cleaned with soap and water like any other porcelain. The trick is to do it so that water is not allowed to soak into old wigs or fabrics or seep into the eye sockets to dissolve the plaster and detach the eyes. A cotton swab or small soft toothbrush is well suited to this task because it will force you to work in one small controllable area at a time. Nevertheless, you should keep a tissue nearby to catch the inevitable drips. If you have never done this, do not try it on your $20,000 A.T. first.

Composition should *never* be washed. You've probably seen the dull, anemic surface of a composition body that has lost its color and patina due to the efforts of a well-meaning laundress.

Dingy human hair wigs should always be removed from the doll's head first, then cleaned by gently swishing in cold water and Woolite® and rinsing (try not to get the cap wet). Strong cotton and linen clothing can be washed in mild soap (Orvis® is a good one that museums use) and lukewarm water, but it's best to leave silks and velvets alone. Even careful dry cleaning can reduce fragile silk to shreds.

REPAIRING

We might all take a lesson from standard museum policy on restoration: Never do anything to a doll that can't be undone later. A hundred years from now someone may discover a superior method of filling in a missing piece of bisque, but if no one can get your Plastic Rock off the doll's head, the improvement will be useless. You could easily lose a sale tomorrow because the prospective buyer doesn't like the permanent repair you have made.

With a little practice most people can learn how to restring a doll, comb out a tangled wig, or even reset eyes. It's best to stick to such maintenance tasks unless the doll is otherwise unsalvageable.

REDRESSING

Unless a doll's clothes are literally falling off, please don't redress it. If you want to give it a new dress while it's in your charge, that's okay, but at least keep the original clothes labeled and safe so that they can be passed along to the next owner. The same goes for rewigging. A slightly threadbare mohair wig cut short by some small long-ago owner has more charm and originality than a perfect modern French finger-curled human hair wig or, heaven forbid, a Saran one.

Before redressing a doll purchased without clothes, a part of your job is to research the period of its manufacture so that you know how a baby or a child or an adult doll would have been dressed at that time. Your Simon & Halbig 1079 girl won't look her best in a replica of Mary Todd Lincoln's inaugural ball gown. With a little extra research you can also match the style of the fabric and trim to the era of the doll. As eye-catching as the neon green silk polyester may appear on the bolt, you will soon see that it would be best to leave it there and go for something more subdued. By the way, you can still buy *old* fabrics and trimmings at doll shows and flea markets. Just examine them carefully to make sure they are sturdy enough to last another fifty years or so.

WHERE TO FIND DOLLS

SHOPS

There are two types of specialty shops where you will find old dolls. General antique shops most often have a doll or two for sale, but gone are the days when a dealer would tell you, "Yeah, I think I have a box of old dolls in the back. You can have your pick for $5." Most dealers know a bit about dolls and take the time to try to identify the ones that come into their hands. Unfortunately, when they err in price, it is almost always on the high side, but you may find an unmarked French doll that is still a good buy even though it's marked triple the value of the German doll the proprietor thinks it is. If you become friendly with your local dealers, they will probably be glad to call you when dolls come in.

If you have an antique doll shop in your area, you are fortunate. You won't find any bargains, but there will be many dolls to choose from, and you are sure to find one now and then that you feel is reasonably priced or that you must have regardless of the price. If you are a relatively new collector, you may find a mentor in the shop owner; if you are more advanced, perhaps he or she will become a friend with whom to share information. The shop may also be a place to meet other collectors, find out about doll clubs, and learn about local shows and other events.

SHOWS

There's nothing more exciting than a big doll show if you want the widest variety of dolls to choose from for purchase or simply to look and learn. The number of doll shows has multiplied so rapidly over the past twenty years that no matter where you live you should be able to attend one or two a year without traveling more than a few hours from home. Prices at shows are generally a bit higher than they are in the shops because of dealer overhead, transportation, and lodging. Dealers also feel, and rightly so, that with a high concentration of buyers they can up their prices and still sell dolls. The plus side is that on the last day of the show (or during the last hour if it is a one-day event) you may be able to get a healthy discount on that big Jumeau you've been eyeing. The dealers aren't looking forward to packing up all of their unsold dolls and carting them back to the shop. Of course, if you wait till the last moment, you take the chance that the doll you want has already been sold to someone else.

Because there are so many dolls at a show, you have a greater chance of uncovering a bargain; unfortunately, that chance is somewhat offset by the fact that the dealers have been merrily buying, selling, and trading among themselves for at least two hours before you get through the front door. But believe me, the dealers haven't seen all of the good buys.

Since many dealers are from out of town or state, be sure to get a receipt with the dealer's name and address on it for anything you purchase. If you discover a new-looking crack in the doll's head after you get home, you shouldn't count on taking it back for a refund. But if you find that your big German all-bisque doll is incised "Nippon" under its sewn-on clothes, the dealer should be willing to take it back. It was more than likely an honest mistake, and the dealer's reputation is worth more than one doll in any case. At the risk of making a nuisance of yourself, the more you can get a dealer to write about the doll on your receipt, the better off you are. If he or she swears the doll was Marie Antoinette's most cherished childhood plaything, handed down by loving hands through generations of exiled French aristocrats, ask that it be written down. And signed.

A big show is also a wonderful place to learn. There is usually at least one doll book seller represented, so it's a fine opportunity to browse. You can see for yourself if that book on the history of Mr. Potatohead you saw in the catalog is really worth $85.

Because the dealers are stuck at their tables all day, they often become bored and lonely, and it's a great time to chat with them. You can also give them your name and address and ask them to keep an eye out for any unusual dolls you've been searching for. But use tact—don't ask a dealer to expound on the difference between cold- and hot-pressed composition just as twenty drooling potential buyers invade the booth.

AUCTIONS

Many collectors think auctions are scary. The main difference between buying at auction and buying from a shop is that *you* decide how much you want to pay. If you set firm price limits for yourself before the bidding begins, you are not going to skulk out of the gallery carrying a $4500 Barbie doll under your arm.

In fact most dolls at auction sell well below retail, so even with the 10% buyer's premium many galleries add to your bill, your price will average 25% less than a dealer would charge. It's usually the surprise or record-breaking prices that makes news.

Before the auction begins, there is a viewing period during which you have the opportunity to examine any of the dolls that interest you. If you are not allowed to make as thorough an examination as you would like—without harming the doll, of course—see the manager or take your business elsewhere. This is important, as some galleries still have a strict no-return policy once the hammer has fallen.

The catalog will have a description of each lot with an estimate of what range the gallery feels the doll will sell within. This is only a guideline but should help you in deciding what you will have to pay. If the owner has placed a reserve on the doll, it is probably no more than 75% of the low estimate ($300 on a doll estimated at $400 to $600) and most likely less.

After you register on sale day, you will probably be given a numbered paddle with which to bid, so have no fear that you must learn some mysterious sign language or that you could buy something when you adjust your collar. You might feel most comfortable watching a full session before plunging in yourself. This is usually not necessary; within half an hour you will have the auctioneer's rhythm down pat. Still, when the lot you want comes up, the previous two hundred lots will seem to have taken twenty minutes apiece to sell, and yours will pass by at the speed of light. So get your paddle up, and don't take it down until you have successfully purchased the lot you want or the auctioneer has passed your maximum.

If you don't live near the auction gallery and wish to bid by mail or phone, it is very important that you satisfy yourself about the condition of the lots on which you bid. Most auction catalogs now list the major flaws, and many are even more thorough. If you have any specific questions, write or call in and ask to speak to one of the specialists. Most will be happy to talk with you. They want you to be happy with your purchases so that you will come back again.

If your bid is successful, and you can't pick up your winnings in person, the gallery will pack them and send them to you; but you will be charged for this service.

The best thing about buying at auction is that you have the opportunity to purchase a wide variety of "fresh" dolls at prices well below retail. The worst thing about buying at auction is that the one doll you want is always the same doll the heir to the Kellogg's fortune wants.

BUYING BY MAIL

Most doll collectors' publications contain classified ads from which you can order dolls and lists of dolls for sale. This armchair method of buying is great for collectors who do not have easy access to specialty shops or shows and also for those who are hunting for specific dolls they have been unable to locate elsewhere. The main drawback, obviously, is that you cannot see the doll until it arrives on your doorstep, paid for in full. Some dealer lists include photos (tiny but adequate), but most likely the dealer will offer to send you color Polaroids at $1 to $3 a shot. Regardless, each written description on the list should be thorough and accurate and should include any defects the doll may have. If a list of 75 dolls mentions no defects, something is awry.

The mailing list works best for modern dolls, which do not vary nearly as much in quality within one model or type as the antique dolls do. Therefore, if the condition is accurately described, you have a good idea of what the doll will look like. If you have any questions about any of the dolls on the list, it is worth investing in a long distance phone call to ask the advertiser before you order.

You should also make sure you understand the terms of sale before you order. If the fine print tells you that everything is sold "as is" or that all sales are final, buy elsewhere. You should be able to return a doll for full refund within a reasonable amount of time as long as the doll is in the same condition in which you received it. By the way, if your doll arrives damaged, stop unpacking right away and call the carrier for instructions. The doll is insured in transit by the shipper, not the seller.

YARD SALES, HOUSE SALES,
AND FLEA MARKETS

For those who enjoy a hunt with long odds but the chance for a big payoff, your best bet is a flea market, house sale, or yard sale.

Nearly every town has at least one weekly flea market at the local drive-in, schoolyard, or church basement. Among the pots and pans, costume jewelry, and horse heads painted on black velvet, you will find a few dolls. Most will be modern plastic or cheap souvenir dolls, and most will be overpriced (not many flea market dealers know anything about dolls, so they employ that old logic "I don't know what it is, but it's gotta be worth at least $50"). Of course, you could find a little grubby, but valuable, unstrung French-type all-bisque doll in with the basket of Japanese bisque figurines marked $50 each. Just don't expect the dealer to be there next week when you want to make a return. At a flea market, most sales are final.

House sales, especially estate properties, hold the most promise for the seeker of antique dolls. Nearly every old house contains at least a few old dolls or toys that have been left to be sold with the furnishings and personal belongings after the more valuable antiques have been removed. House sales are usually run by energetic local amateurs who might know something about silver, glass, and books but price everything else the best they can. House sales are advertised in the local papers and are nearly always held on weekends. However, if you see one advertised to open its doors at 10 A.M., don't expect to saunter in at noon and find anything interesting left. Dealers and serious collectors know about house sales, too, and nowadays lines will begin forming at 8 A.M. or earlier outside a promising house. Prospective buyers will be handed numbers and allowed in fifteen at a time every ten minutes or so. If you are number 16, you could be out of luck.

The garage or lawn sale is your best bet for getting a good buy, but you will have to wade through many boxes of broken appliances, magazines, baby clothes, and empty jars before you find even one scraggly-looking Chatty Cathy. If you collect vinyl dolls, you'll have more success than other collectors will, since most lawn sales are held by young families who are either moving or cleaning out their closets. But the prices are nearly always rock bottom, so if you persevere through thirty or forty sales before finding six perfect Alexanderkins lined up in a row for $2 each, it will still be worthwhile, and you'll have had fun looking.

TIPS FOR SELLING

As mentioned earlier, the prices in this book are those a private collector would have to pay for the dolls listed, not what a private collector should expect to receive for selling them. Dealers pay rent and utilities on their shops and must sit in them all day or pay someone else to. They also must pay transportation and travel expenses to acquire new stock and often pay thousands of dollars per year for advertising. Even then many dolls sit unsold in shops for a year or more, taking up space. Obviously, dealers cannot pay you the same amount they ask for the doll or they would soon go broke. They will pay anywhere from half to two-thirds of the doll's retail value, or they might offer to sell the doll on your behalf for a 30 to 50% commission.

This is the easiest way to dispose of your dolls, but with a little effort on your part you can probably get a better return by a method other than selling directly to a dealer. For example, you can pay for a table at a doll show and sell the dolls yourself at retail prices. If you enjoy meeting people and watching crowds and like the idea of being on the other side of the table for a change, this can be an entertaining experience. There are two things to keep in mind, however: First, you will not sell all of your dolls at the show. I know, it's hard to believe that you will actually be packing up that giant clothespin family and taking it home with you, but if you sell 30% of your dolls, you can consider that a success. Second, the most common mistake a novice salesperson makes is overpricing his or her wares. If this is a one-shot event for you, you would be wise to price your dolls at an attractive level somewhat beneath the going rate. The satisfaction you feel at having had a successful day will more than make up for the few dollars extra you might have gotten.

You also can sell your dolls through classified ads in doll-related publications (as mentioned earlier as a method for buying). Except for trips to the post office, this can be done entirely from your home. You will have to pay for the ads, for printing your list, and for postage, and the rate of returns will be higher than that for sales made in person; but if you take care with the descriptions on your list, the returns will be low.

Selling through auction is another very viable option for the private collector. You can turn the whole business over to a gallery, which will store your dolls, catalog them, advertise and promote them, sell them, collect the money, and send it on to you—minus a commission.

The one drawback is that you can't set an exact selling price for your dolls beforehand—it wouldn't be an auction if there weren't some risk involved. You and the gallery *can* set reserves (prices below which your dolls will not be sold), which are normally half to three-quarters of the low estimate in the catalog. And if you choose a large, well-known gallery, you can be assured of enough competition to bring healthy prices. Your dolls will probably sell somewhere between the price a dealer would pay you and the price that dealer would ask in his or her shop. This is called "fair market value." If your collection is extremely fine, however, it may very well sell at or above retail value. At any rate, you'll be so thrilled when the doll with the smashed leather face you paid $5 for at the school bazaar sells for $600 that you'll forgive the ignorant buyers for not putting a premium price on "Brenda," your childhood composition baby.

Often you will have better luck selling run-of-the-mill dolls at small country auctions where buyers are less sophisticated. Before you turn your dolls over to anyone, though, be sure you understand what the terms of your agreement are and that you have them in writing. It is also your responsibility to assure yourself that the dealer or auction gallery is reputable.

And unless you have made an extremely good buy, you should not, as a private collector, expect to turn a profit on a doll until you have held it for at least three to five years.

PART 1

DOLLS AND PRICES ·
BY MATERIAL

PART 1

DOLLS AND PRICES
BY MATERIAL

ALL-BISQUE

Although most all-bisque dolls were produced in Germany during the late 19th and early 20th centuries, relatively few were marked with manufacturers' names or initials. In recent years certain groups of all-bisque dolls have been attributed to their proper factories; however, most of the makers are still unknown. Prices for the German dolls average from $50 to $250; those of probable French make cost three to four times more and are worth every cent if you can afford them. Even at 4 to 6 inches in height, they radiate quality and charm.

If your budget is small, you may decide to look for sets of little Japanese painted-bisque figurines. Most were made in the 1930s and were often given as prizes at fairs or as party favors. If the decoration is neatly applied, they can be awfully cute and are frequently found in their original boxes.

Perfect for collectors with limited display space, all-bisque dolls are plentiful and relatively inexpensive, and they average only 3 to 6 inches in height. Even the most inexpert seamstress can fashion simple clothes for them, and they can be displayed in imaginative groupings.

PRICE ADJUSTMENTS FOR CONDITION

Crack in head	−50 to −70%
Minor chips at shoulder or hip joints	−25% or more
Lacking wig	−20%
Obvious discoloration or faded facial features	−30 to −50%
Crack in body	−30%
Wearing original commercial clothes	+30% or more

FRENCH TYPE

These dolls are French in appearance and most were probably made in France at the end of the 19th century; however, because they are unmarked or marked only with numbers, they are called "French type."

CHILD

All-bisque, bald head or cut-out crown, mohair wig, fixed glass eyes, closed mouth, swivel neck, jointed at shoulders and hips (some with additional joints at elbows and knees), long arms and legs, molded boots or bare feet

- Molded boots

4–5 ″ (10–13 cm)	350–400
6–7 ″ (15–18 cm)	600–700

- Bare feet

6–7 ″ (15–18 cm)	750–850

- Joints at elbows and knees

6 ″ (15 cm)	1750–2200

Pair of French-type all-bisque dolls, 6 ¼ ″. *Courtesy of Christie's East.*

GERMAN MANUFACTURERS

HERTEL & SCHWAB

OUR FAIRY: GM 1913

All-bisque, wig, glass eyes, smiling mouth, jointed at neck and shoulders; made for Louis Wolf & Co.
Mold number: 222

6″ (15 cm)	800–1200
9″ (23 cm)	1500–1650

TYPICAL MARK:

222

WITH SIZE NUMBER

HERTWIG & CO.

CHILD: 1920s

All-bisque, molded and painted hair, painted features, molded and painted clothes, jointed at shoulders

6″ (15 cm)	150–200

All-bisque Hertwig boy, 3 1/2″. *Julie Collier.*

GEBRÜDER HEUBACH

CHIN-CHIN BABY

All-bisque, molded and painted cap and queue, painted features, jointed at shoulders

4″ (10 cm)   200–250

TYPICAL MARK:

TRIANGULAR STICKER
ON CHEST

GIRL: CA. 1910+

All-bisque, molded and painted hair (short bob, some with bangs), painted eyes, closed mouth, jointed at shoulders and hips, molded and painted shoes and socks

6″ (15 cm)   375–450
8″ (20 cm)   750–900

Gebrüder Heubach all-bisque girl with molded hair, incised *10490*, 9″.
Courtesy of Christie's East.

30

PIANO BABIES: LATE 19TH CENTURY +

One-piece, all-bisque seated or reclining figure, molded and painted hair, painted eyes, molded and painted clothes or nude

5–6 ″ (13–15 cm)	200–250
8 ″ (20 cm)	400–500

TYPICAL MARK:

Gebrüder Heubach piano baby, incised *3102 1,* 5 ½ ″. *Courtesy of Christie's South Kensington*.

VARIOUS GERMAN MANUFACTURERS

CHILD WITH PAINTED EYES

All-bisque, bald head or small hole cut in crown, mohair wig, painted features, jointed at shoulders and/or hips

- Early (round face, plump proportions, molded bootines): late 19th century

3–5 ″ (8–13 cm)	150–200

- Late (slimmer proportions, molded shoes and socks, generally medium quality): 1900–1930

5–7 ″ (13–18 cm)	100–150

TYPICAL MARKS FOR ALL:

(MADE IN) GERMANY,
SOMETIMES SIZE NUMBER
AND/OR
MOLD NUMBER

- Mold 130
   - 4" (10 cm)   **70–90**
   - 5" (13 cm)   **100–150**
- Mold 150
   - 5–6" (13–15 cm)   **165–185**

CHILD WITH GLASS EYES

All-bisque, mohair wig, sleep or fixed glass eyes, open or closed mouth, one-piece head and body or swivel neck, jointed at shoulders and hips, molded and painted footwear

All-bisque boy with painted eyes, 7 1/2". *Courtesy of Christie's South Kensington.*

- Early (plump proportions, molded boots): late 19th century
   - Type I: One-piece head and body
      - 5–6" (13–15 cm)   **275–325**
      - 8–9" (20–23 cm)   **500–600**
   - Type II: Swivel neck
      - 5" (13 cm)   **375–425**
      - 6" (15 cm)   **500–600**
      - 7" (18 cm)   **600–700**
      - "Wrestler" 8–9" (20–23 cm)
      -               **950–1100**

All-bisque glass-eyed "Wrestler," 10". *Courtesy of Richard W. Withington, Inc.*

- Late (one-piece head and body, molded and painted shoes and socks): 1900–1930

  4–6″ (10–15 cm)　　200–250

- Mold 102 (open mouth, jointed at neck, shoulders, and hips; "Wrestler")

  8″ (20 cm)　　1000–1200

- Mold 130 (open mouth, jointed at shoulders and hips)

  4–6″ (10–15 cm)　　200–250

- Mold 133 (swivel neck, jointed at shoulders and hips)

  5–6″ (13–15 cm)　　550–650

- Mold 150 (open or open/closed mouth, jointed at shoulders and hips)

  4″ (10 cm)　　120–160

  5–7″ (13–18 cm)　　250–300

  9–10″ (23–25 cm)　　650–750

- Mold 160 (closed mouth, jointed at shoulders and hips)

  6″ (15 cm)　　240–280

- Mold 178 (open/closed mouth, jointed at neck, shoulders, and hips)

  6″ (15 cm)　　450–550

  8″ (20 cm)　　750–850

- Mold 180 (open mouth, jointed at neck, shoulders, and hips)

  11″ (28 cm)　　400–500

- Mold 184 (closed mouth, jointed at shoulders and hips)

  5″ (13 cm)　　150–200

Late all-bisque girl with sleep eyes, 4 3/4″. *Julie Collier.*

33

- Mold 208 (closed mouth, jointed at neck, shoulders, and hips)
  6–7″ (15–18 cm)   **500–600**

- Mold 257 (open/closed mouth, jointed at shoulders and hips)
  4–5″ (10–13 cm)   **225–275**
  7″ (18 cm)   **300–350**

- Mold 508 (open mouth, jointed at neck, shoulders, and hips)
  6–7″ (15–18 cm)   **250–300**

- Mold 886 (open mouth, jointed at neck, shoulders, and hips)
  5–6″ (13–15 cm)   **300–400**
  8″ (20 cm)   **450–500**

CHILD WITH MOLDED HAIR

All-bisque, molded hair (usually blond), painted features, jointed at shoulders and hips, molded and painted shoes and socks

Simon & Halbig all-bisque girl with swivel neck and sleep eyes, incised 886 S5H, 9″. Courtesy of Christie's East.

- Early (short molded and painted curls, good quality, molded and painted boots or heeled slippers): 1880s–1900
  4″ (10 cm)   **100–150**
  6–8″ (15–20 cm)   **275–350**

- Late (medium-length molded and painted curls or bobbed hair, sometimes with a molded ribbon): 1900–1930
  4–5″ (10–13 cm)   **50–75**

German all-bisque dolls with molded hair, 4–5″. Courtesy of Marvin Cohen Auctions.

- "Flappers" (short molded and
  painted bobbed hair, small painted
  features, slim proportions, often pink
  bisque): 1920s–1930s
  3–4″ (8–10 cm)   40–60

- "Penny Dolls" (small white bisque,
  molded and painted blond hair,
  jointed at shoulders and/or hips):
  late 19th–early 20th century
  1–2″ (3–5 cm)   20–30

All-bisque "flapper"-type with
molded hair, 3″. *Courtesy of
Christie's South Kensington.*

BABY
All-bisque, molded and painted or
brush-stroked hair, painted features,
bent-limb baby body, jointed at shoulders and hips

- Early: ca. 1900
  3–5″ (8–13 cm)   100–150

- Character (face similar to larger
  bisque-head character babies): ca.
  1915
  3–4″ (8–10 cm)   125–175

- Pink bisque (often found wearing
  original pink or blue commercial
  dress and bonnet): 1920s
  2–3″ (5–8 cm)   50–60

NODDERS: 1920s
Head strung to immobile body with
elastic, painted features, molded and
painted clothing, often comic characters

- Children
  3–4″ (8–10 cm)   40–60

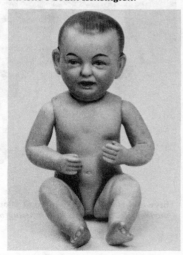

All-bisque character baby, incised
*229 17, 7″. Courtesy of Christie's
South Kensington.*

35

- Comic characters
  4″ (10 cm)   **85–125**

CHILD WITH MOLDED CLOTHES

All-bisque, molded and painted hair (sometimes including hat), painted features, most often jointed at shoulders, molded and painted street clothing or undergarments

- Early (wearing undergarments)
  4–6″ (10–13 cm)   **175–225**

- Late (wearing 1910s or 1920s play-clothes)
  3–4″ (8–10 cm)   **100–150**
  6–7″ (15–18 cm)   **175–225**

DRESSED ANIMALS: EARLY 20TH CENTURY

All molded and painted bisque, usually jointed at shoulders and sometimes hips; animals stand on two legs, often wear crocheted costumes

2–3″ (5–8 cm)   **75–125**

Three all-bisque bears, jointed at shoulders and hips, 1 ¼–2 ¼″,
Courtesy of Christie's South Kensington.

BATHING BEAUTIES: 1920s

One-piece reclining ladies, molded and painted hair or mohair wig, painted features, molded swimsuits or nude

3–4″ (8–10 cm)	30–50
5–6″ (13–15 cm)	80–110
Unusual pose or very fine quality	
	150–200

Bisque "bathing beauty" with molded hair, 3″. *Courtesy of Christie's South Kensington.*

PIANO BABIES: LATE 19TH CENTURY

One-piece seated or reclining children, molded hair, painted features, usually with molded clothing

2–3″ (5–8 cm)	80–110
6–8″ (13–20 cm)	225–250
12″ (31 cm)	400–500

SNOW BABIES: CA. 1900+

All-bisque, immobile, sometimes jointed, painted features, rough-textured bisque snowsuits

- Immobile
  1–2″ (3–5 cm) 30–50
- Jointed
  2–3″ (5–8 cm) 200–250
- Baby with snow animal
  2–3″ (5–8 cm) 120–150
- Other characters
  150+

Two bisque "snow babies," 1 and 4″. *Courtesy of Sotheby's, New York.*

IMMOBILES

TYPE I: FROZEN CHARLOTTES

All-white or pink bisque one-piece figures, much like their glazed china counterparts in design but with a greater variety of hairstyles (frequently blond), usually undressed

- White bisque
  3–4″ (8–10 cm)   **60–90**

- Pink bisque ("Alice" hairstyle with headband or luster boots): ca. 1880
  5″ (13 cm)   **200–300**

- Molded chemise and bonnet
  4–5″ (10–13 cm)   150–200

TYPE II: DRESSED IMMOBILES: 1920s–1930s

All-bisque, molded and painted clothing, usually painted after firing

- Children
  3″ (8 cm)   **30–40**

- Gnomes and Santas
  2–3″ (5–8 cm)   **50–75**

- Tiny "cake" figures
  1–2″ (3–5 cm)   **20–30**

AMERICAN MANUFACTURERS

NANCY ANN DRESSED DOLLS

Nancy Ann Abbott's career in the doll business began with Japanese bisque dolls that she imported, dressed, and sold. With more orders than she could fill, Miss Abbott opened two of her own doll potteries; the first in Berkeley, California, in 1939, and the second in Stockton, California, in 1944. The dolls produced in these factories were not porcelain but "bisque" in its broader sense, an unglazed ceramic. By the time Miss Abbott switched to hard plastic in 1949, she had sold over 1 million dolls.

STORYBOOK DOLLS: 1939–1948

All-bisque, mohair wig, painted eyes, painted mouth; all jointed at shoulders, some also jointed at neck and/or hips

3 ¹/₂–7 ″ (9–18 cm)   **45–60**

MARK:

> STORY
> BOOK
> DOLL
> U.S.A.

ON BACK

"Bisque" Storybook doll. *Courtesy of Marvin Cohen Auctions.*

39

AMERICAN DISTRIBUTORS OF GERMAN-MADE DOLLS

GEORGE BORGFELDT & CO.

BONNIE BABE: TRADEMARK 1926

All-bisque, molded and painted hair, glass eyes, smiling open mouth, pink or blue molded and painted shoes and socks; jointed at neck, shoulders, and hips

5 ″ (13 cm)   450–550

TYPICAL MARK:

LABEL ON CHEST

HAPPIFATS: TRADEMARK 1914

All-bisque, one-piece head and body, jointed arms, painted forelock, painted features, molded and painted clothes on roly-poly body, painted shoes and socks

4–5 ″ (10–13 cm)   125–175

TYPICAL MARK:

HAPPIFAT
GERMANY

ENCLOSED IN A CIRCLE. LABEL ON CHEST OR UNMARKED

MIMI: TRADEMARK 1922

All-bisque, wig, painted eyes, open/closed mouth, jointed at shoulders and hips; designed by J. I. Orsini, made by Alt, Beck & Gottschalck

5″ (13 cm)   **950–1150**

VIVI: TRADEMARK 1922

All-bisque, wig, painted eyes, smiling mouth, jointed at shoulders and hips; designed by J. I. Orsini, made by Alt, Beck & Gottschalck

5″ (13 cm)   **1000–1200**

E. I. HORSMAN CO.

HEbee-SHEbee: CA. 1925 +

All-bisque, bald head, painted features, molded chemise and booties, jointed at shoulders and hips; designed from drawings of Charles Twelvetrees

4″ (13 cm)   **300–400**
8″ (20 cm)   **750–1000**

TYPICAL MARK:

IN CIRCULAR LABEL ON CHEST

TYNIE BABY: 1920s

All-bisque, painted hair, glass sleep eyes, closed mouth, bent-limb baby body, jointed at neck, shoulders, and hips

6″ (15 cm)   **800–1100**

TYPICAL MARK:

Germany
E. I. Horsman

JAPANESE MANUFACTURERS

Japanese all-bisques appeared in the United States during World War I and continued to be imported until well into the 1950s. Most are obvious copies of German products but are not nearly so well made.

QUEUE SAN BABY: CA. 1916+

All-bisque, molded and painted cap and queue, painted features, usually jointed at shoulders; made by Morimura Brothers

4–5 ″ (10–13 cm)	60–80

CHILD IMMOBILE WITH MOLDED CLOTHES

All-bisque, molded and painted hair, features, and clothes

2–3 ″ (5–8 cm)	5–10
Boxed set 4–5 ″ (10–13 cm)	30–50

TYPICAL MARK:

> QUEUE
> SAN
> BABY

IN DIAMOND SHAPE LABEL ON CHEST

TYPICAL MARKS FOR ALL:

> NIPPON
> or
> (Made in) Japan

INCISED OR STAMPED

COPIES OF GERMAN CHARACTERS

3–4″ (8–10 cm)　　　　　**30–60**

"BETTY BOOP" GIRL

All-bisque, undressed, jointed at shoulders

3–4″ (8–10 cm)　　　　　**10–20**
7″ (18 cm)　　　　　　　**25–35**

Japanese bisque immobile with molded clothes. *Courtesy of Dorothy Balz.*

Morimura Bros. all-bisque "Dolly," 3 1/4″. *Courtesy of Christie's South Kensington.*

43

AMERICAN, ENGLISH, AND JAPANESE BISQUE

When imports of German bisque dolls were drastically cut during World War I, a number of foreign porcelain factories attempted to fill the void. The results were surprisingly poor in general, demonstrating to any doubters the degree of technical knowledge and experience necessary to produce fine bisque heads.

While the American, English, and Japanese products project a certain amount of charm—especially those made by the American firm of Fulper—their quality is still weak. The healthy prices they command are due mainly to their novelty, rarity, and historical interest.

PRICE ADJUSTMENTS FOR CONDITION

Hairline crack in head, front	−50%
Hairline crack in head, back	−30%
Large crack or repair to head	−50 to −70%
Replaced wig	−10 to −15%
Body in poor condition	−25%
Replaced body	−30%
Wearing exceptional original clothes	+30 to +50%
With original clothes and box	+50 to +100%

AMERICAN BISQUE

FULPER

Founded in the early 1800s by Samuel Hill, the Fulper Pottery Co. (originally Hill's Pottery) was purchased from Hill's executors in 1860 by Abraham Fulper, a company employee. After Fulper's death in 1881, the firm was directed by his sons until it was sold to the Stangl Pottery Co. in 1930. The Fulper name is well known to collectors of Art Nouveau or Deco pottery. It wasn't until 1915, however, that Fulper, hoping to cash in on the demand for bisque dolls during World War I, began the production of doll heads. The Flemington, New Jersey, factory made dolls for only six years but was the most successful of the American companies that worked with bisque during this period.

CHILD DOLL
Bisque socket head, mohair wig, sleep eyes, open mouth, jointed composition body

14″ (36 cm)	350–400
17–19″ (43–48 cm)	425–475
21–24″ (53–61 cm)	475–550
42″ (107 cm)	3000

Crib Note: Bisque shoulderhead model on kid body runs about $50 less than the same size socket-head model.

TYPICAL MARK:

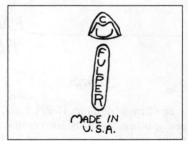

45

CHARACTER BABY

Bisque socket head, mohair wig, sleep eyes, open mouth, composition bent-limb baby body

16–17″ (43–46 cm)	350–400
20–21″ (51–53 cm)	550–650
23–24″ (58–61 cm)	650–750

Fulper character baby, 16″. *Courtesy of Marvin Cohen Auctions.*

Rookwood character baby shoulderhead, 5 1/2″. Produced in 1918 by the American art pottery firm, possibly as a prototype. Sold at auction for $3700. *Courtesy of Marvin Cohen Auctions.*

ENGLISH BISQUE

GOSS

The firm of William Henry Goss, like many other Staffordshire ceramic factories, was encouraged to try its hand at producing dolls during World War I. The modeling of the resulting heads is quite good, but one must assume their molds were taken directly from German heads, since in all other respects the quality and decoration of these dolls are very poor.

CHILD DOLL: CA. 1912+

Bisque shoulderhead, wig, inset or sleep glass eyes, closed mouth (lips painted dark red), cloth body

18–20″ (46–51 cm)   **150–250**

CHARACTER BABY: CA. 1918

Bisque head with flange neck, painted hair and eyes, open-closed mouth painted dark red, cloth body

15–18″   **300–400**

Crib Note: Other British marks to look for are Willow (Hewitt Brothers) and D.P. Co. (Doll Pottery Company), also using Staffordshire-made heads.

TYPICAL MARK:

GOSS

Goss bisque shoulderheaded girl, 17″. *Courtesy of Christie's South Kensington*.

JAPANESE BISQUE

MORIMURA BROTHERS

Morimura Brothers was one of the companies that found success making and distributing bisque dolls during World War I when imports were cut off from Germany. The Japanese unabashedly set out to imitate the German products, and this New York–based firm distributed the best of them, as well as dolls made in the United States. Today collectors do not seek out the M B mark, finding these dolls inferior to their German counterparts; however, they were certainly popular with grateful American buyers during World War I. According to research by the Colemans, the doll import branch of the company was taken over by the New York City firm of Langfelder, Homma and Hayward in 1922.

CHILD DOLL
Bisque socket head, wig, glass sleep eyes, open mouth, jointed composition body

21–25″ (53–64 cm)   **300–400**

TYPICAL MARK:

Morimura Bros. child doll, incised *O*, 14″. *Courtesy of Christie's East*.

CHARACTER BABY

Bisque socket head, painted hair or wig,
glass sleep eyes, open mouth, composition bent-limb baby body

9–12″ (23–31 cm)	125–175
16–19″ (41–48 cm)	250–300
20–24″ (51–61 cm)	350–450

FRENCH BISQUE

Between 1860 and 1900, France produced some of the most beautiful dolls ever made, and today these dolls, as a group, are the most sought-after and expensive of all collectible dolls.

The elegant lady dolls of the 1860s to 1880s (called "French fashions" by early collectors, with the mistaken notion that they were not playthings but small portable fashion mannequins) made the French manufacturers' reputations as the world's finest doll-makers. These bisque ladies, with their pale, flawless complexions, deep blown-glass eyes, shaded lids, feathered brows, faint smiles, and exquisitely made bodies of kid leather or articulated wood, were expensive when they were new and had couture-quality wardrobes that could cost ten times the price of the dolls.

When child dolls became popular in the late 1870s, the French again produced the finest and most costly examples, and these dolls—by Bru, Jumeau, A. T., Steiner, and other revered makers—form the cream of the French crop.

One rather disturbing phenomenon that has surfaced with the immense popularity of French dolls is that inexperienced collectors are paying high prices indiscriminately for *any* French dolls they find. Collectors should note that after 1899, when the S.F.B.J. was formed and when the French could no longer stand up against their German competition, the quality of most French products took a nosedive, and the industry never recovered. So take a good look at any late French doll you are considering and don't be blinded by its origin. Look out for mottled, poor-quality bisque and stiff, masklike faces. Is the doll really worth 50 to 100% more than its German counterpart?

PRICE ADJUSTMENTS FOR CONDITION

Hairline crack in head	−30 to −60%
Large crack or repair to head	−50 to −70%
Replaced wig	−15%
Poor body condition	−20%
Replaced body	−30%
Wearing original commercial chemise	+10 to +15%
Wearing original couture-quality clothes	+30 to +50%
With original wardrobe and box or trunk	+60 to +100%

A. T.

These rare and beautiful bébés are known by the initials found incised on the backs of their heads. To date there is no proof as to who the maker was, but the most likely candidate seems to be A. Thullier, who bought some bisque doll heads from François Gaultier.

BÉBÉ

Bisque head, cork pate, mohair wig, paperweight eyes, pierced ears, closed or open mouth; bisque socket-head model has ball-jointed composition body; bisque swivel-head model has shoulderplate on leather body with bisque lower arms

- Closed-mouth model
  18–21″ (46–53 cm)
  22,000–28,000

- Open-mouth model
  16–18″ (41–46 cm)
  10,000–12,000

TYPICAL MARK:

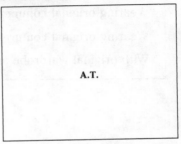

A.T.

WITH SIZE NUMBER BETWEEN THE INITIALS

A. T. bébé, incised 7, 18″. *Courtesy of Christie's East.*

BRU JEUNE & CIE

One of the leading French doll companies, Bru Jeune & Cie was founded by Casimir Bru Jeune in 1866. Succeeding owners, before the firm joined the S.F.B.J. in 1899, were H. Chevrot from 1883 to 1889 and Paul Eugene Girard from 1889 to 1899. Both the Bru lady dolls and the bébés are highly prized by collectors. Two particularly distinctive features found on many Bru dolls are beautifully modeled shoulderplates and graceful bisque hands.

LADY DOLL TYPE I: 1868+

Bisque swivel head on shoulderplate, cork pate, mohair wig, paperweight eyes, pierced ears, closed or closed-smiling mouth, kid body with kid or wooden arms, all-wooden body, or cloth body with kid or bisque lower arms

13–14″ (33–36 cm)	2000–2500
15–16″ (38–41 cm)	3400–3700
18–19″ (46–48 cm)	4400–4800
36″ (91 cm)	7250+

TYPICAL MARK:

HEAD MARKED WITH LETTER TO INDICATE SIZE

Bru smiling lady doll, incised *E*, 16″.
Courtesy of Christie's East.

LADY DOLL TYPE II

Bisque shoulderhead, fixed glass eyes, mohair wig, gusseted kid body; a doll of lower quality than Type I and probably of a later date

14–15″ (35.5–38 cm)   1200–1500

TYPICAL MARK:

FOR TYPE II

Bru lady doll, incised *B. Jne ET CIE*, 14″. *Courtesy of Christie's East*.

BÉBÉ MARKED WITH LETTER OR SIZE NUMBER: 1870s

Bisque head, skin wig, paperweight eyes, pierced ears, closed mouth. Swivel head model has bisque shoulderplate on gusseted kid body with bisque lower arms. Socket-head model has jointed all-wooden body

14–15″ (36–38 cm)	**7000–8000**
24″ (61 cm)	**9000–11,000**

TYPICAL MARK:

BÉBÉ BREVÉTE S.G.D.G.

PAPER LABEL ON CHEST

Bru "Bébé Brevété," incised *2*, 18″.
Courtesy of Christie's East.

BÉBÉ MARKED CIRCLE AND DOT OR CRESCENT: 1870s

Bisque swivel head on shoulderplate with molded bosom, cork pate, skin or mohair wig, paperweight eyes, pierced ears, open/closed mouth, gusseted kid body with bisque lower arms

13″ (33 cm)	6500–8000
16–18″ (41–46 cm)	9000–12,000
21–22″ (53–56 cm)	12,000–15,000

TYPICAL MARKS:

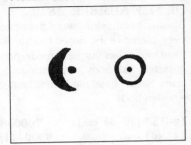

Bru bébé, incised with a circle and dot, 16″. *Courtesy of Christie's East.*

BÉBÉ MARKED BRU JEUNE: 1880s

Bisque swivel head on shoulderplate with molded bosom, cork pate; skin, mohair, or human hair wig; paperweight eyes, pierced ears, open/closed mouth (some with molded tongue tip), kid body, kid or kid-over-wood upper arms, bisque lower arms, kid or kid-over-wood upper legs, kid or wood lower legs; some have jointed composition bodies

13″ (33 cm)	6000–7000
16–18″ (41–46 cm)	8500–10,000
20–22″ (51–56 cm)	11,000–13,000
24–25″ (61–64 cm)	16,500–18,500
30–32″ (76–81 cm)	22,000–25,000

TYPICAL MARK:

Bru Jeune bébé, incised 7, 20″.
Courtesy of Christie's East.

57

BÉBÉ TETEUR: 1870s–1890s+

Bisque swivel head on shoulderplate, kid body with kid-covered metal upper arms and legs, bisque lower arms and kid or wood lower legs, skin or mohair wig, paperweight eyes, pierced ears, open mouth with round opening for nipple; key suctions liquid from bottle into a container in the head and then back to bottle; also called "nursing Bru"

13″ (33 cm)   3500–4500

TYPICAL MARK:

BRU Jᴺᴱ

Bru "Bébé Teteur," 16″. *Courtesy of Christie's East.*

BÉBÉ MARKED BRU JEUNE R

Bisque socket head, mohair wig or human hair wig, paperweight eyes, pierced ears, open or open/closed mouth, jointed composition body

- Open-mouth model
    20–21″ (51–53 cm)   2000–3000
    27″ (69 cm)   3000+

- Closed-mouth model
    17″ (43 cm)   2200–2800

TYPICAL MARK:

BRU Jᴺᴱ R

| 21″ (53 cm) | 4000–5000 |
| 27″ (69 cm) | 7000–8500 |

Crib Note: The quality of these late dolls runs from high to very poor; hence, prices can be erratic.

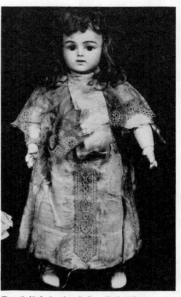

Bru bébé, incised *Jne R 7, 18″*.
Courtesy of Christie's East.

WALKING AND KISS-THROWING BÉBÉ

Bisque socket head, mohair or human hair wig, glass sleep eyes, pierced ears, open mouth, jointed composition body with pull-string mechanism to activate kiss-throwing arm

| 22–23″ (56–58 cm) | 3500–4000 |

━━━ DANEL & CIE ━━━

In 1889, Danel, former director of the Jumeau factory, and Jean Marie Guepratte, another Jumeau employee, founded this Montreuil-sois-Bois and Paris doll company. They were in business for only six years. Perhaps a contributing factor to the early demise of the firm was the lawsuit the Colemans write about: Jumeau apparently claimed that Danel had taken Jumeau molds when he left to start his own company. Danel denied this but lost the case.

PARIS-BÉBÉ:
TRADEMARK 1889
Bisque socket head, cork pate, mohair or human hair wig, paperweight eyes, pierced ears, closed mouth, jointed composition body

23″ (58 cm)   3800–4200

TYPICAL MARK:

PARIS BEBE

BÉBÉ FRANÇAIS:
TRADEMARK 1891
Bisque socket head, cork pate, mohair or human hair wig, paperweight eyes, pierced ears, closed mouth, jointed composition body

15″ (38 cm)   2200–2600
18″ (46 cm)   3000–3250

TYPICAL MARK:

B 8 F

"Paris Bébé," probably Danel & Cie, 26″. *Courtesy of Sotheby's, New York.*

E. D.

The origin of E. D. dolls is not known; however, the most likely manufacturer is considered to be Etienne Denamur, a Paris dollmaker who was in business during the last half of the 19th century. To add to the mystery, a similar E. D. mark is found on dolls bearing a strong resemblance to the products of Jumeau; these dolls may have been made by Danel et Cie.

TYPICAL MARK:

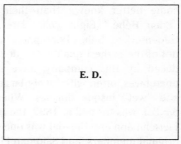

E. D.

WITH SIZE NUMBER BETWEEN THE INITIALS

BÉBÉ MARKED E. D.: CA. 1890s

Bisque socket head, cork pate, mohair or human hair wig, paperweight eyes, open or closed mouth, jointed composition body

- Closed-mouth model

13–14″ (33–36 cm)	1400–1600
16″ (41 cm)	1800–2000
20–22″ (51–56 cm)	2200–2600
26″ (66 cm)	3400–3600

- Open-mouth model

21–22″ (53–56 cm)	1600–1800
24″ (61 cm)	2200–2400

Crib Note: *These dolls have a slightly cross-eyed look that makes them easy to recognize. Many of their bisque heads have lovely "wet" finishes.*

E. D. bébés, open and closed mouth versions, 16 and 22″. *Courtesy of Marvin Cohen Auctions.*

FLEISCHMANN & BLOEDEL

Saloman Fleischmann and Jean Bloedel founded this company in 1873. The firm had offices in Furth, Bavaria, Sonneberg, Thur, Paris, and London. On March 31, 1890, Fleischmann and Bloedel trademarked the name that has become better known than their own, "Eden Bébé." Eight years later they trademarked Bébé Triomphe. Though not of the highest quality, the dolls produced by this company have sweet, open faces, often with lovely large eyes and "wet" bisque finishes. When the S.F.B.J. was formed in 1899, the firm of Fleischmann and Bloedel was one of the original members, and Saloman Fleischmann became its director. With the outbreak of World War I, Fleischmann, a German citizen, was forced to leave France and give up his holdings in the S.F.B.J. He died a few years later in Spain.

EDEN BÉBÉ: TRADEMARK 1890

Bisque socket head, cork pate, mohair or human hair wig, large paperweight eyes, pierced ears, open or open/closed mouth, jointed composition body

- Closed-mouth model

13″ (33 cm)	1200–1600
19–21″ (48–53 cm)	1900–2300
23″ (58 cm)	2400–2800

TYPICAL MARK:

EDEN BEBE
PARIS

• Open-mouth model

15″ (38 cm)	900–1200
18″ (46 cm)	1250–1400
23–24″ (58–61 cm)	1500–1800
25–26″ (64–66 cm)	1800–2100

"Eden Bébé," incised *11, 24″*.
Courtesy of Marvin Cohen Auctions.

FRANÇOIS GAULTIER

In 1867, François Gaultier built a porcelain factory in St. Maurice. For the next thirty-two years the Gaultier family made bisque doll heads and other bisque doll parts. Among Gaultier's customers were Gesland, Jullien, Petit & Dumontier, Rabery & Delphieu, Simonne and Thullier. In 1899 the firm joined the S.F.B.J.

LADY DOLL: 1868+

Bisque swivel head and shoulderplate, cork pate; skin, mohair, or human hair wig, paperweight eyes, pierced ears, closed mouth, gusseted kid body (some with bisque lower arms)

10″ (25 cm)	800–950
12–14″ (31–36 cm)	1200–1400
15–16″ (38–41 cm)	1300–1500
17–18″ (43–46 cm)	1600–1800
20–22″ (51–56 cm)	2200–2500

F. G. lady, marked on shoulder, 13″.
Courtesy of Christie's East.

27–28" (69–71 cm)	2750–3000
31–34" (79–86 cm)	4200–4500

Crib Note: *F. G. ladies have square faces that make them fairly easy to recognize.*

BÉBÉ MARKED F. G. (IN BLOCK LETTERS)

Bisque head, cork pate, skin wig, paper-weight eyes, pierced ears, closed mouth; socket-head model on jointed composition body with straight wrists; swivel-head model with shoulderplate on gusseted kid body with bisque lower arms or cloth body with composition limbs

11" (28 cm)	2200–2500
14–16" (36–41 cm)	2750–3000
17–20" (43–53 cm)	3000–3250
27–28" (69–71 cm)	3500–4000
32–35" (81–89 cm)	6000–7000

BÉBÉ MARKED F. G. (IN A CARTOUCHE)

Bisque socket head, cork pate, mohair or human hair wig, paperweight eyes, pierced ears, open or closed mouth (some closed-mouth models with molded tongue tip), jointed composition body with straight wrists

- Closed-mouth model

11–13" (28–33 cm)	1750–1900
15–18" (38–46 cm)	2000–2200

TYPICAL MARK:

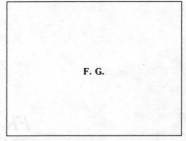

F. G.

WITH SIZE NUMBER BETWEEN THE INITIALS

TYPICAL MARK:

22–24″ (56–61 cm)	2600–2800
29″ (74 cm)	3800–4200

- Open-mouth model
19″ (48 cm)	1400–1600
23–24″ (58–61 cm)	1600–1750
26″ (66 cm)	1900–2100

F. G. bébé, incised with cartouche, 28″. *Courtesy of Christie's East.*

GESLAND

The Gesland family of Paris made doll bodies from 1860 to 1915. The firm remained in business under various successors until 1928. Gesland used bisque heads made by François Gaultier, and by World War I the company was also using J. Verlingue heads. The typical Gesland cloth body has a wire frame covered with cotton padding and a top layer of stockinette.

LADY DOLL: 1868+
Bisque swivel head on shoulderplate, mohair or human hair wig, paperweight eyes, pierced ears, closed mouth, Gesland cloth body with bisque hands and lower legs

22″ (56 cm)	3000–3500
26″ (66 cm)	3800–4200

TYPICAL MARK:

E. GESLAND

STAMP ON BODY

BÉBÉ

Bisque swivel head, composition shoulderplate, cork pate, mohair wig, paperweight eyes, pierced ears, closed mouth, Gesland cloth body with composition hands and lower legs

13″ (33 cm)	**2100–2300**
22–23″ (56–58 cm)	**3200–3500**
32″ (81 cm)	**5500–6500**

TYPICAL MARK:

BÉBÉ E.GESLAND
BRE⁼ S.G.D.G.
5.RUE BÉRANGER5
PARIS

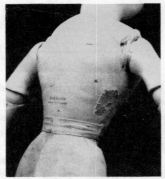

Gesland body showing stamp and part label. (See "Bodies" section for complete doll.)

— HURET —

The Parisian doll and toy company, Maison Huret, was already long established when Mlle Calixte Huret apparently emerged as its creative force during the mid-19th century. She is credited with producing the fashionably plump-faced ladies with almond eyes, in both china and bisque, so sought after by today's collectors, as well as with patenting a number of inventions, including the important swivel neck. A succession of new owners took over the company beginning in 1885, and although some bébés were produced when child dolls became popular, it is Calixte Huret's lady dolls for which Maison Huret is best known.

LADY DOLL: 1850+

Bisque shoulderhead or swivel head on shoulderplate, skin or mohair wig, painted or glass eyes, some with pierced ears, closed mouth, kid or wooden body with bisque or metal hands, some cloth bodies with leather arms

16″ (41 cm)	3800–4200
18–19″ (46–48 cm)	5000–6000

Crib Note: Huret dolls are often confused with those produced by Mme Rohmer. Both used bisque and china heads with glass or painted eyes and were made during the same period. The easiest way to tell them apart is by looking for the marks stamped on their torsos.

TYPICAL MARK:

**BREVETE DEP. S.G.D.G.
MAISON HURET
Boulevart Montmartre
PARIS**

STAMPED ON TORSO

Late Huret lady with painted eyes, 18″. *Courtesy of Richard W. Withington, Inc.*

67

JULLIEN

Jullien may well have been one of the earliest French doll companies; however, not enough records have been found to give more than periodic glimpses of the firm's activities. According to research done by the Colemans, when Jullien Jr. advertised his "indestructible bébé" in 1892, he was at least the third generation to head the firm. His father had been serving as foreman of the jury for the doll and toy section of the Paris Exposition when he died in 1889. Since the existing dolls with the known Jullien mark could not date much earlier than the 1880s, it seems very probable that a group of the unmarked lady dolls from the preceding two decades was made by this firm. Jullien joined the S.F.B.J. shortly after the turn of the century.

BÉBÉ: 1875+

Bisque socket head, mohair or human hair wig, paperweight eyes, pierced ears, closed or open mouth, jointed composition body

- Closed-mouth model
  - **18–20" (46–50.5 cm)** 3200–3500
  - **24" (61 cm)** 3800–4100

- Open-mouth model
  - **24" (61 cm)** 1800–2100
  - **27–28" (69–71 cm)** 2300–2500
  - **30" (76 cm)** 2600–2850

TYPICAL MARK:

JULLIEN

Jullien bébé dressed as a boy, incised 7, 18". *Courtesy of Sotheby's New York.*

JUMEAU

The best known of the French manufacturers, Jumeau is a favorite with collectors because its dolls are not only plentiful but of fine quality as well. Pierre François Jumeau opened his Paris doll company in 1842. By 1859, he was selling dolls with porcelain heads; however, these heads may have been china ones, made by another factory. Though Jumeau had established a factory for making bisque heads at Montreuil-sous-Bois by 1873, the company entered its greatest period of success when Emil Jumeau took over the directorship from his father in the latter part of the decade. Under the younger Jumeau's management, production was greatly increased, the lovely child dolls with ball-jointed bodies were introduced, and a number of inventions were patented. Emile Jumeau, a master of self-promotion, never missed an opportunity to extoll the virtues of his own products while pointing out the supposed defects in his competitors'. It is likely that a number of anonymous but very flattering contemporary brochures about Jumeau and his dolls were, in fact, written by Jumeau himself.

LADY DOLLS: 1860s+

Bisque swivel head on shoulderplate, mohair wig, paperweight eyes, pierced ears, closed mouth, kid body (some gusseted)

13–16″ (33–41 cm)	2200–2500
19″ (48 cm)	3200–3500
25–26″ (64–66 cm)	4500–5000
34″ (86 cm)	13,000–16,000

TYPICAL MARK:

JUMEAU
MEDAILLE D'OR
PARIS

ON BODY, HEAD MARKED WITH SIZE NUMBER

Jumeau lady doll, incised *5*, 19 ½″.
Courtesy of Sotheby's, New York.

BÉBÉ "PORTRAIT": 1870s

Bisque socket head, cork pate, mohair wig, large paperweight eyes, pierced ears, closed mouth, ball-jointed wood and composition body with straight wrists

12–14″ (31–36 cm)	4300–4500
15–16″ (38–41 cm)	4500–5000
17–18″ (43–46 cm)	5100–5300
20–22″ (51–56 cm)	5500–6000

Early, large-eyed Jumeau bébé (called "Portrait" by collectors), incised *6*, 18″. *Courtesy of Christie's East*.

BÉBÉ: "LONG FACE"

Bisque socket head, cork pate, mohair wig, paperweight eyes, pierced ears, closed mouth, ball-jointed composition body with straight wrists

20″ (51 cm)	13,000–15,000
25–26″ (64–66 cm)	16,500–18,000
28″ (71 cm)	19,000

BÉBÉ MARKED EJ

Bisque socket head, cork pate; skin, mohair, or human hair wig, paperweight eyes, pierced ears, closed mouth, ball-jointed composition or wood and composition body with straight wrists

11–13″ (28–33 cm)	3800–4000
14–16″ (36–41 cm)	4200–4500
17–19″ (43–48 cm)	4800–5200
20–22″ (51–56 cm)	5500–5800
26″ (66 cm)	6500–7500

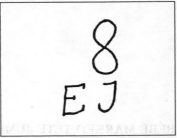

Jumeau "long-faced" bébé, incised *9*, 20″. *Courtesy of Sotheby's, New York.*

TYPICAL MARK:

E. J. bébé, incised *8*, 18″. *Courtesy of Christie's East.*

71

BÉBÉ MARKED DEPOSÉ JUMEAU

Bisque socket head, mohair or human hair wig, paperweight eyes, pierced ears, closed mouth, ball-jointed wood and composition body, straight wrists

12 ″ (31 cm)	2200–2600
15–16 ″ (38–41 cm)	3100–3300
18–20 ″ (46–51 cm)	3500–3800
21–23 ″ (53–58 cm)	3800–4200
26–27 ″ (66–69 cm)	5200–5600

TYPICAL MARK:

DEPOSE
JUMEAU
7

Jumeau bébé, incised *Deposé Jumeau 8, 18″. Courtesy of Sotheby's, New York.*

BÉBÉ MARKED TÊTE JUMEAU

Bisque socket head, mohair or human hair wig, paperweight eyes, pierced ears, open or closed mouth, ball-jointed wood and composition body

• Closed-mouth models

10–11 ″ (25–28 cm)	2500–2800
13–14 ″ (33–36 cm)	2100–2300
15–17 ″ (38–43 cm)	2500–2700
18–20 ″ (46–51 cm)	2800–3100

TYPICAL MARK:

TETE JUMEAU
B^{TE} SGDG

21–23 ″ (53–58 cm)	3100–3300
24–26 ″ (61–66 cm)	3400–3600
30–34 ″ (76–86 cm)	5000–5500

• Open-mouth models

18–20 ″ (46–51 cm)	1600–1800
21–22 ″ (53–56 cm)	1950–2100
24–26 ″ (61–66 cm)	2200–2400
27–29 ″ (69–74 cm)	2600–2800
30–31 ″ (76–79 cm)	2900–3200

Closed mouth Tête Jumeau bébé, incised *13, 28 ″. Courtesy of Christie's East.*

BÉBÉ MARKED 1907

Bisque socket head, mohair or human hair wig, sleep or fixed glass eyes, pierced ears, open mouth, ball-jointed composition body

16 ″ (41 cm)	800–1100
19–20 ″ (48–51 cm)	1100–1300
21–23 ″ (53–58 cm)	1350–1500
27 ″ (69 cm)	1700–1800
31–33 ″ (79–84 cm)	2000–2500
34–36 ″ (86–91 cm)	2800–3200

TYPICAL MARK:

$$1907$$
$$15$$

Jumeau bébé, incised *1907 12, 26 ″.* *Courtesy of Christie's East.*

PRINCESS DOLLS: 1938

Bisque socket head, wig, flirty glass sleep eyes, pierced ears, closed mouth, jointed composition body; designed to represent France (for the country) and Marianne (for the republic); a pair was given to the British princesses Elizabeth and Margaret Rose

18″ (46 cm)
32″ (84 cm)

TYPICAL MARK:

UNIS
FRANCE
71 306 149

JUMEAU
1938

**THE WORDS "UNIS FRANCE" ARE
ENCLOSED IN A POINTED OVAL**

Jumeau "Princess Doll," 32″.
Courtesy of Marvin Cohen Auctions.

74

221 LADIES: 1940s–1950s

Bisque socket head, mohair wig in period hairstyle, fixed glass eyes, closed mouth, five-piece composition body with stand affixed to foot; a series of eight famous women of history

10″ (25 cm)   **300–400**

TYPICAL MARK:

221

Jumeau "Empress Eugenie" from the "Great Ladies" series, 10″. *Courtesy of Christie's East*.

LADY DOLLS
(UNKNOWN MANUFACTURERS)

    Because most early bisque dolls were marked with only a letter or number indicating size, the makers of many fine lady dolls of the late 19th century are now a mystery. These ladies have been called "fashion dolls" by collectors because they were often dressed with great skill in the latest Paris styles.

LADY DOLL

Bisque shoulderhead or swivel head on shoulderplate; mohair, skin, or human hair wig, paperweight eyes, pierced ears, closed mouth, kid body with kid or bisque lower arms, cloth body with kid arms, or all-wood body

10–12 ″ (25–31 cm)	1000–1300
13–15 ″ (33–38 cm)	1400–1600
16–18 ″ (41–46 cm)	1750–2000
19–21 ″ (48–53 cm)	1900–2200
22–23 ″ (56–58 cm)	2400–2700

Bisque-headed lady doll, incised *E Deposé 1 B*, possibly for E. Barrois, 14 ″. *Courtesy of Christie's East*.

—— *LANTERNIER* ——

A late arrival on the French doll scene, A. Lanternier made bisque dolls from 1914 to 1924. Many of his doll heads have interesting and distinctive modeling, while others are unattractive and garishly decorated. The quality of the bisque is surprisingly uneven too, considering his factory was located in Limoges, a city renowned for its porcelain products.

CHILD DOLL

Bisque socket head, mohair or human hair wig, sleep or fixed glass eyes, open mouth, jointed composition or composition and wood body

11–13 ″ (28–33 cm)	300–400
16–17 ″ (41–43 cm)	350–500
20–23 ″ (51–58 cm)	600–750
26–28 ″ (66–71 cm)	900–1200

TYPICAL MARK:

FABRICATION
FRANCAISE
A L & CIE
LIMOGES

Lanternier doll, incised *"Favorite No. 1,"* 14 ″. Courtesy of Sotheby's, New York.

TOTO

Bisque socket head, mohair or human hair wig, sleep or fixed glass eyes, pierced ears, open/closed mouth with molded teeth, jointed composition body

18 ″ (46 cm)	800–900
22–24 ″ (56–61 cm)	900–1150

TYPICAL MARK:

DEPOSÉ TOTO
LIMOGES

LADY DOLL

Adult bisque socket head, mohair or human hair wig, glass eyes, open/closed mouth, jointed composition body

| 13–14″ (33–36 cm) | 550–650 |
| 24″ (61 cm) | 850–1100 |

MOTHEREAU

Not a great deal is known about the Paris firm of Alexandre Mothereau, which produced, at the end of the 19th century, the rare and lovely "Bébé Mothereau." These dolls have rather poorly proportioned, jointed composition bodies. The heads were probably purchased from another factory.

BÉBÉ: 1880+

Bisque socket head, cork pate, human hair wig, paperweight eyes, pierced ears, closed mouth, jointed composition body

22–23″ (56–58 cm)   12,000–14,000

TYPICAL MARK:

B. M.

WITH SIZE NUMBER

Bébé Mothereau, incised *9 B.M.*, 22″.
Courtesy of Sotheby's, New York.

A. MARQUE

Born in Nanterre, France, July 14, 1872, sculptor Albert Marque first

78

exhibited his work in 1899 at the Salon de la Société Nationale. Although many of his sculptures were heads of children, at what point in his career he modeled the doll head incised with his name is unknown. With less than fifty of these dolls known to exist, they are the most expensive of any made in the last century.

CHARACTER CHILD

Bisque socket head, mohair wig, paperweight eyes, pierced ears, closed mouth, jointed composition body with bisque lower arms; the prominent ears and tiny, pointed chin give the doll an elfin appearance

22″ (56 cm)   **35,000–45,000**

MARK:

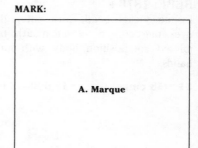

A. Marque

IN SCRIPT

Marque bébé, incised *A. Marque*, *22″. Courtesy of Margaret Woodbury Strong Museum.*

PETIT & DUMONTIER

Frederic Petit and Andre Dumontier of Paris made bisque dolls with heads supplied by François Gaultier from 1878 to 1890.

BÉBÉ: 1878+

Bisque socket head, cork pate, glass eyes, pierced ears, closed mouth, ball-jointed composition body with metal hands

21″ (53 cm)   12,000–15,000

TYPICAL MARK:

> P. D.

WITH SIZE NUMBER BETWEEN INITIALS

PHENIX

First used by Henri Alexandre as early as 1888, the name "Bébé Phenix" was trademarked by Alexandre's successor, Widow LaFosse, in 1895. At that time she was also the owner of Jules Steiner's company, which accounts for the fact that Bébé Phenix dolls are attributed to both Steiner and Alexandre.

BÉBÉ PHENIX: 1888+

Bisque socket head, cork pate, mohair or human hair wig, paperweight eyes, pierced ears, closed mouth, jointed composition or composition and wood body

11–14″ (28–36 cm)   1800–2200
17–18″ (43–46 cm)   2600–2800
20–22″ (51–56 cm)   3000–3250

TYPICAL MARK:

> BEBE PHENIX

PINTEL & GODCHAUX

Henri Pintel and Ernest Godchaux of Montreuil-sous-Bois, France, made bisque dolls from 1887 until they joined the S.F.B.J. in 1899.

BÉBÉ: 1887+

Bisque socket head, cork pate, mohair or human hair wig, paperweight eyes, open or closed mouth, jointed composition body with straight wrists

• Open-mouth model

20″ (51 cm)	**1400–1600**
23″ (58 cm)	**1750–2000**

• Closed-mouth model

23″ (58 cm)	**2800–3200**

Crib Note: For many years the PG mark was thought to belong to Bru, standing for its director Paul Girard.

TYPICAL MARK:

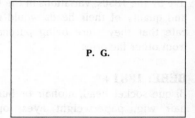

P. G.

WITH SIZE NUMBER BETWEEN INITIALS

Pintel & Godchaux bébé, incised *P G*, 18 ½″. *Courtesy of Sotheby's, New York.*

RABERY & DELPHIEU

Rabery & Delphieu dolls rank with the better French products of the late

19th century, the typical bébé having pale creamy bisque, with large dark eyes under long feather-edged brows and a well-made composition body. Though the company was already active by the 1850s, variations in the look and quality of their heads would indicate that they were being purchased from other factories.

BÉBÉ: 1881+

Bisque socket head, mohair or human hair wig, paperweight eyes; open, open/closed, or closed mouth; ball-jointed composition body

- Closed-mouth models

12–13″ (31–33 cm)	2200–2300
15–16″ (38–41 cm)	2400–2600
24–25″ (61–64 cm)	3000–3350

- Open-mouth models

16″ (41 cm)	800–1000
18–20″ (46–51 cm)	1000–1200
22″ (56 cm)	1300–1500
25–27″ (64–69 cm)	1700–2000

TYPICAL MARK:

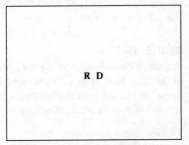

R D

WITH SIZE NUMBER BETWEEN INITIALS

Rabery & Delphieu bébé, 19″. *Private collection*.

— ROHMER —

Mme Marie Rohmer, whose career closely paralleled that of Calixte Huret, produced lady dolls of bisque and china from the middle to late 19th century in Paris. During a period when most doll and toy companies were directed by men, Mme Rohmer appears to have been quite successful. Among the patents she was granted was one for articulated joints for kid bodies, probably the ball-type knee joints that distinguish Rohmer bodies.

LADY DOLL: 1857+

Bisque swivel head with flange-type joint on shoulderplate, cork pate, mohair or human hair wig, fixed glass or painted eyes, closed mouth, kid body with Rohmer stamp; some with pierced ears; some arms partly wood, guttapercha, or bisque

14″ (36 cm)	3000–3300
18″ (46 cm)	3500–5000

Crib Note: Many Rohmer kid bodies have strings at the waist that can be pulled to adjust the lower legs into a seated position.

TYPICAL MARK:

> **MME ROHMER**
> **BREVETE SGDG PARIS**

IN OVAL STAMP ON BODY

Rohmer glass-eyed lady doll, stamp on chest, 18″. *Courtesy of Christie's East.*

ROSTAL

Very little is known about Henri Rostal. He was working in Paris in 1914 when he trademarked the names "Mon Tresor" and "Bébé Mon Tresor," but there is no information to indicate at what date he opened his business or for how long he manufactured dolls.

BÉBÉ MARKED MON TRESOR

Bisque socket head, mohair or human hair wig, sleep glass eyes, open mouth, jointed composition body

19″ (48 cm)	500–600
23″ (58 cm)	800–1000

TYPICAL MARK:

MON
TRESOR

SCHMITT & FILS

The Schmitt family of Nogent-sur-Marne and Paris was in the doll business from 1854 to 1891, and its dolls are among the finest and costliest on the market today. It is interesting to note that both this family and Franz Schmidt of Germany used crossed blacksmith's hammers in their trademarks as symbols of their surnames.

BÉBÉ: 1877+

Bisque socket head with round face, mohair or human hair wig, paperweight eyes, pierced ears, closed mouth, ball-jointed composition or wood-and-composition body with straight wrists

11″ (28 cm)	4200–4800
15–17″ (38–43 cm)	6000–7000
23″ (58 cm)	8000–11,000

TYPICAL MARK:

Crib Note: *The Schmitt body is a distinctive one, having long feet, gauntlet-shaped forearms, and a flat rear end, on which the crossed hammers are stamped.*

Bébé Schmitt, incised *Sch* with a shield 4.5, 23″. Courtesy of Sotheby's, New York.

SOCIÉTÉ FRANÇAISE DE FABRICATION DE BÉBÉS & JOUETS (S.F.B.J.)

The French Society for the Manufacture of Dolls and Toys was formed in 1899 by a group of French dollmakers, including Bru, Jumeau, Fleischmann & Bloedel, Pintel & Godchaux, and Rabery & Delphieu, in order to compete effectively with the German companies in the world doll market. As the members pooled their resources, the rights to many of the individually trade-marked names were transferred to the Society. After 1915, the Society also used the UNIS (Union Nationale Inter-Syndicale) mark on some of the dolls they sold.

CHILD DOLL
Bisque socket head, mohair or human hair wig, glass sleep eyes, open mouth, jointed or five-piece composition body

- Mold 60

8–10″ (20–25 cm)	175–250
13–14″ (33–36 cm)	400–500
18–20″ (46–51 cm)	550–650

- Mold 230

13″ (33 cm)	400–600
22″ (56 cm)	1000–1200
27″ (69 cm)	1500–1800

- Mold 301

7–9″ (18–23 cm)	200–300
10–11″ (25–28 cm)	300–400
16–17″ (41–43 cm)	600–700
19″ (48 cm)	750–850
21–23″ (53–58 cm)	800–1000
25–26″ (64–66 cm)	950–1200
27–29″ (69–74 cm)	1000–1300
32–33″ (81–84 cm)	1500–1750

- Walking, talking, and kiss-throwing

22–23″ (56–58 cm)	1200–1400

- Without Mold Number

10″ (25 cm)	300–400
18″ (46 cm)	550–650
22–24″ (56–61 cm)	700–850
26–27″ (66–69 cm)	900–1100
30–34″ (76–86 cm)	1400–1700

TYPICAL MARK:

S.F.B.J.
301
PARIS

S.F.B.J. child, incised *15*, 32″.
Courtesy of Sotheby's, New York.

CHARACTER CHILD
Bisque socket head, jointed composition body

- Mold 226 (molded and painted hair, fixed glass eyes, open/closed mouth)
  20″ (51 cm)   **1800–2000**

- Mold 227 (flocked or painted hair, fixed glass eyes, open smiling mouth)
  21″ (53 cm)   **2300–2500**

- Mold 235 (flocked or painted hair, fixed glass eyes, open or open/closed smiling mouth with two upper teeth)
  15–17″ (38–43 cm)   **1800–2100**

- Mold 236 (wig, glass sleep eyes, smiling open/closed mouth with molded upper teeth)
  13″ (33 cm)   **1400–1600**

- Mold 237 (flocked hair, fixed glass eyes, open mouth)
  14–15″ (36–38 cm)   **1700–1800**
  16–18″ (41–46 cm)   **2100–2300**

- Mold 238 (wig, fixed glass eyes, open mouth)
  16″ (41 cm)   **1900–2200**
  22″ (56 cm)   **2800–3200**

- Mold 239 (Poulbot, trademark 1913; wig, distinctive character face with no eyebrows, fixed almond-shaped glass eyes, closed smiling mouth; often found in pairs; designed by Francisque Poulbot)
  13–14″ (33–36 cm)   **20,000 pair**

TYPICAL MARK:

S F B J
252
PARIS

S.F.B.J. 238 character girl, 22″.
Courtesy of Marvin Cohen Auctions.

S.F.B.J. 239 character boy, incised
Poulbot, 13 ½″. *Courtesy of Sotheby's, New York.*

- Mold 247 (wig, glass sleep eyes, open/closed mouth with molded upper teeth)
  16" (41 cm)   **1800–2200**

- Mold 252 (wig, sleep glass eyes, pouty closed mouth)
13" (33 cm)	**4200–4800**
28" (71 cm)	**7000–9000**

CHARACTER TODDLER
Bisque socket head, jointed composition toddler body

- Mold 226 (molded and painted hair, glass eyes, open/closed mouth)
  15–16" (38–41 cm)   **1000–1250**

- Mold 236 (wig, sleep glass eyes, smiling open/closed mouth with molded upper teeth)
15" (38 cm)	**1200–1500**
18–19" (46–48 cm)	**1400–1600**
20–22" (51–56 cm)	**1600–1800**
23–25" (58–64 cm)	**1800–2050**
27–28" (69–71 cm)	**2200–2500**

- Mold 247 (wig, sleep glass eyes, open/closed mouth with molded upper teeth)
13" (33 cm)	**1200–1500**
16" (41 cm)	**2000–2200**
27" (69 cm)	**2350–2500**

TYPICAL MARK:

> S.F.B.J.
> 236
> PARIS

S.F.B.J. 236 character toddler, 13".
Courtesy of Christie's East.

- Mold 251 (wig, sleep glass eyes, open mouth, some with molded upper teeth)

12–15 " (31–38 cm)	800–900
18 " (46 cm)	1000–1200
20–21 " (51–53 cm)	1200–1500
24–25 " (61–64 cm)	1600–1800
26–27 " (66–69 cm)	1900–2200

- Mold 252 (wig, sleep glass eyes, pouty closed mouth)

20–21 " (51–53 cm)	5000–6000
28 " (71 cm)	6500–7500

CHARACTER BABY

Bisque socket head, bent-limb baby body

- Mold 236 (wig, sleep glass eyes, smiling open/closed mouth with molded upper teeth)

9 " (23 cm)	650–750
13–14 " (33–36 cm)	800–1000
17 " (43 cm)	1200–1400
21–25 " (53–64 cm)	1500–2000

- Mold 272 (molded and painted hair, fixed glass eyes, open mouth)

17 " (43 cm)	550–700

S.F.B.J. 251 toddler, 15 ". *Courtesy of Marvin Cohen Auctions.*

TYPICAL MARK:

S.F.B.J. 236 PARIS

— STEINER —

From the early round-faced dolls with their two rows of strange pointed teeth to the uncontested charm of the later bébés with their characteristic quirky eyebrows, Steiner produced some of the most distinctive high-quality dolls of the 19th century. Jules Nicholas Steiner, the founder, under whom the company's finest dolls were made, headed the Paris firm from 1855 until 1892. His successor, Amédée La Fosse, apparently died in 1893; his widow took over the directorship and was followed by Jules Mettais in 1899 and Edmond Daspres in 1904.

ROUND-FACED BÉBÉS: 1870s+

Bisque socket head, mohair or skin wig, pale coloring with mauve-shadowed lids, paperweight eyes, some with pierced ears, closed mouth or open mouth with one or two rows of teeth, composition body or bisque body with cloth joints; head unmarked

- Open mouth with teeth
  17–19″ (43–48 cm)   2400–2600

- Taufling-type body
  18″ (46 cm)   4500–5000

Steiner round-faced bébé on taufling-type body, 17 ¼″. *Courtesy of Sotheby's, New York*.

KICKING AND CRYING: 1870s–1890s

Same mold as round-faced bébé; later examples have pinker tint and heavier brows, carton body with clockwork mechanism, composition arms and lower legs

18–22″ (46–56 cm)   1400–1600

Steiner "Bébé Parlant Automatique," 20″. *Courtesy of Sotheby's, New York*.

BÉBÉ MARKED BOURGOIN: 1880s

Bisque socket head, cardboard pate, mohair or human hair wig, paperweight eyes or sleep eyes operated by a lever protruding from head, pierced ears, closed mouth, ball-jointed composition body with straight wrists; Bourgoin mark found on A & C series dolls

8″ (20 cm)	4900
14″ (36 cm)	3400–3600
17–18″ (43–46 cm)	3750–4000
20–22″ (51–56 cm)	4200–4600
24–25″ (61–64 cm)	4700–5000
28″ (71 cm)	5300–5800

TYPICAL MARK:

STE C
J. Steiner. Bté S. g. D. g. J. Bourgoin

Steiner Bourgoin bébé, incised *Ste C 5, 24″. Courtesy of Christie's East.*

BÉBÉ MARKED C: 1880s+

Bisque socket head, cardboard pate, mohair or human hair wig, paperweight eyes or sleep eyes operated by a lever protruding from head, pierced ears, closed mouth, ball-jointed composition body

8″ (20 cm)	2500–2800
14–16″ (36–41 cm)	3100–3500
18–20″ (46–51 cm)	3800–4200
21–24″ (53–61 cm)	4300–4600
30″ (76 cm)	7500–7800

TYPICAL MARK:

> **FIGURE C**
> **J. STEINER BTE S.G.D.G.**
> **PARIS**

Steiner C series bébé, incised *Figure C No. 3, 21″. Courtesy of Marvin Cohen Auctions.*

BÉBÉ MARKED A: 1880s+

Bisque socket head, cardboard pate, mohair or human hair wig, paperweight eyes, closed mouth, pierced ears, ball-jointed composition body

10–11″ (25–28 cm)	2300–2500
15–17″ (38–43 cm)	3200–3600
18–20″ (46–51 cm)	3400–3800
21–23″ (53–58 cm)	4000–4500
25–28″ (64–71 cm)	5200–5800

TYPICAL MARK:

> **J. STEINER**
> **BTE SGDG**
> **PARIS**
> **FIRE A**

32–34″ (81–86 cm)	6000–7000
38″ (96 cm)	8500–9000

Steiner A series bébé, 14″. *Courtesy of Christie's East.*

BÉBÉ MARKED LE PARISIEN: 1892+

Bisque socket head, cardboard pate, wig, paperweight eyes, pierced ears, closed or open mouth, jointed composition body

• Closed-mouth model

11″ (28 cm)	1200–1400
17–19″ (43–48 cm)	1800–2200
20–24″ (51–61 cm)	2800–3200
28–32″ (71–81 cm)	4000–4500

• Open-mouth model

18–21″ (46–53 cm)	1500–2100

TYPICAL MARK:

LE PARISIEN
A 21
PARIS

Steiner Bébé Le Parisien, incised *A 9*, 16½″. *Courtesy of Richard W. Withington, Inc.*

J. VERLINGUE

J. Verlingue of Boulogne-sur-Mer, Paris, and Montreuil-sous-Bois was a dollmaker from 1915 until some time in the 1920s. Typical of late French dolls, the coloring and decoration of Verlingue's heads are not as delicate as that found on earlier bébés.

BÉBÉ: 1915+

Bisque socket head, mohair or human hair wig, sleep or fixed glass eyes (sometimes painted eyes), open mouth, jointed composition body

14″ (36 cm)	300–400
17–19″ (43–48 cm)	450–525
24–25″ (61–64 cm)	550–650

TYPICAL MARK:

PETITE FRANCAISE
FRANCE
J V

WITH ANCHOR

GERMAN BISQUE

By far the most abundant of antique dolls, German bisques offer more variety, both in price and in quality, than any other category. Almost any collector can afford a German doll, as their prices range roughly from $50 to $5000, and most of them are attractive and well made. Many of the pre-1900 children, by such makers as Kestner, Simon & Halbig, and Alt, Beck & Gottschalck, can compete with their French counterparts in quality and beauty; but because they are German, they can be purchased for a good deal less.

While the quality of both French *and* German dolls seemed to falter between about 1900 and 1910, the Germans revived the whole European doll-making community with their innovative "character" dolls—babies and children modeled with wonderfully naturalistic features and expressions. Today the prices of the best of these character dolls rival those of late 19th-century bébés.

World War I was a disaster for German bisque doll makers, whose biggest customers stopped doing business with them. After the war, the industry came back briefly to compete with American composition dolls during the 1920s and 1930s, then died out for all intents and purposes with the advent of World War II.

PRICE ADJUSTMENTS FOR CONDITION

Hairline crack in head, front	−50%
Hairline crack in head, back	−30%
Large crack or repair to head	−50 to −70%
Replaced wig	−10 to −15%
Body in poor condition	−25%
Replaced body	−30%
Wearing exceptional original clothes	+30 to +50%
With original clothes and box	+50 to +100%

ALT, BECK & GOTTSCHALCK

Gottlieb Beck and Theodor Gottschalck founded this porcelain factory in Nauendorf, Germany, in 1854. By the time Friedrich and Johann G. Alt became co-owners in 1881 and 1882, doll production had begun. By 1885 all four men had died, and the company then passed through a succession of new owners, though it retained its original name until 1920. C. M. Bergmann; Wagner & Zetsche; Nockler & Tittel; George Borgfeldt; Fischer, Naumann & Co; and Wiesenthal, Schindel & Kallenberg all bought doll heads from Alt, Beck & Gottschalck.

CHILD DOLL, SHOULDERHEAD: BY 1888

Bisque head slightly turned or swivel head on shoulderplate, mohair or human hair wig, sleep or fixed glass eyes, open or closed mouth, bisque lower arms, kid (occasionally cloth) body and legs.

Typical mold numbers: 639, 698, 870, 911, 1064, 1123, 1237 (GM 1899)

TYPICAL MARKS:

639 # 9

1123 ½ in Germany № 10 Made

96

- Closed-mouth models

12–15″ (31–38 cm)	450–550
16–18″ (41–46 cm)	575–650
19–21″ (48–53 cm)	700–750
22–24″ (56–61 cm)	800–900
28″ (71 cm)	1100–1400

- Open-mouth models

15″ (38 cm)	300–325
22–24″ (56–58 cm)	400–500

Crib Note: These early dolls are of excellent quality, with fine pale bisque, delicate coloration, and paperweight eyes. Longtime favorites with collectors, it was not until a few years ago that research by the Ciesliks attributed them to AB&G.

A B G turned shoulderheaded doll, incised *639, 26″*. *Courtesy of Christie's East.*

CHILD DOLL, SOCKET HEAD: CA. 1912

Bisque head, mohair or human hair wig, sleep or fixed glass eyes, open mouth, jointed composition body.
Typical mold number: 1362

17–19″ (43–48 cm)	325–375
20–22″ (51–56 cm)	375–425
23–25″ (58–64 cm)	450–550
37″ (94 cm)	1400–1600

TYPICAL MARK:

WITH MOLD NUMBER IMPRESSED BENEATH

A B G 1362 child, 35″. *Courtesy of Christie's South Kensington.*

CHARACTER BABY: 1910+

Bisque socket head, mohair wig, glass sleep eyes, open mouth, composition bent-limb baby body.

Typical mold numbers: 1322 (GM 1910), 1352, 1361, 1363, 1367

9–11″ (23–28 cm)	250–300
14–16″ (36–41 cm)	325–375
17–19″ (43–48 cm)	350–425
21–23″ (53–58 cm)	450–550
24–27″ (61–69 cm)	600–700

TYPICAL MARK:

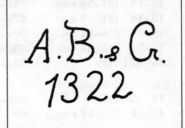

WITH MOLD NUMBER IMPRESSED BENEATH

BAEHR & PROESCHILD

Georg Baehr and August Proeschild founded their porcelain factory in 1871. After the death of Proeschild in 1888 and of Baehr in 1894, the company passed through various ownerships, including that of Baehr's son Hans. In 1918, Bruno Schmidt bought the factory. Besides making its own doll heads, the Ohrdorf company also made heads for Bruno Schmidt, Adolf Wislizenus, Josef Bergmann, Heinrich Steir, Kley & Hahn, Nockler & Tittel, and Wiesenthal, Schindel & Kallenberg.

CHILD DOLL: BY 1888

Bisque head, mohair or human hair wig, sleep or fixed glass eyes, open mouth; shoulderhead model has kid body; socket-head model has jointed composition body.

Typical mold numbers: 224 (GM 1888), 247 (GM 1889), 269, 281 (GM 1892), 289 (GM 1892), 297 (GM 1893), 320 (GM 1894), 325

12–13" (31–33 cm)	275–325
15–18" (38–46 cm)	350–450
22" (56 cm)	500–550
26–27" (66–69 cm)	650–750

Crib Note: Add 25% for socket head with composition body.

TYPICAL MARK:

THE MOLD NUMBER IMPRESSED IN THE BACK OF THE HEAD

Baehr & Proeschild child, incised *269, 23". Courtesy of Christie's South Kensington.*

AMERICAN INDIAN: CA. 1889

Bisque socket head, black mohair wig, fixed glass eyes, pierced ears, closed mouth, stern expression, jointed composition body.

Mold number: 244

12–13″ (31–33 cm)	**400–600**
16″ (41 cm)	**700–900**

TYPICAL MARK:

244

THE MOLD NUMBER IMPRESSED IN THE BACK OF THE HEAD

Baehr & Proeschild Indian character, incised *244*, 13″. *Courtesy of Christie's East*.

100

CHARACTER BABY: 1910+

Bisque socket head, mohair wig, glass sleep eyes, open mouth, composition bent-limb baby body.
Typical mold numbers: 585, 619, 624, 678

10–12″ (25–31 cm)	325–375
13–15″ (33–38 cm)	400–450
18–19″ (46–48 cm)	475–550
25″ (64 cm)	750–1000

TYPICAL MARKS:

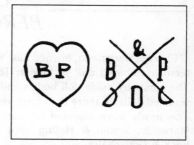

WITH MOLD NUMBER IMPRESSED BENEATH

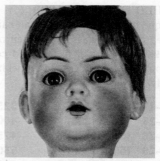

Baehr & Proeschild 678 character baby, 18½″. *Courtesy of Christie's South Kensington.*

CHARACTER CHILD: 1910+

Bisque socket head, mohair or human hair wig, glass sleep eyes or painted eyes, open/closed mouth, jointed composition body.
Mold number: 536

13″ (33 cm)	2400–2600

TYPICAL MARKS:

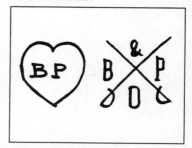

WITH MOLD NUMBER IMPRESSED BENEATH

C. M. BERGMANN

Charles Bergmann opened his Waltershausen-based doll factory in 1888. The company made doll bodies and assembled dolls for more than forty years. The heads were supplied by Armand Marseille, Simon & Halbig, and Alt, Beck & Gottschalck.

CHILD DOLL: BY 1889

Bisque head, mohair or human hair wig, sleep or fixed glass eyes, open mouth; socket-head model has jointed composition body; shoulderhead model has kid body

17–19″ (43–48 cm)	325–375
20–23″ (51–58 cm)	400–450
24–26″ (61–64 cm)	475–550
27–29″ (69–74 cm)	550–650
30–32″ (76–81 cm)	800–950

TYPICAL MARK:

C. M. BERGMANN

SOME WITH S & H OR SIMON & HALBIG

Bergmann child doll, 26″. *Courtesy of Marvin Cohen Auctions.*

CHARACTER BABY: BY 1914

Bisque socket head, mohair wig, glass sleep eyes, open mouth, composition bent-limb baby body.

Typical mold number: 612

12″ (31 cm)	350–400
18″ (46 cm)	500–600
30″ (76 cm)	1800–2200

Crib Note: Allow 30% more for mold 612 with open/closed mouth.

TYPICAL MARK:

C. M. BERGMANN

CATTERFELDER PUPPENFABRIK

This Waltershausen-area factory was active at the beginning of this century, and though it had several directors during its lifetime, the best known is Carl Trautmann, its founder. During his ownership it was called Puppenfabrik Finsterbergen, according to research by the Ciesliks, and then took its new name in 1906 when Trautmann sold out. Most, if not all, of the heads used by this company after Trautmann left were supplied by Kestner.

CHILD DOLL

Bisque socket head, mohair or human hair wig, glass sleep eyes, pierced ears, open mouth, jointed composition body; heads by Kestner.
Typical mold number: 264

19" (48 cm)   **400–500**

TYPICAL MARKS FOR ALL:

C.P.

OR

Catterfelder
Puppenfabrik

WITH MOLD NUMBER BENEATH

CHARACTER BABY

Bisque socket head, mohair or human hair wig, glass sleep eyes, open mouth, composition bent-limb baby body.
Typical mold numbers: 208, 263

20–24" (51–61 cm)   **600–700**

CUNO & OTTO DRESSEL

One of the longest-running family doll and toy businesses in Germany, the Dressel company was founded by Johann Georg Dressel as a trading house

104

in the early 18th century. The Sonneberg firm remained in the Dressel family for six generations. Cuno and Otto, the best-known brothers, were the owners when doll production began in the 1870s. Bisque doll heads were supplied by Armand Marseille, Simon & Halbig, Ernst Heubach, and Gebruder Heubach.

CHILD DOLL WITH TRADEMARK OR COD MARK: FIRST GM 1892

Bisque head, mohair or human hair wig, sleep or fixed glass eyes, open mouth; socket-head model has jointed composition body; shoulderhead model has kid body

16–19″ (41–48 cm)	275–325
20–23″ (51–58 cm)	350–400
24–26″ (61–66 cm)	400–500

Crib Note: Allow 25% extra for socket-head models with composition bodies.

TYPICAL MARKS:

CHILD DOLL WITH JUTTA MARK: REGISTERED TRADEMARK 1906

Bisque socket head, mohair or human hair wig, glass sleep eyes, some with pierced ears, open mouth, jointed composition body; heads by Simon & Halbig.
Mold numbers: 1348, 1349

18″ (46 cm)	500–550

TYPICAL MARK:

1348
JUTTA
S & H

24″ (61 cm)	650–750
30″ (76 cm)	1000–1200

"Jutta" child, incised *1349*, 26″.
Courtesy of Christie's South Kensington.

CHARACTER DOLLS: PORTRAIT SERIES

- Uncle Sam: GM 1895
  Bisque caricature socket head, mohair wig and goatee, glass eyes, smiling closed mouth, jointed composition body, dressed as Uncle Sam

- American Military Heroes: GM 1898
  William McKinley, Admiral William T. Sampson, Admiral George Dewey, Major General Nelson A. Miles; bisque portrait socket head, molded and painted hair, intaglio or glass eyes, jointed composition body, dressed in military uniform

14″ (36 cm)	1600–1850

Crib Note: Dressel may have made others, including Admiral Charles D. Sigsbee, Admiral Winfield S. Schley, and Admiral Richmond P. Hobson.

TYPICAL MARK:

> LETTER AND SIZE
> NUMBER IMPRESSED IN
> BACK OF HEAD

Group of Dressel portrait dolls.
Courtesy of Marvin Cohen Auctions.

BABY OR TODDLER WITH JUTTA MARK: 1914+

Bisque socket head, mohair or human hair wig, glass sleep eyes, open mouth, composition bent-limb baby body or jointed composition toddler body; heads made by Simon & Halbig and Ernst Heubach

- Baby
16–17" (41–43 cm)	**550–650**
19–22" (48–56 cm)	**650–750**

- Toddler
7" (18 cm)	**350–400**
14–15" (36–38 cm)	**650–750**
22" (56 cm)	**900–1100**

TYPICAL MARK:

JUTTA
1914

"Jutta" character baby, incised *1920 50 12, 21". Courtesy of Christie's South Kensington.*

LADY: CA. 1920

Bisque socket head, mohair wig, glass sleep eyes with inset lashes, pierced ears, closed mouth, ball-jointed composition body; body and face are that of young, slender woman; heads by Simon & Halbig.
Mold number: 1469

14" (36 cm)   1200–1500

TYPICAL MARK:

*1469.
C.& O. Dressel.
Germany.*

Crib Note: *Simon & Halbig made a version of Mold 1469 for themselves. The S&H heads are usually superior, both in sharpness and decoration.*

Dressel 1469 young lady, 14".
Courtesy of Christie's East.

EISENMANN & CO.

In 1881, Gabriel and Josef Eisenmann started an export business with offices in Furth and London. By 1895, they were selling dolls along with toys and household goods. Some of the Eisenmann bisque doll heads were made by Gebruder Heubach.

CHARACTER BABY: CA. 1912

Bisque socket head, painted hair, painted eyes, open-closed mouth, composition bent-limb baby body

14–16″ (36–41 cm)   **650–800**

EINCO

Eisenmann character baby head, incised *Einco 2, 5″. Courtesy of Christie's South Kensington.*

GANS & SEYFARTH

Otto Gans and Hugo Seyfarth of Waltershausen, Germany, were partners in the doll business from 1908 to 1922, when Gans started his own company and Seyfarth founded Seyfarth & Reinhardt with Hugo Reinhardt. Otto Gans is credited with the invention in 1901 of "flirting eyes" for dolls.

109

CHILD DOLL: 1908+

Bisque socket head, mohair or human hair wig, glass sleep eyes with lashes, open mouth, jointed composition body

15–19″ (38–48 cm)	300–350
24–25″ (61–64 cm)	400–450

TYPICAL MARK:

G & S
Germany

GOEBEL

Franz Goebel and his son William founded their company as a pottery in 1879. By 1887 the firm was making dolls. When William became the sole owner in 1893, the name of the company was changed from F & W Goebel to William Goebel. William continued as head of the company until his death in 1911. At that time his son Max took over the operation. Besides making their own doll heads, Goebel made the Bébé Elite and other heads for Max Handwerck. The company is probably best known for its production of Hummel figurines.

CHILD DOLL: 1887+

Bisque head, mohair or human hair wig, glass sleep eyes, open mouth; sockethead model has jointed composition body; shoulderhead model has kid body

12–13″ (31–33 cm)	200–250
18–19″ (46–48 cm)	300–400
24″ (61 cm)	450–500

TYPICAL MARK:

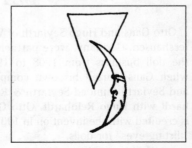

CHARACTER CHILD: CA. 1914

Bisque socket head, molded and painted hair, painted eyes, open/closed mouth, jointed composition body

6–7″ (15–18 cm)   **250–300**

HEINRICH HANDWERCK

Handwerck's Waltershausen factory was in business by 1885. Composition and leather bodies were manufactured on the premises; nearly all bisque heads were purchased from Simon & Halbig. The early, less common shoulderheads may have been obtained from Ernst Heubach. When Handwerck died in 1902, the business was taken over by the Waltershausen Puppenfabrik, a subsidiary of Kämmer & Reinhardt.

CHILD DOLL

Bisque socket head, mohair or human hair wig, glass sleep eyes, pierced ears, open mouth, ball-jointed composition body.
Typical mold numbers: 99, 109, 119

16″ (41 cm)	**275–325**
17–19″ (43–48 cm)	**375–425**
20–22″ (51–56 cm)	**425–475**
23–25″ (58–64 cm)	**480–550**

TYPICAL MARK:

Germany
KEINRICH KANDWERCK
SIMON &KALBIG
2 1/4

111

26–28″ (66–71 cm)	600–650
30–32″ (76–81 cm)	800–900
33–35″ (84–89 cm)	1100–1400
36–38″ (91–97 cm)	1500–1800
39–41″ (99–104 cm)	1800–2200

Heinrich Handwerck child doll, incised *Heinrich Handwerck Simon & Halbig, 21″. Martie Cook.*

MAX HANDWERCK

Max Handwerck's Waltershausen doll factory was in operation by 1899. The Goebel company supplied many doll heads, including those for Handwerck's Bébé Elite line.

CHILD DOLL: 1900+

Bisque socket head, human hair or mohair wig, glass sleep eyes, open mouth, ball-jointed composition body

24–26″ (61–66 cm)	500–600
28–30″ (71–76 cm)	800–1000

TYPICAL MARK:

> MAX
> HANDWERCK

Max Handwerck "Bébé Elite," 15″.
Private collection.

KARL HARTMANN

Karl Hartmann owned a doll factory in Upper Franconia from 1911 to 1926.

CHILD DOLL: 1911+

Bisque socket head, mohair or human hair wig, glass sleep eyes, open mouth, jointed composition body

20" (51 cm)	275–325
23–25" (58–64 cm)	350–450

TYPICAL MARK:

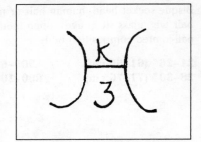

Karl Hartmann child, incised *K H*, *25". Courtesy of Marvin Cohen Auctions*.

HERTEL, SCHWAB & CO.

August Hertel, Heinrich Schwab, and Friedrich Muller, all sculptors, opened a porcelain factory in Stutzhaus with Hugo Rosenbusch in 1910. The firm was relatively unknown until recently, when the Ciesliks discovered that many doll heads that previously had been credited to other firms were, in fact, made by Hertel & Schwab. The company made doll heads for Kley & Hahn, Koenig & Wernicke, George Borgfeldt, Louis Wolf,

Strobel & Wilken, and Wiesenthal, Schindel & Kallenberg. Most Hertel & Schwab dolls have finely painted eyelashes and thin, feathered eyebrows.

CHARACTER BABY: 1910+

Bisque socket head, molded and painted hair or mohair wig, glass sleep eyes, open or open/closed mouth, composition bent-limb baby body.

Typical mold numbers: 142, 150, 151, 152

11–12″ (28–31 cm)	275–350
13–15″ (33–38 cm)	350–400
16–18″ (41–46 cm)	425–475
19–20″ (48–51 cm)	500–550
22–24″ (56–61 cm)	575–650

TYPICAL MARK:

> **MOLD NUMBER INCISED IN BACK OF HEAD**

Hertel & Schwab 152 character baby, 14″. *Courtesy of Christie's East.*

115

CHARACTER CHILD OR TODDLER: 1910+

Bisque socket head, molded and painted hair or mohair wig, glass sleep eyes or painted eyes, closed or open/closed mouth, jointed composition body or composition toddler body.

Typical mold numbers: 127, 141, 149, 157

13–14″ (33–36 cm)	**1200–1600**
16″ (41 cm)	**2500–3000**
18–19″ (46–48 cm)	**3500–3800**

TYPICAL MARK:

MOLD NUMBER INCISED
IN BACK OF HEAD

Hertel & Schwab 149 character girl, 18″. *Courtesy of Marvin Cohen Auctions.*

ERNST HEUBACH

Ernst Heubach opened his porcelain factory in Koppelsdorf, Germany, in 1887. His son, also named Ernst, joined the firm in 1915. The Marseille and Heubach factories merged in 1919. Heubach made doll heads for Cuno & Otto Dressel, Seyfarth & Reinhardt, Gebrüder Ohlhaver, Adolf Wislizenus, and possibly some shoulderheads for Heinrich Handwerck. Ernst Heubach manufactured inexpensive dolls of unremarkable design and should not be confused with Gebruder Heubach, whose product showed greater artistry and much wider variety.

CHILD DOLL, SHOULDERHEAD: 1888+

Bisque head, mohair or human hair wig, glass sleep eyes, open mouth, kid body with bisque lower arms.
Typical mold number: 275

11" (28 cm)	140–170
14" (36 cm)	175–200
17–18" (43–46 cm)	200–250
20–23" (51–58 cm)	250–325

TYPICAL MARK:

Heubach-Köppelsdorf
321·510
Germany

SAME FOR ALL DOLLS, BUT MOLD NUMBERS VARY AND *KOPPELSDORF* IS SOMETIMES INCISED BENEATH

CHILD DOLL, SOCKET HEAD: CA. 1912+

Bisque head, mohair or human hair wig, glass sleep eyes, open mouth, jointed composition body.
Typical mold numbers: 250, 251, 302, 312, 342

6–8" (15–20 cm)	150–200
13" (33 cm)	220–260
16–18" (41–46 cm)	275–325
20–23" (51–58 cm)	350–400
25–27" (64–69 cm)	400–500
32–33" (81–84 cm)	650–750

CHARACTER BABY: CA. 1914+

Bisque socket head, mohair or human hair wig, glass sleep eyes, some with pierced nostrils, open mouth, composition bent-limb baby body.
Typical mold numbers: 267 (GM 1914), 300, 320, 321, 342

6–7″ (15–18 cm)	175–225
9–11″ (23–28 cm)	250–300
14–16″ (36–41 cm)	325–375
19–23″ (48–58 cm)	450–525
24–26″ (61–66 cm)	550–650
29″ (74 cm)	700–800

Ernst Heubach 300 character baby, 24″. *Courtesy of Christie's East*.

CHARACTER TODDLER: CA. 1914+

Bisque socket head, mohair or human hair wig, glass sleep eyes, some with pierced nostrils, open mouth, composition toddler body.
Typical mold numbers: 267 (GM 1914), 300, 320, 342

11″ (28 cm)	300–350
16–18″ (41–46 cm)	475–550
19–20″ (48–51 cm)	575–625
23–26″ (58–66 cm)	650–800

Ernst Heubach 342 toddler, 19″. *Courtesy of Marvin Cohen Auctions*.

GEBRÜDER HEUBACH

Known for its wide array of imaginative character dolls, Gebrüder Heubach is one of the most popular firms with today's collectors. Christoph and Philipp Heubach started this company with the purchase of a Lichte porcelain factory in 1840. Philipp's grandsons,

Richard, Philipp, Jr., and Ottokar, ran the company from 1888 to 1919, when Richard's son Richard and his cousin Eduard took over. The factory made doll heads for Cuno & Otto Dressel, Hamburger & Co., Wagner & Zetsche, Gebrüder Ohlhaver, Eisenmann & Co., and others.

CHARACTER DOLLS: 1910+

Because of the lack of similarity between mold numbers, each model will be listed and described separately; all have bisque heads

- Mold 5730 (socket head, wig, glass sleep eyes, open mouth, jointed composition body)
  33″ (84 cm)   **3600–4200**

- Mold 6894 (socket head, painted hair, painted eyes, closed mouth)
  15″ (38 cm)   **350–400**

- Mold 6969 (socket head, wig, glass sleep eyes or painted eyes, closed mouth, ball-jointed composition body)
  12″ (31 cm)   **1900–2100**
  16″ (41 cm)   **2200–2500**

- Mold 6970 (socket head, wig, glass eyes, closed mouth, ball-jointed body)
  11–12″ (28–31 cm)   **1000–1500**

- Mold 6971 (socket head, wig, painted eyes, closed mouth; jointed composition body)
  11″ (28 cm)   **300–350**

- Mold 7072 (boy, shoulderhead, molded and painted hair, painted

TYPICAL MARKS:

7246
Germany

HEU:
BACH
Germany

WITH MOLD NUMBER INCISED ON EITHER SIDE OR ABOVE THE TRADEMARK

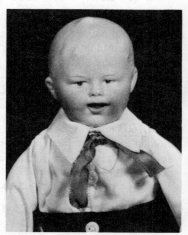

Gebrüder Heubach 8221 smiling character boy, 10″. *Courtesy of Christie's East.*

119

eyes, closed mouth, kid body with
bisque lower arms)

  13″ (33 cm)   **225–275**

- Mold 7109 (baby, socket head,
  molded and painted hair, painted
  eyes, open/closed mouth, composition bent-limb baby body)

  15″ (38 cm)   **350–450**

- Mold 7246 (socket head, wig, glass
  sleep eyes, pouty closed mouth,
  jointed composition body)

  11–14″ (28–36 cm)   **1200–1600**
  27″ (69 cm)   **4300–4500**

- Mold 7247 (socket head, wig, glass
  sleep eyes, closed mouth, ball-jointed
  composition body)

  11″ (28 cm)   **700–800**

- Mold 7407 (socket head, glass or
  painted eyes, open/closed mouth,
  jointed composition body)

  15″ (38 cm)   **1200–1500**

- Mold 7602 (baby, socket head,
  molded and painted hair, painted
  eyes, closed mouth, composition
  bent-limb baby body)

  7–8″ (18–20 cm)   **275–325**
  10–11″ (25–28 cm)   **350–400**
  16″ (41 cm)   **475–525**

- Mold 7603 (baby, socket head,
  molded and painted hair, painted
  eyes, open/closed mouth, composition bent-limb baby body)

  12–14″ (31–36 cm)   **350–400**

- Mold 7604 (socket head, molded and
  painted hair or wig, painted eyes,

**Gebrüder Heubach 7604 smiling
character boy, 12″.** *Courtesy of
Christie's East.*

smiling open/closed mouth, jointed
composition body)

8″ (20 cm)	**175–225**
13″ (33 cm)	**350–450**

• Mold 7605 (socket head, molded and
painted hair, painted eyes, open/
closed mouth, jointed composition
body)

12″ (31 cm)	**350–450**

• Mold 7622 (boy, socket head,
molded and painted hair, painted
eyes, closed mouth, ball-jointed composition body)

17″ (43 cm)	**700–900**

• Mold 7631 (baby, socket head,
molded and painted hair, painted
eyes, closed mouth, composition
bent-limb baby body)

9″ (23 cm)	**250–300**

• Mold 7644 (boy, shoulderhead,
molded and painted hair, painted
eyes, open/closed mouth, cloth
body, composition arms and legs)

10″ (25 cm)	**250–300**

• Mold 7711 (socket head, glass sleep
eyes, open mouth, jointed composition body)

8″ (20 cm)	**500–600**

• Mold 7759 (baby, socket head,
molded and painted hair, painted
eyes, closed mouth, composition
bent-limb baby body)

8″ (20 cm)	**250–300**

• Mold 7852 (girl)

17″ (43 cm)	**1500–1800**

• Mold 7911 (boy, socket head,
molded and painted hair, painted

**Gebrüder Heubach 7763 character
girl, 11½″. *Courtesy of Christie's
East*.**

eyes, laughing open/closed mouth,
jointed composition body)

    14–15″ (36–38 cm)   **950–1000**
    17″ (43 cm)   **1200–1500**

• Mold 7975 (Baby Stuart, socket head,
molded removable bonnet, glass
sleep eyes, closed mouth, composition bent-limb baby body)

    12″ (31 cm)   **2800–3200**

• Mold 7977 (Baby Stuart, socket head,
molded bonnet, painted eyes, closed
mouth, composition bent-limb baby
body)

    9–12″ (23–31 cm)   **800–1000**

**Gebrüder Heubach "Baby Stuart,"
incised 7977, 10″. *Courtesy of
Christie's East.***

• Mold 8035 (boy, socket head,
molded and painted hair, painted
eyes, closed mouth, jointed composition body)

    17″ (43 cm)   **3800–4100**

• Mold 8191 (molded and painted hair,
painted eyes, laughing open/closed
mouth, composition bent-limb baby
body or composition toddler body)

    8″ (20 cm)   **300–350**
    12″ (31 cm)   **550–650**
    15″ (38 cm)   **650–750**

• Mold 8192 (socket head, wig, glass
sleep eyes, open mouth, jointed composition body)

    9–11″ (23–28 cm)   **475–525**
    16″ (41 cm)   **750–900**

**Gebrüder Heubach 8192 glass-eyed
character girl, 10½″. *Courtesy of
Christie's East.***

• Mold 8306 (shoulderhead, molded
and painted hair, pierced ears,
open/closed laughing mouth with
molded teeth and tongue, kid body
with bisque lower arms)

    13″ (33 cm)   **350–400**

- Mold 8420 (socket head, glass sleep
  eyes, pouty open/closed mouth,
  composition toddler body)
  14–15″ (36–38 cm)   1800–2200

- Mold 8724 (boy, shoulderhead,
  painted eyes, closed mouth, kid
  body)
  14″ (36 cm)   150–200

- Mold 8774 ("Whistling Jim," molded
  and painted hair, painted eyes,
  mouth shaped to whistle)
  13″ (33 cm)   900–1100

- Mold 9457 (shoulderhead, wig,
  painted eyes, closed mouth, cloth
  body, bisque arms, composition legs;
  Old Man, Indian, or Eskimo)
  13″ (33 cm)   1500–1750

- Mold 10633 (shoulderhead, mohair
  wig, glass sleep eyes, open mouth,
  kid body with bisque lower arms)
  22″ (56 cm)   550–700

— *ADOLF HÜLSS* —

In operation by 1915, this Waltershausen factory is best known for its
character babies and toddlers. Doll
heads were supplied by Simon & Halbig.

CHARACTER BABY: 1926+

Bisque socket head, human hair wig, feathered eyebrows, glass sleep eyes with inset lashes, open mouth, composition bent-limb baby body.
Mold number: 156 (GM 1926)

14″ (36 cm)	250–300
17″ (43 cm)	350–375
20–22″ (51–56 cm)	400–450

TYPICAL MARK:

WITH MOLD NUMBER INCISED BENEATH AND "SIMON & HALBIG" ABOVE

Hülss 156 character baby, 23″.
Courtesy of Christie's East.

KÄMMER & REINHARDT

This revered Waltershausen doll factory was founded in 1885 by Ernst Kämmer, a sculptor, and Franz Reinhardt, a businessman. By 1890 the factory was selling bisque-head dolls. In 1902 the company bought Heinrich Handwerck's factory and began to purchase doll heads from Simon & Halbig. Unlike most other firms that purchased their doll heads from outside sources, Kämmer & Reinhardt employed their own

124

talented designers. It is evident in the resulting quality and variety of their product. The first bisque character dolls were introduced by Kämmer & Reinhardt in 1909.

CHILD DOLL: 1890+

Bisque socket head, human hair or mohair wig, glass sleep eyes, open mouth, ball-jointed composition body; typical size numbers: 46, 53, 55, 62, 66, 68. Typical mold numbers: 192, 403

6–9 ″ (15–23 cm)	250–300
10–12 ″ (25–31 cm)	350–400
14–16 ″ (36–41 cm)	400–450
18–20 ″ (46–51 cm)	475–525
21–22 ″ (53–56 cm)	550–600
24–26 ″ (61–66 cm)	650–750
27–29 ″ (69–74 cm)	750–850
30–34 ″ (76–86 cm)	1000–1250

Crib Note: Mold 192 is one of the few heads not supplied to Kämmer & Reinhardt by Simon & Halbig. It also comes in a closed-mouth version, for which the price should be doubled.

CHARACTER BABY: 1909+

Bisque socket head, bent-limb baby body

- Mold 100 (molded and painted hair, painted eyes, open/closed mouth): GM 1909

10–12 ″ (25–31 cm)	375–425
14–15 ″ (36–38 cm)	450–500
18–20 ″ (46–51 cm)	650–750

TYPICAL MARK:

Kämmer & Reinhardt child doll, incised *38*, 15 ″. *Courtesy of Sotheby's, New York*.

TYPICAL MARK:

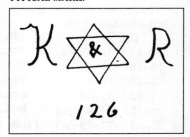

125

- Mold 115A (wig, glass sleep eyes, closed mouth): GM 1911

11" (28 cm)	1750–2000
16" (41 cm)	3000–3500

- Mold 116 (molded and painted hair, glass sleep eyes, open/closed mouth): GM 1911

14" (36 cm)	1500–1750

- Mold 116A (wig, glass sleep eyes, open or open/closed mouth): GM 1911

10" (25 cm)	800–1000
13" (33 cm)	1200–1400
15–19" (38–48 cm)	1700–2100
24" (61 cm)	2600–2800

Kämmer & Reinhardt 100 "Baby," **14". *Courtesy of Christie's East.***

Crib Note: *Allow 25% more for open/ closed mouth version.*

- Mold 121 (wig, glass sleep eyes, open mouth): GM 1912

10" (25 cm)	350–400
14–15" (36–38 cm)	550–600
16–17" (41–43 cm)	650–750
23–25" (58–64 cm)	900–1200

- Mold 122 (wig, glass sleep eyes, open mouth): GM 1912

10–12" (25–31 cm)	425–475
13–15" (33–38 cm)	500–550
16–18" (41–46 cm)	600–650
19–21" (48–53 cm)	675–725

Kämmer & Reinhardt 116 A character baby, 16". *Courtesy of Christie's East.*

- Mold 126 (wig, glass sleep eyes, open mouth): GM 1914

11" (28 cm)	275–325
13–14" (33–36 cm)	375–450
16–18" (41–46 cm)	550–600
19–20" (48–51 cm)	600–650
21–22" (53–56 cm)	675–750
25–26" (64–66 cm)	800–900
28–31" (71–79 cm)	1100–1400

Kämmer & Reinhardt 121 character baby, 23". *Courtesy of Christie's East.*

- Mold 128 (wig, glass sleep eyes, open mouth): GM 1914

10″ (25 cm)	**450–500**
18″ (46 cm)	**800–1000**
23″ (58 cm)	**1200–1500**

CHARACTER CHILD: 1909+
Bisque socket head, ball-jointed composition body

- Mold 101 (wig, painted eyes, closed mouth): GM 1909

7–10″ (18–25 cm)	**1200–1500**
12–14″ (31–36 cm)	**1600–1800**
15–17″ (38–43 cm)	**2000–2500**
18–20″ (46–51 cm)	**2800–3200**

- Mold 107 (wig, painted eyes, closed mouth): GM 1909

14″ (36 cm)	**6000–7000**

- Mold 109 (wig, painted eyes, closed mouth): GM 1909

15–16″ (38–41 cm)	**6500–7000**

- Mold 112 (wig, painted eyes, closed mouth): GM 1909

17″ (43 cm)	**7500–8000**

- Mold 114 (wig, painted or glass sleep eyes, closed mouth; designed by Karl Krausser): GM 1909

7–9″ (18–23 cm)	**800–1100**
10–11″ (25–28 cm)	**1750–2200**
14″ (36 cm)	**2400–2600**
18–19″ (46–48 cm)	**4200–4600**
22″ (56 cm)	**5500–6000**
25–26″ (64–66 cm)	**7500–8500**

TYPICAL MARK:

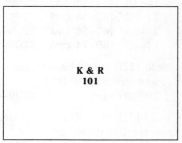

K & R
101

Kämmer & Reinhardt 101 character boy, 11″. *Courtesy of Christie's East.*

- Mold 114X (flocked hair, painted eyes, closed mouth)
  - **15" (38 cm)**   **2800–3200**

- Mold 117 (wig, glass sleep eyes, closed mouth): GM 1911
  - **12" (31 cm)**   **2500–2800**
  - **16–18" (41–46 cm)**   **3500–4000**
  - **21–22" (53–58 cm)**   **4400–4800**
  - **24–26" (61–66 cm)**   **5000–5500**
  - **27–29" (69–74 cm)**   **6200–6800**

- Mold 117A (wig, glass sleep eyes, closed mouth): GM 1911
  - **20" (51 cm)**   **4200–4600**

Kämmer & Reinhardt 114 character girl, 22". *Courtesy of Marvin Cohen Auctions.*

- Mold 117N (wig, flirty eyes, open mouth): GM 1916
  - **16" (41 cm)**   **900–1100**
  - **18–21" (46–53 cm)**   **1200–1600**
  - **22–24" (56–61 cm)**   **1500–2000**
  - **26–27" (66–69 cm)**   **2100–2300**
  - **30–31" (76–79 cm)**   **2400–2600**
  - **36" (91 cm)**   **3000–3300**

- Mold 120 (wig, glass sleep eyes, open mouth)
  - **23–24" (58–61 cm)**   **1500–1800**

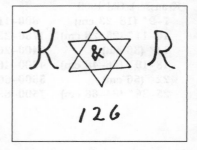

Kämmer & Reinhardt 117n flirty-eyed character girl, 30". *Courtesy of Christie's South Kensington.*

CHARACTER TODDLER: 1911+

Bisque socket head, glass sleep eyes, jointed composition toddler body

- Mold 115 (molded and painted hair, closed mouth): GM 1911
  - **15" (38 cm)**   **3200–3500**

- Mold 115A (wig, closed mouth): GM 1911
  - **13" (33 cm)**   **2400–2600**
  - **17" (43 cm)**   **3500–4000**
  - **25" (64 cm)**   **5000**

TYPICAL MARK:

- Mold 116A (wig, open/closed mouth): GM 1911

12–13" (31–33 cm)	**1200–1600**
16" (41 cm)	**2200–2500**

- Mold 117N (wig, flirty eyes, open mouth): GM 1916

30–32" (76–81 cm)	**2500–3000**

- Mold 117X (wig, flirty eyes, open mouth): GM 1911

15" (38 cm)	**1500–1800**

- Mold 118A (wig, open mouth): GM 1911

10" (25 cm)	**1000–1250**

- Mold 121 (wig, open mouth): GM 1912

13" (33 cm)	**800–1100**
21–22" (53–56 cm)	**1300–1600**
25" (64 cm)	**1750–1850**
28" (71 cm)	**1900–2200**

- Mold 126 (wig, open mouth): GM 1914

8–10" (20–25 cm)	**400–450**
16" (41 cm)	**550–600**
19–21" (48–53 cm)	**650–750**
22–23" (56–58 cm)	**800–900**
26–28" (66–71 cm)	**1200–1500**
33" (84 cm)	**1800–2200**

- Mold 127 (molded and painted hair, open mouth)

11–12" (28–31 cm)	**1100–1300**
18" (46 cm)	**1500–1800**
27–28" (69–71 cm)	**2500–2800**

Kämmer & Reinhardt 126 character toddler, 19". *Courtesy of Sotheby's, New York.*

Kämmer & Reinhardt character toddler, 12". *Courtesy of Sotheby's, New York.*

KESTNER

Ask any collector to list the foremost German bisque doll factories, and one of the first names you will hear is Kestner. The prolific and long-lived company produced bisque dolls of appealing design and consistent high quality throughout the late 19th and early 20th centuries. And its toy-making history goes back much farther than that.

Johann Daniel Kestner opened a factory in Waltershausen, Germany, in 1816. By 1823 he was making wooden and papier-mâché dolls. After Kestner's death in 1858, his widow directed the company until a grandson, Adolf Kestner, was old enough to assume leadership. During this period (in 1860) the firm purchased its first porcelain factory. In 1863 Adolf became the company's director, a job he held until his death in 1918. Production of bisque-head dolls began under Adolf Kestner. Kestner made bisque doll heads for Kley & Hahn, Catterfelder Puppenfabrik, George Borgfeldt, and others.

CHILD DOLL, SHOULDERHEAD WITHOUT MOLD NUMBERS: 1888+

Bisque head, mohair or human hair wig, glass eyes, open or closed mouth, kid body with bisque lower arms

- Closed mouth

14–16″ (36–41 cm)	**500–600**
18–20″ (46–51 cm)	**650–700**
23″ (58 cm)	**700–800**
26″ (66 cm)	**900–1100**

- Swivel head on shoulderplate

19–20″ (48–51 cm)	**2500–3000**

- Open mouth

21″ (53 cm)	**400–500**
26–28″ (66–71 cm)	**650–750**

CHILD DOLL, SHOULDERHEAD WITH MOLD NUMBERS: CA. 1892+

Bisque head, mohair or human hair wig, sleep eyes, open mouth, kid body with bisque lower arms.
Typical mold numbers: 148, 154, 156 (GM 1898), 166 (GM 1898)

14″ (36 cm)	225–275
16–18″ (41–46 cm)	350–400
19–21″ (48–53 cm)	410–450
22–24″ (56–61 cm)	450–500
25–27″ (64–69 cm)	525–625
29–32″ (74–81 cm)	700–850

TYPICAL MARK:

7½ 154 Dep.

Kestner 154 shoulderhead child, 22″. *Courtesy of Christie's East.*

CHILD DOLL, SOCKET HEAD WITH CLOSED MOUTH: CA. 1888

Bisque head, mohair or human hair wig, paperweight or glass sleep eyes, some with straight wrists, ball-jointed composition body

- Without mold numbers, mold 169, or X and XI

10–13″ (25–33 cm)	1200–1500
15–17″ (38–43 cm)	1800–2100
18–21″ (46–53 cm)	2250–2500
24–25″ (61–64 cm)	2700–3000
30–32″ (76–81 cm)	3200–3600

Child doll incised *VIII*, probably a Kestner. *Courtesy of Marvin Cohen Auctions.*

CHILD DOLL, SOCKET HEAD WITH OPEN MOUTH: CA. 1888+

Bisque head, mohair or human hair wig, glass sleep eyes, ball-jointed composition body

- Without mold numbers: ca. 1888+

8" (20 cm)	375–450
14" (36 cm)	500–550
17" (43 cm)	650–700
24" (61 cm)	1000–1200

- "A. T." type

16" (41 cm)	2200–2500
21" (53 cm)	3000–3500

- With mold numbers: 1892+
  Molds 129 (GM 1897), 136 (GM 1897), 152, 155, 156 (GM 1898), 164, 167, 168, 171, 174, 196, 214

8–9" (20–23 cm)	300–350
11–13" (28–33 cm)	350–400
14–16" (36–41 cm)	400–430
17–18" (43–46 cm)	450–475
19–20" (48–51 cm)	475–525
21–22" (53–56 cm)	500–550
23–24" (58–61 cm)	550–600
25–26" (64–66 cm)	600–650
27–29" (69–74 cm)	650–750
30–32" (76–81 cm)	800–1050
33–36" (84–91 cm)	1100–1400

- Mold 143: GM 1897

9–12" (23–31 cm)	525–575
14–16" (36–41 cm)	600–700
17–19" (43–48 cm)	800–900
21" (53 cm)	950–1050

TYPICAL MARK:

made in Germany 129

Kestner 171 child, 16". *Courtesy of Christie's East.*

Kestner 143 child, 18". *Courtesy of Christie's East.*

CHARACTER CHILD: 1908+

Bisque socket head, mohair or human hair wig, ball-jointed composition body

- Mold 178 (painted eyes, closed mouth): 1908+
  12″ (31 cm)   1500–1750

- Mold 183 (glass eyes, open/closed mouth)
  16″ (41 cm)   2500–3000

- Mold 185 (painted eyes, open/closed mouth)
  11″ (28 cm)   1700–1900

- Mold 220 (glass sleep eyes, open mouth)
  17″ (43 cm)   1200–1400
  (Price doubles for closed-mouth version)

Kestner 260 girl, 19 ½″. *Courtesy of Christie's East.*

- Mold 249 (glass sleep eyes, open mouth)
  20–21″ (51–53 cm)   1000–1250
  24–25″ (61–64 cm)   1400–1600
  30–32″ (76–81 cm)   1750–2000

- Mold 260 (glass sleep eyes, open mouth)
  16–17″ (41–43 cm)   700–800
  20–22″ (51–56 cm)   900–1050
  25″ (64 cm)   1100–1400
  36″ (91 cm)   1800–2200
  41–42″ (104–107 cm)
  **   2700–3000**

Kestner 220 character boy, 17″. *Courtesy of Richard W. Withington, Inc.*

CHARACTER BABY: 1912+

Bisque socket head, glass sleep eyes, composition bent-limb baby body

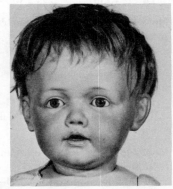

- JDK (molded and painted hair, open or open/closed mouth)

10–13″ (25–33 cm)	**400–450**
14–16″ (36–41 cm)	**525–600**
17–19″ (43–48 cm)	**750–850**
26″ (66 cm)	**950–1200**

- Molds 211, 226 (wig, open or open/closed mouth)

11–14″ (28–36 cm)	**400–450**
15–17″ (38–43 cm)	**500–575**
18–21″ (46–53 cm)	**650–750**
22–24″ (56–61 cm)	**1000–1250**
26″ (66 cm)	**1400–1600**

- Hilda (molds 237, 245; molded and painted hair or wig, open mouth): GM 1914

11–13″ (28–33 cm)	**1900–2100**
14–16″ (36–41 cm)	**2200–2500**
17–19″ (43–48 cm)	**2800–3200**
20–21″ (51–53 cm)	**3600–4100**
24″ (61 cm)	**4800–5200**
26″ (66 cm)	**5500–6500**

Kestner "Hilda" baby, incised *237,* 19 ½″. *Courtesy of Christie's South Kensington.*

- Mold 247 (wig, open mouth): GM 1915

12–13″ (31–33 cm)	**1000–1200**
16″ (41 cm)	**1600–1800**

- Mold 257 (wig, open mouth)

10–11″ (25–28 cm)	**400–450**
13–15″ (33–38 cm)	**450–550**
16–18″ (41–46 cm)	**600–700**
23–26″ (58–66 cm)	**900–1100**

Kestner 247 baby, incised *K 14 247 JDK 14,* 17″. *Courtesy of Christie's South Kensington.*

CHARACTER TODDLER: 1912+

Bisque socket head, mohair or human hair wig, glass sleep eyes, open or open/closed mouth, jointed composition toddler body.
Typical mold numbers: 211, 220, 235, 247 (GM 1915), 257, 260

- Mold 211
16–18″ (41–46 cm)	**900–1100**

- Mold 220
17″ (43 cm)	**2000–2500**

- Mold 235
16″ (41 cm)	**800–900**

- Mold 247
16–17″ (41–43 cm)	**1600–1800**

- Mold 257
15″ (38 cm)	**650–750**

- Mold 260
10″ (25 cm)	**400–450**
13–14″ (33–36 cm)	**550–650**
17″ (43 cm)	**700–800**
21–22″ (53–56 cm)	**850–900**
24″ (61 cm)	**1000–1200**

LADY: CA. 1898+

Bisque socket head, mohair or human hair wig, glass sleep eyes, jointed composition lady body.
Mold number: 162

18–20″ (46–51 cm)	**1400–1600**

TYPICAL MARK:

ℬ made in Germany. 6 J.D.K. 211.

Kestner 260 character toddler, 18″. *Courtesy of Christie's South Kensington.*

Kestner 162 lady, 17″. *Courtesy of Christie's East.*

135

GIBSON GIRL: CA. 1905 +

Bisque shoulderhead, mohair or human hair wig, glass sleep eyes, closed mouth, kid body with bisque lower arms; doll has very distinctive look; chin is tilted up and face is elegant with haughty expression.

Mold number: 172

10″ (25 cm)	950–1100
12–14″ (31–36 cm)	1300–1500
15–17″ (38–43 cm)	1900–2200
20–21″ (51–53 cm)	3300–3800

Kestner "Gibson Girl," 10″. *Courtesy of Christie's East.*

KLEY & HAHN

Albert Kley and Paul Hahn were the founders and owners of their company from 1902 until 1922, when Kley died. The heads for their bisque dolls came from Kestner, Baehr & Proeschild and Hertel & Schwab.

CHILD DOLL WITH WALKÜRE
MARK: REGISTERED 1903

Bisque socket head, mohair or human hair wig, glass sleep eyes, open mouth, jointed composition body; heads by Kestner

21–23″ (53–58 cm)	375–450
24–26″ (61–66 cm)	450–550
27–30″ (69–76 cm)	600–700
34–36″ (86–91 cm)	1000–1200
42″ (107 cm)	2400–2600

TYPICAL MARK:

Kley & Hahn girl, marked "Walküre," 27″. *Courtesy of Marvin Cohen Auctions.*

CHARACTER BABY: 1910+

Bisque socket head, composition bent-limb baby body

- Mold 167 (heads by Hertel & Schwab; wig, glass sleep eyes, open mouth)

11–12″ (28–31 cm)	350–400
13–15″ (33–38 cm)	450–500

- Mold 525 (heads by Baehr & Proeschild; molded and painted hair, painted eyes, open/closed mouth)

TYPICAL MARK:

10–12″ (25–31 cm)	400–450
13–14″ (33–36 cm)	450–500
15–16″ (38–41 cm)	550–650

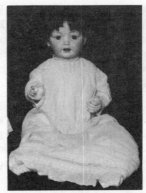

Kley & Hahn 176 character baby, 24″. *Courtesy of Christie's East.*

CHARACTER CHILD: 1910+

Bisque socket head, ball-jointed composition body

TYPICAL MARK:

- Mold 166 (heads by Hertel & Schwab; molded and painted hair, glass sleep eyes, open mouth
     | 21″ (53 cm) | 900–1100 |
     | 30″ (76 cm) | 1500–1800 |
     (Price doubles for closed mouth version)

- Molds 520, 526 (heads by Baehr & Proeschild; wig, painted eyes, closed mouth)
     | 18–19″ (46 cm) | 3500–3750 |
     | 20–22″ (51–56 cm) | 3900–4200 |

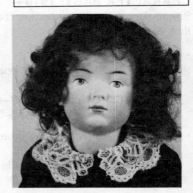

Kley & Hahn character boy with painted eyes, 19″. *Courtesy of Christie's East.*

CHARACTER TODDLER

Bisque socket head, wig, glass sleep eyes, open/closed mouth, jointed composition toddler body; heads by Hertel & Schwab.

Mold number: 169

17″ (43 cm)	**2800–3100**
21″ (53 cm)	**3400–3600**

KOENIG & WERNICKE

This Waltershausen doll factory was founded by Max Koenig and Rudolf Wernicke in 1912. Hertel & Schwab and Baehr & Proeschild supplied most of the bisque doll heads used by Koenig & Wernicke.

CHARACTER BABY: 1910+

Bisque socket head, mohair or human hair wig, glass sleep eyes, open mouth, composition bent-limb baby body.
Typical mold numbers: 98, 99

9″ (23 cm)	275–325
16–18″ (41–46 cm)	400–500
20″ (51 cm)	550–600
23″ (58 cm)	650–700
24–27″ (61–69 cm)	800–1100
34″ (86 cm)	1800–2200

TYPICAL MARK:

K & W

Koenig & Wernicke character baby, incised *99*, 22″. *Courtesy of Christie's South Kensington*.

GEBRÜDER KÜHNLENZ

Three brothers, Julius, Cuno, and Bruno Kühnlenz, opened their Kronach porcelain factory in 1884. By 1889 they were making bisque doll heads. Cuno became the sole owner in 1901 and remained in charge of the company until his death in 1929. This factory produced dolly faces almost exclusively. Many are particularly vacuous-looking and are recognizable by their fleshy look and tiny, almost receding chins. Until the Ciesliks published their research, the dolls from this firm were assigned to Gebrüder Krauss.

CHILD DOLL: 1889+

Bisque socket head, sleep or set glass eyes, open or closed mouth, jointed composition body.
Typical mold numbers: 29 (GM 1891), 32, 44, 76 (GM 1889) 165

- Mold 32 (closed mouth)
22″ (56 cm)	**1250–1500**

- Molds 29, 44, 76 (open mouth)
16–18″ (41–46 cm)	**625–675**
20–24″ (51–61 cm)	**700–800**
27–30″ (69–76 cm)	**950–1200**

- Mold 165 (open mouth)
8″ (20 cm)	**140–180**
12″ (31 cm)	**200–250**
22–23″ (26–58 cm)	**450–500**

TYPICAL MARK:

Gbr 44 K

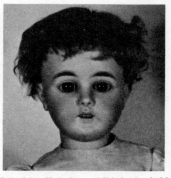

Gebrüder Kuhnlenz child, incised *44-30, 22″. Courtesy of Richard W. Withington, Inc.*

LOUIS LINDNER & SÖHNE

Although the Lindners never produced any dolls themselves, several generations of this family were in the doll business in Sonneberg from 1840 until 1930. The Ciesliks credit Edmund Lindner with the introduction of the

Taufling to the German toy industry in 1850.

CHARACTER CHILD: CA. 1910+

Bisque socket head, mohair or human hair wig, glass sleep eyes, open mouth, ball-jointed composition body; made by Simon & Halbig.
Mold number: 1339

18–21" (46–53 cm)	**600–700**
29–32" (74–81 cm)	**1500–2000**

TYPICAL MARK:

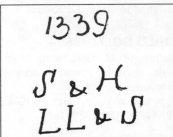

Lindner 1339 child, 20". *Courtesy of Christie's South Kensington.*

ARMAND MARSEILLE

The ubiquitous A.M. 390 is the most common of all German bisque dolls. Its creator, Armand Marseille, was born in Russia of Huguenot parents in 1856. Immigrating to Germany, Marseille had purchased a porcelain factory by 1885. His dolls were inexpensive, and aside from one or two of the early molds and some of the later characters, they were also very ordinary in design. However, Marseille was successful for the sheer numbers of dolls he produced, and because many of them are sweet-faced with creamy complexions, they are still popular with numerous collectors today.

Between 1917 and 1919, Marseille retired, and his son Hermann became director. In 1919, the Marseille factory merged with the Ernst Heubach factory under the name The United Köppelsdorfer Porzellanfabrik; however, each factory continued to manufacture heads separately under the old names.

Armand Marseille made doll heads for everybody. (Not really, it just seems like it.) Among the many were Cuno & Otto Dressel, Louis Wolfe, Seyfarth & Reinhardt, Peter Scherf, C. M. Bergmann, George Borgfeldt, E. U. Steiner, and Arranbee.

CHILD DOLL, SHOULDERHEAD WITH MOLD NUMBER: 1890+

Bisque head, mohair or human hair wig, sleep or fixed glass eyes, open mouth, kid body with bisque lower arms.
Typical mold numbers: 370, 1894, 3200 (GM 1896), 3500 (GM 1899)

10″ (25 cm)	125–175
14–15″ (36–38 cm)	200–225
16–18″ (41–46 cm)	225–250
19–21″ (48–53 cm)	250–275
22–24″ (56–61 cm)	300–350
26–28″ (66–71 cm)	375–450

TYPICAL MARK:

1894.
AM.DEP
germany

CHILD DOLL, SHOULDERHEAD WITH NAME: 1898+

Bisque head, mohair or human hair wig, sleep or fixed glass eyes, open mouth, kid body with bisque lower arms (occasionally cloth body).

Typical names: Alma (made for George Borgfeldt), Lilly, Mabel, Princess, Rosebud

12–14″ (31–36 cm)	140–160
20–23″ (51–58 cm)	250–300
25–26″ (64–66 cm)	325–375

TYPICAL MARK:

> **NAME OF DOLL INCISED ON BACK OF HEAD**

CHILD DOLL, SOCKET HEAD WITH MOLD NUMBER: 1890+

Bisque head, mohair or human hair wig, sleep or fixed glass eyes, open mouth, ball-jointed composition body.
Mold numbers: 390, 1894

• Mold 390

7–8″ (18–20 cm)	120–160
11–12″ (28–31 cm)	140–160
15–17″ (38–43 cm)	225–275
18–20″ (46–51 cm)	300–350

TYPICAL MARK:

> *1894.*
> *A.M. D E P*
> *germany*

Armand Marseille 390 girl, 21″.
Courtesy of Marvin Cohen Auctions.

21–23″ (53–58 cm)	350–400
24–26″ (61–66 cm)	400–450
27–29″ (69–74 cm)	475–525
30–33″ (76–84 cm)	600–700

• Mold 1894

10–12″ (25–31 cm)	225–275
14–16″ (36–41 cm)	285–325
19–21″ (48–53 cm)	350–400
23–24″ (58–61 cm)	450–500

Crib Note: *Occasionally 1894 molds of exceptional quality can be found. Expect to pay 50% more for these dolls, which were produced 10 to 15 years before the first 390.*

Armand Marseille 1894 boy, 14 1/2″.
Courtesy of Christie's East.

FLORODORA: 1901+

Bisque head, human hair or mohair wig, glass sleep eyes, open mouth; shoulderhead model has kid body with bisque lower arms; socket-head model has jointed composition body; made for George Borgfeldt; registered trademark 1901

• Shoulderhead

| 14–15″ (36–38 cm) | 200–250 |
| 20–23″ (51–58 cm) | 300–350 |

TYPICAL MARK:

Made in Germany.
Florodora
A. O. M.

27″ (69 cm)   400–450

• Socket head
    14–16″ (36–41 cm)   225–275
    20–22″ (51–56 cm)   350–450
    26–28″ (66–71 cm)   550–600

Armand Marseille "Florodora," 13″. *Martie Cook.*

QUEEN LOUISE: TRADEMARK 1910

Bisque socket head, mohair or human hair wig, glass sleep eyes with inset lashes, open mouth, ball-jointed composition body; made for Louis Wolf & Co.

20–23″ (51–58 cm)   350–450
24–26″ (61–66 cm)   475–525
27–30″ (69–76 cm)   550–650

TYPICAL MARK:

Queen Louise
Germany

Armand Marseille "Queen Louise," 24 1/2″. *Courtesy of Sotheby's, New York.*

CHARACTER CHILD: 1910+

Bisque socket head, mohair or human hair wig, jointed composition body

- Mold 231, Fany: GM 1912
  16" (41 cm)   **3800–4200**

- Mold 310, Just Me (side-glancing glass sleep eyes, rosebud mouth)
  7–9" (18–23 cm)   **1000–1200**
  12" (31 cm)   **1500–1700**
  Painted bisque   **600–700**

- Mold 550 (painted or glass sleep eyes, dimples, closed mouth)
  15" (38 cm)   **1500–1800**
  18" (46 cm)   **2500–3000**

- Mold 560a (glass sleep eyes, dimples, open mouth): GM 1910
  9" (23 cm)   **200–250**

- Mold 590 (glass sleep eyes, open/ closed mouth)
  17" (43 cm)   **1100–1250**

CHARACTER TODDLER: 1910+

Bisque socket head, jointed composition toddler body

- Mold 231, Fany (wig, glass sleep eyes, closed mouth): GM 1912
  13" (33 cm)   **2500–2800**

- Mold 251 (made for George Borgfeldt; wig, glass sleep eyes, open/ closed mouth): GM 1912
  12–15" (31–38 cm)   **1200–1500**

TYPICAL MARK:

590
A3M
Germany
D.R.G.M.

Armand Marseille "Just Me" doll, incised *310*, 11½". *Courtesy of Sotheby's, New York*.

TYPICAL MARK:

590
A3M
Germany
D.R.G.M.

- Mold 560 (molded and painted hair, painted eyes, open/closed mouth) GM: 1910
11" (28 cm)	**350–400**

- Mold 560a (wig, glass sleep eyes, dimples, open mouth): GM 1910
11" (28 cm)	**350–400**

- Mold 590 (wig, glass sleep eyes, open mouth)
17–18" (43–46 cm)	**700–800**

- Mold 971 (wig, glass sleep eyes, open mouth): GM 1913
14" (36 cm)	**375–400**
16–18" (41–46 cm)	**425–475**

- Mold 980 (glass sleep eyes, open mouth)
18" (46 cm)	**450–500**

- Mold 990 (wig, glass sleep eyes, open mouth)
16" (41 cm)	**375–425**
23" (58 cm)	**650–700**

Armand Marseille "Fany" toddler, 14". *Courtesy of Christie's South Kensington*.

CHARACTER BABY: 1910+

Bisque socket head, composition bent-limb baby body

- Mold 233 (wig, glass sleep eyes, open mouth)
12" (31 cm)	**450–500**

- Mold 251 (made for George Borgfeldt; wig, glass sleep eyes, open/closed mouth)
10–12" (25–31 cm)	**1100–1300**

TYPICAL MARK:

Germany
985
A. 7/0. M.

148

- Mold 329 (made for George Borgfeldt; wig, glass sleep eyes, open
  mouth): GM 1913
  - **14–18″ (36–46 cm)   350–450**

- Mold 343 (wig, glass sleep eyes): GM
  1927
  - **12″ (31 cm)   275–325**

- Mold 500 (molded and painted hair,
  painted eyes, closed mouth): GM
  1910
  - **7″ (18 cm)   200–250**
  - **15″ (38 cm)   450–500**

- Mold 518 (molded and painted hair,
  glass sleep eyes, open mouth)
  - **17″ (43 cm)   450–500**
  - **23″ (58 cm)   600–700**

Armand Marseille 985, 18½″.
Courtesy of Marvin Cohen Auctions.

- Mold 590 (wig, glass sleep eyes,
  open mouth)
  - **15″ (38 cm)   500–550**
  - **17″ (43 cm)   850–900**

- Mold 971 (wig, glass sleep eyes,
  open mouth): GM 1913
  - **14″ (36 cm)   375–400**

- Mold 980 (wig, glass sleep eyes,
  open mouth)
  - **11″ (28 cm)   300–325**
  - **25″ (64 cm)   600–650**

- Mold 985 (wig, glass sleep eyes, dimples, open mouth)
  - **18″ (46 cm)   375–425**

- Mold 990 (wig, glass sleep eyes,
  open mouth)
  - **11″ (28 cm)   200–250**
  - **16–18″ (41–46 cm)   325–375**
  - **22″ (56 cm)   500–550**
  - **27″ (69 cm)   675–725**
  - **34–36″ (86–91 cm)   1300–1500**

**Armand Marseille 590 character
baby, 17″.** *Courtesy of Christie's
East.*

BABY GLORIA: 1926+

Bisque head, molded and painted hair, glass sleep eyes, dimples, open mouth, cloth body with composition arms and legs

10″ (25 cm)	**225–275**
14″ (36 cm)	**450–525**
17″ (43 cm)	**800–850**

TYPICAL MARK:

> **Baby Gloria**
> **Germany**

INFANT: 1926+

Bisque head, molded and/or painted hair, glass sleep eyes, open mouth (except for Mold 341, which has closed mouth), composition bent-limb baby body or cloth body with composition or celluloid hands; mold numbers ending in a K denote socket heads; others have flange necks.

Typical mold numbers: 341 (GM 1926) 351, 352 (GM 1930)

9–12″ (23–31 cm)	**200–250**
13–17″ (33–43 cm)	**275–325**
18–20″ (46–51 cm)	**350–450**
21–24″ (53–61 cm)	**500–600**

TYPICAL MARK:

A.M.
Germany
351 2½K

Armand Marseille 351 infant, 22″.
Courtesy of Christie's East.

LADY: 1925+

Bisque socket head, mohair wig, glass sleep eyes, closed mouth, slender composition lady body.

Typical mold numbers: 300, 400 (GM 1926)

- Mold 300 (mark has additional initials MH)

9″ (23 cm)	650–700

- Mold 400

12″ (31 cm)	900–1100
17–19″ (43–48 cm)	1400–1600

TYPICAL MARK:

A 400 M

PORZELLANFABRIK MENGERSGEREUTH

The porcelain factory at Mengersgereuth was founded by Carl Craemer and François Heron in 1908. Doll production apparently began with a new owner, Robert Carl, in 1913. The name "Trebor," found in the mark of some Mengersgereuth child dolls, is "Robert" spelled backward.

CHILD DOLL WITH TREBOR MARK: CA. 1913+

Bisque socket head, mohair or human hair wig, glass sleep eyes, open mouth, jointed composition body

15″ (38 cm)	300–350
25″ (64 cm)	500–600

TYPICAL MARK:

Trebor
Germany
P.M.

CHARACTER BABY: CA. 1920+

Bisque socket head, mohair or human hair wig, glass sleep eyes, open mouth, composition bent-limb baby body.
Typical mold numbers: 914, 924

12″ (31 cm)	325–350
15–16″ (38–41 cm)	400–450
20–22″ (51–56 cm)	500–600

TYPICAL MARK:

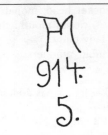

Porzellanfabrik Mengersgereuth 914 character baby, 15″. *Martie Cook.*

GEBRÜDER OHLHAVER

J. P. G. and Hinrich Ohlhaver were producing dolls at their Sonneberg factory by 1913. Their bisque doll heads came from Ernst Heubach, Porzellanfabrik Mengersgereuth, and Gebrüder Heubach. The trade name Revalo, used on many of their dolls, is Ohlhaver spelled backward without the two Hs.

CHILD DOLL: 1913+

Bisque socket head, mohair or human hair wig, glass sleep eyes, open mouth, ball-jointed composition body

15–18″ (38–46 cm)	400–500
23–25″ (58–64 cm)	600–650
27″ (69 cm)	750–800

TYPICAL MARK:

Revalo
3 Dep

CHARACTER BABY: 1913+

Bisque socket head, mohair or human hair wig, glass sleep eyes, open mouth, composition bent-limb baby body

14″ (36 cm)	375–400
20″ (51 cm)	500–550
25″ (64 cm)	650–700

THEODOR RECKNAGEL

Theodor Recknagel opened a porcelain factory in 1886 at Alexandrienthal in Thuringia. The company made dolls for more than forty years.

CHILD DOLL: CA. 1900+

Bisque socket head, mohair or human hair wig, glass sleep eyes, open mouth, ball-jointed composition body.
Typical mold numbers: 1907 (GM 1910), 1909

8″ (20 cm)	115–140
11″ (28 cm)	150–180
14–15″ (36–38 cm)	200–230

TYPICAL MARK:

1909
DEP
R A

17" (43 cm)   250–300
21" (53 cm)   325–350

CHARACTER CHILD: CA. 1910+

Bisque socket head, molded and painted hair, painted eyes, laughing open/closed mouth, jointed composition body

8–9" (20–23 cm)   120–150
13" (33 cm)   250–300

TYPICAL MARK:

R A

CHARACTER BABY

Bisque socket head, molded and painted bonnet, painted eyes, laughing open/closed mouth, composition bent-limb baby body
Mold number: 22 (GM 1912)

10" (25 cm)   275–325

Recknagel character baby with molded bonnet, incised 22, 9", *Courtesy of Christie's East.*

INFANT: CA. 1925+

Bisque head with flange neck, molded and painted hair, glass sleep eyes, closed mouth, cloth body with celluloid hands.
Mold number: 126

14" (36 cm)   375–425

PETER SCHERF

A doll factory was founded in Sonneberg by Peter Scherf in 1879. After Scherf's death in 1887, various members of the family directed the firm into the 1920s. The bisque shoulderheads were probably made by Armand Marseille.

CHILD DOLL: CA. 1899+

Bisque socket or shoulderhead, mohair or human hair wig, glass sleep eyes, open mouth; socket-head model has jointed composition body; shoulderhead model has kid body

15″ (38 cm)   **275–325**

TYPICAL MARK:

P. Sch

Peter Scherf girl, 16″. *Courtesy of Christie's East.*

BRUNO SCHMIDT

Bruno Schmidt opened his Waltershausen doll factory in 1900. In 1918 he purchased Baehr & Proeschild, the

155

porcelain factory that had been supplying Schmidt's bisque doll heads.

CHILD DOLL: 1900+

Bisque socket head, mohair or human
hair wig, glass sleep eyes, open mouth,
ball-jointed composition body

19–22" (48–56 cm)	400–500
28" (71 cm)	700–750
33" (84 cm)	900–1100

TYPICAL MARK FOR ALL DOLLS:

CHARACTER CHILD: 1911+

Bisque socket head, glass sleep eyes,
ball-jointed composition body

- Mold 2096 (molded and painted hair,
  open mouth)
    15" (38 cm)   700–750

- Mold 2097 (wig, open/closed mouth):
  GM 1911
    28" (71 cm)   1100–1250

Bruno Schmidt 2096 character boy,
called "Tommy Tucker," 16".
Courtesy of Marvin Cohen Auctions.

CHARACTER TODDLER: CA. 1911+

Bisque socket head, glass sleep eyes, open mouth, jointed composition toddler body

- Molds 2048, 2068 (molded and painted hair)

14" (36 cm)	750–800
19–20" (58–51 cm)	1100–1200

- Mold 2085 (mohair or human hair wig)

16" (41 cm)	550–600

CHARACTER BABY: 1911+

Bisque socket head, mohair wig, glass sleep eyes, open mouth, composition bent-limb baby body.
Mold number: 2087 (GM 1911)

18" (46 cm)	450–500

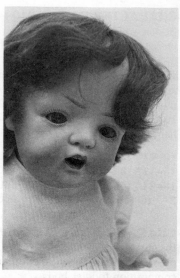

Bruno Schmidt 2085 toddler, 16".
Courtesy of Marvin Cohen Auctions.

FRANZ SCHMIDT

Franz Schmidt founded his Thuringia doll factory in 1890 and headed the company until his death in 1942. The Ciesliks credit him with many inventions, including pierced nostrils and movable tongues for dolls. Although Simon & Halbig supplied the bisque doll heads Schmidt used, evidently the designs for the heads came from the sculptors at Schmidt's factory.

CHARACTER BABY: 1910+

Bisque socket head, glass sleep eyes, pierced nostrils, open mouth, composition bent-limb baby body.

Typical mold numbers: 1255 (molded and painted hair), 1271 (GM 1910, molded and painted hair), 1272 (GM 1910, wigged, or molded and painted hair), 1295 (wigged)

10–11″ (25–28 cm)	325–375
15–17″ (38–43 cm)	450–550
18–21″ (46–53 cm)	600–700
27″ (69 cm)	900–950

CHARACTER TODDLER: 1910+

Bisque socket head, glass sleep eyes, pierced nostrils, open mouth, jointed composition toddler body.

Typical mold numbers: 1255 (molded and painted hair), 1272 (GM 1910, wigged)

18–22″ (46–56 cm)	750–850

CHILD: 1890s+

Bisque socket head, glass sleep eyes, open mouth, jointed composition body

16–18″ (41–46 cm)	400–500
24–27″ (61–69 cm)	600–700

TYPICAL MARK:

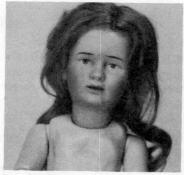

F. S. & C°
1272/40 Z
Deponient

Franz Schmidt painted-eye character child, incised *1409*, 12″. *Courtesy of Christie's East.*

Franz Schmidt girl, 31″. *Courtesy of Christie's South Kensington.*

SCHOENAU & HOFFMEISTER

The initials SPBH, so commonly seen in doll marks from this firm, come from the owners' surnames and the name of their factory. *S* and *H* stand for Arthur Schoenau and Carl Hoffmeister, founders of the company in 1901, and *P B* (usually found enclosed in a star) stands for Porzellanfabrik Burggrub. After Hoffmeister left the concern in 1907, the Schoenau family continued to direct the company until 1930.

CHILD DOLL: 1901+

Bisque socket head, mohair or human hair wig, glass sleep eyes, open mouth, ball-jointed composition body; typical name: Viola.

Typical mold numbers: 1906, 1909

13–14″ (33–36 cm)	200–250
17–20″ (43–51 cm)	300–400
21–23″ (53–58 cm)	400–475
24–26″ (61–66 cm)	475–550
27–28″ (69–71 cm)	600–650
32–33″ (81–84 cm)	800–900
38–39″ (97–99 cm)	1500–1800

TYPICAL MARK:

WITH MOLD NUMBER INCISED BENEATH

Schoenau & Hoffmeister 1909 girl, 21″. *Courtesy of Christie's East.*

PRINCESS ELIZABETH: CA. 1932

Bisque socket head, blond curly wig, glass sleep eyes, smiling open mouth, jointed composition toddler body; very distinctive character face; head often appears too large for its body; designed by Casar Schneider

| 16–17″ (41–43 cm) | 1500–1750 |
| 20–24″ (51–61 cm) | 2500–2800 |

TYPICAL MARK:

Porzellanfabrik
Burggrub
Princess Elizabeth

Schoenau & Hoffmeister "Princess Elizabeth," 23″. *Courtesy of Marvin Cohen Auctions.*

SCHÜTZMEISTER & QUENDT

Philipp Schützmeister and Wilhelm Quendt founded a porcelain factory in Boilstadt in 1889. Philipp was the sole owner from 1908 until the company joined the Bing concern in 1918. Schützmeister & Quendt made bisque doll heads for Kämmer & Reinhardt and Welsch & Co.

CHILD DOLL: CA. 1900

Bisque socket head, mohair wig, glass sleep eyes, open mouth, jointed composition body.

Mold number: 101

24″ (61 cm)	**450–500**
31″ (79 cm)	**650–700**

TYPICAL MARK:

S & Q
(Intertwined)

Schützmeister & Quendt 301 girl, 24″. *Courtesy of Christie's South Kensington.*

CHARACTER BABY: CA. 1920+

Bisque socket head, mohair wig, glass sleep eyes, open mouth, composition bent-limb baby body.

Mold number: 201

12″ (31 cm)	**250–300**
17″ (43 cm)	**350–375**

SIMON & HALBIG

Probably the loveliest of all German bisque dolls were manufactured in this Gräfenhain factory founded by Wilhelm

161

Simon and Carl Halbig in 1879. After Simon's death in 1894, the Halbigs directed the firm until 1920, when they sold it to Kämmer & Reinhardt. Simon & Halbig had the first German patent for inset eyelashes in 1893. This prosperous factory turned out millions of first-rate bisque doll heads over its long history, a large portion of them for other factories including Cuno & Otto Dressel, Kämmer & Reinhardt, Adolf Hülss, Heinrich Handwerck, Hamburger & Co., Franz Schmidt, Louis Lindner, Adolf Wislizenus, George Borgfeldt, and Wiesenthal, Schindler & Kallenberg. These heads are easy to identify, as most of them prominently bear the Simon & Halbig name along with the name of the company for which they were made.

CHILD DOLL, SHOULDERHEAD WITH CLOSED MOUTH: 1888+

Bisque shoulderhead or swivel head on shoulderplate, mohair or human hair wig, glass eyes, pierced ears, kid body with bisque lower arms

- Mold 719
  15″ (38 cm)   **1200–1500**
- Mold 905
  16″ (41 cm)   **1750–2000**
- Mold 939
  30″ (76 cm)   **2800–3200**
- Mold 940
  13″ (33 cm)   **800–1000**
- Mold 949
  18″ (46 cm)   **1000–1200**

TYPICAL MARKS FOR ALL DOLLS:

SIMON × HALBIG

S & H

WITH MOLD NUMBER

• Mold 950
   19" (48 cm)   **1200–1500**

CHILD DOLL, SHOULDERHEAD WITH OPEN MOUTH: 1889+

Bisque shoulderhead or swivel head on shoulderplate, mohair or human hair wig, glass eyes, pierced ears, kid body with bisque lower arms

• Mold 949
   31" (79 cm)   **1300–1400**

• Mold 1009: GM 1889
   18" (46 cm)   **550–600**

• Mold 1080: GM 1892
   15" (38 cm)   **350–400**
   19" (28 cm)   **450–500**
   27" (69 cm)   **625–650**

• Mold 1250: GM 1898
   14–15" (36–38 cm)   **425–475**
   23–25" (58–64 cm)   **650–750**

• Mold 1260
   21" (53 cm)   **600–650**

SMALL LADY DOLL: 1894+

Bisque shoulderhead, period-style mohair wig, fixed glass eyes, closed mouth, cloth or leather body with bisque lower arms.
Mold number 1160: GM 1894

6–7" (15–18 cm)   **275–325**
10" (25 cm)   **400–450**
14" (36 cm)   **1100–1200**

Crib Note: *Collectors sometimes refer to these dolls as "Little Women," although their hair styles are much more representative of the 1680s than the 1860s. For the same reason, the term "rococo wig," though often used, is also inaccurate.*

Because of their diminutive size, these dolls were often used in doll houses. They could also be purchased without bodies and used for pincushion or powder puff tops.

CHILD DOLL, SOCKET HEAD WITH CLOSED MOUTH: 1887 +

Bisque head, mohair or human hair wig, pierced ears, glass eyes, ball-jointed composition body

- Mold 905
18 ″ (46 cm)	2400–2600

- Mold 919
16 ″ (41 cm)	4000–4500

- Mold 929
16 ″ (41 cm)	1500–1750

- Mold 939
14 ″ (36 cm)	1000–1200
24 ″ (61 cm)	2400–2700
29 ″ (74 cm)	3100–3400

- Mold 949
15 ″ (38 cm)	1200–1500
21–22 ″ (53–56 cm)	2000–2200
24 ″ (61 cm)	2350–2500
27–28 ″ (69–71 cm)	3000–3200

- Mold 989: GM 1889
15 ″ (38 cm)	1400–1600

Simon & Halbig 949 closed-mouth girl, 22 ″. *Courtesy of Christie's East.*

CHILD DOLL, SOCKET HEAD WITH OPEN MOUTH: 1887+

Bisque head, mohair or human hair wig, sleep glass eyes, pierced ears, ball-jointed composition body

- Molds 530, 540, 550, 570, 1009 (GM 1889), 1078 (GM 1892), 1079 (GM 1892), 1248 (GM 1898), 1269

7–9 " (18–23 cm)	225–275
12–14 " (31–36 cm)	400–425
15–18 " (38–46 cm)	425–475
20–23 " (51–58 cm)	500–550
25–28 " (64–71 cm)	600–700
29–31 " (74–79 cm)	750–850
32–33 " (81–84 cm)	900–1100
35–36 " (89–91 cm)	1400–1600
39 " (99 cm)	2500–2700
46 " (117 cm)	4400–4800

Simon & Halbig 1079 girl, 34 ".
Courtesy of Christie's South Kensington.

- Molds 719, 949, 979

10 " (25 cm)	400–450
20–23 " (51–58 cm)	900–1100
27–29 " (69–74 cm)	1400–1700
30 " (76 cm)	2200–2500
33–35 " (84–89 cm)	2650–2850
43 " (109 cm)	3800–4100

- Mold 908

14 " (36 cm)	1300–1500

- Mold 1039 (key wound): GM 1891

22 " (56 cm)	1300–1550
26 " (66 cm)	1900–2100

- Mold 1249: GM 1898

12–13 " (31–33 cm)	450–500
16–19 " (41–48 cm)	650–750
22–24 " (56–61 cm)	800–950
27–29 " (69–74 cm)	1100–1400
37 " (94 cm)	1900–2200

Simon & Halbig 1249 girl, 27 ".
Courtesy of Christie's East.

LADY: 1894+

Bisque socket head, mohair or human hair wig, sleep glass eyes, pierced ears, open mouth, ball-jointed composition lady body.

Mold number 1159: GM 1894

17–18″ (43–46 cm)	**1200–1400**
19–21″ (48–53 cm)	**1500–1750**
24–25″ (61–64 cm)	**2000–2350**

Simon & Halbig 1159 lady, 25″.
Courtesy of Sotheby's, New York.

CHARACTER BABY: CA. 1912+

Bisque socket head, mohair or human hair wig, glass sleep eyes, open mouth, composition bent-limb baby body

- Mold 1294

19″ (48 cm)	**600–650**
22–24″ (56–61 cm)	**700–800**
29″ (74 cm)	**1400–1600**

- Mold 1299

10″ (25 cm)	**500–550**

- Mold 1489

12″ (31 cm)	**1900–2100**
25″ (64 cm)	**2800–3100**

CHARACTER CHILD

Bisque socket head, mohair or human hair wig, glass sleep eyes or painted eyes, open or open/closed mouth, ball-jointed composition body

- Mold 151 (painted eyes)
  - 19" (48 cm)   **6400–6700**

Glass sleep eyes:

- Mold 1279: GM 1899
  - 10" (25 cm)   **700–750**
  - 22–23" (56–58 cm)   **2200–2400**
  - 25" (64 cm)   **2700–2800**
  - 29" (74 cm)   **3000–3100**

- Mold 1294
  - 26" (66 cm)   **1100–1250**

- Mold 1299
  - 18" (46 cm)   **700–750**

- Mold 1488
  - 24" (61 cm)   **4750–5000**

CHARACTER TODDLER:
CA. 1912+

Bisque socket head, mohair or human hair wig, glass sleep eyes, open/closed mouth or open mouth, jointed composition toddler body

- Mold 600
  - 11" (28 cm)   **700–750**

- Mold 1299
  - 10–13" (25–33 cm)   **600–650**

- Mold 1428
  - 18" (46 cm)   **1700–1800**
  - 25" (64 cm)   **2400–2600**

- Mold 1488
  - 14" (36 cm)   **2750–2850**
  - 22" (56 cm)   **3300–3500**

E. U. STEINER

Edmund Ulrich Steiner of Sonneberg was in the doll business by 1902, when he registered the name "Steiner's Majestic Doll."

CHILD DOLL MARKED MAJESTIC: TRADEMARK NAME REGISTERED 1902

Bisque head, mohair or human hair wig, glass sleep eyes, open mouth; shoulderhead model has kid body; sockethead model has jointed composition body

- Shoulderhead (heads made by Armand Marseille)

22" (56 cm)	**250–300**
27" (69 cm)	**375–425**

- Socket head

13" (33 cm)	**175–225**
19" (48 cm)	**300–350**
23" (58 cm)	**425–475**
33–36" (84–91 cm)	**900–1100**

TYPICAL MARK:

E. U. St.

ENCLOSED IN A DIAMOND-SHAPED EMBLEM

HERMANN STEINER

Hermann Steiner opened his Tann/Rhon toy company in 1911; however, he didn't make bisque dolls until 1920. Because he came on the scene so late, dolls bearing his mark are mainly the infants and characters popular during the closing years of bisque doll production.

CHILD DOLL: 1920+

Bisque socket head, mohair or human hair wig, glass sleep eyes, open mouth, jointed composition body

7–8 ″ (18–20 cm)	115–140
11 ″ (28 cm)	175–200
16 ″ (41 cm)	275–300
25 ″ (64 cm)	375–425

INFANT: 1925+

Solid-dome bisque socket head, glass sleep eyes, closed mouth, cloth body, celluloid or bisque hands

7–9 ″ (18–23 cm)	125–175

CHARACTER BABY: 1925+

Bisque socket head, mohair or human hair wig, glass sleep eyes, open mouth, composition bent-limb baby body

13 ″ (33 cm)	450–500

TYPICAL MARK:

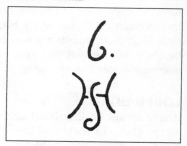

Hermann Steiner infant, 10 ″.
Courtesy of Christie's East.

SWAINE & COMPANY

The Swaine family opened its first porcelain factory near Sonneberg in 1810. One hundred years later, William Swaine was the owner of the company, and dolls were mentioned for the first time. According to the Ciesliks, the factory produced dolls for only a brief period. Most Swaine dolls are recognized by their narrow, uptilted eyes, which many collectors find appealing.

LORI BABY

Bisque socket head, painted hair, glass sleep eyes, open/closed or closed mouth, composition bent-limb baby body

22–23″ (56–58 cm)	2600–2800
25″ (64 cm)	2900–3100

TYPICAL MARK:

Swaine "Lori" baby, incised *232*, 18″. *Courtesy of Christie's East.*

CHARACTER BABY

Bisque socket head, composition bent-limb baby body

- DI (molded and painted hair, painted eyes, closed mouth)
12″ (31 cm)	**500–550**
15–16″ (38–41 cm)	**750–850**

- DIP (wig, glass eyes, open or closed mouth)

- Open mouth
9″ (23 cm)	**400–450**
11–12″ (28–31 cm)	**550–600**

TYPICAL MARKS:

D.V.

OR

D I

OR

D I P

- Closed mouth
  16″ (41 cm)   1200–1400

- DV (molded and painted hair, glass
  eyes, closed mouth)
  10″ (25 cm)   650–700

**Swaine DIP baby, 11 ½″. *Courtesy of
Christie's South Kensington*.**

HERMANN VON BERG

In 1904, Hermann von Berg opened
his doll factory at Huttensteinach,
where he worked for nine years before
moving to Köppelsdorf. He was still in
business in 1938, when the firm of
Schoenau & Hoffmeister was supplying
von Berg with doll heads.

INFANT: 1925+

Bisque head with flange neck, painted hair, glass sleep eyes, open mouth, cloth body or composition bent-limb baby body

18″ (46 cm)   **200–250**

TYPICAL MARK:

H.v.B.

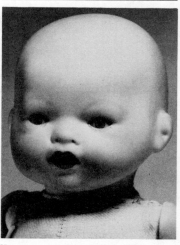

Hermann von Berg infant, 13″.
Courtesy of Christie's South Kensington.

WAGNER & ZETSCHE

Richard Wagner and Richard Zetsche were the founders of the Ilmenau doll factory in 1875. The factory produced doll bodies and finished dolls from 1886 until 1930. The heads were supplied by Gebrüder Heubach and Alt, Beck & Gottschalck.

173

CHILD DOLL, SHOULDERHEAD: BY 1888

Bisque head slightly turned, mohair wig, fixed glass eyes, open mouth, kid body with bisque or composition lower arms; heads by Alt, Beck & Gottschalck

9″ (23 cm)	**100–130**
19″ (48 cm)	**200–225**

TYPICAL MARKS:

OR

W. u. Z.

WELSCH & COMPANY

Ferdinand Welsch and Otto Muhlhauser founded this Sonneberg doll and toy factory in 1911. The Welsch dolls most commonly found today have heads made by Max Oskar Arnold, although the company also used doll heads from Simon & Halbig and Schützmeister & Quendt.

CHILD DOLL WITH MOA MARK: 1920+

Bisque socket head, mohair wig, sleep or set eyes, open mouth, jointed composition body; heads by Max Oskar Arnold

14″ (36 cm)   160–200
23–25″ (58–64 cm)   350–450

TYPICAL MARK:

MOA
Welsch

(MOA enclosed in a star; Welsch in script)

ADOLF WISLIZENUS

Adolf Wislizenus owned a doll and toy factory in Waltershausen from 1878 to 1894. Most of the dolls found today were made during the period that the Heineke family owned the firm, from 1894 to 1931. The bisque doll heads used by the Wislizenus company were supplied by Baehr & Proeschild, Simon & Halbig, and Ernst Heubach.

CHILD DOLL

Bisque socket head, mohair or human hair wig, glass sleep eyes, open mouth, ball-jointed composition body; some marked "Special"

14" (36 cm)	210–240
17–18" (43–46 cm)	300–350
21–23" (53–58 cm)	375–400
24–25" (61–64 cm)	400–450
28–29" (71–74 cm)	550–600
32" (81 cm)	1000–1100

TYPICAL MARK:

AWs
Germany
II

CHARACTER CHILD

Bisque socket head, molded and painted hair, painted eyes, open/closed mouth, ball-jointed composition body.
Mold number: 110

12" (31 cm)	300–350
17–18" (43–46 cm)	950–1150

Wislizenus girl, 24". *Courtesy of Christie's South Kensington.*

AMERICAN DOLLS WITH GERMAN BISQUE HEADS

LOUIS AMBERG & SON

I n 1898, after twenty years of building his toy business in Cincinnati, Louis Amberg moved to New York City, where he worked until his death in 1915. His son Joshua, who had been a partner in the firm since 1912, directed the firm until 1927. The Amberg company is known for its winsome character dolls. One of them, New Born Babe, is also a landmark, having come out nearly ten years before the more famous Bye-Lo.

BABY PEGGY: 1923–1924

Bisque shoulderhead, wig, glass sleep eyes, closed mouth, kid body with bisque lower arms; portrait of child star Baby Peggy Montgomery; head made by Armand Marseille

18–19″ (46–48 cm)	2200–2400
21–22″ (53–56 cm)	2550–2700

TYPICAL MARK:

19©24
LA & S NY
Germany

WITH MOLD NUMBER BENEATH

NEW BORN BABE: 1914+

Bisque socket head with flange neck, painted hair, glass sleep eyes, open mouth, cloth body with composition lower arms or cloth body with celluloid hands; designed by Jeno Juszko; heads made by Theodor Recknagel, Limbach, Armand Marseille, and perhaps others

11–12″ (28–31 cm)	350–400
14–16″ (36–41 cm)	500–600

TYPICAL MARK:

LA & S
RA 241
GERMANY

Amber "New Born Babe," 12 ½".
Courtesy of Christie's East.

GEO. BORGFELDT & CO.

A native of Germany, George Borgfeldt immigrated to America in 1853 at the age of twenty. Starting as a bookkeeper, Borgfeldt worked in several different businesses before becoming a partner in the toy firm of Strasburger, Ffeiffer & Co. in 1873. With two other

Strasburger employees, Marcell and Joseph Kahle, Borgfeldt formed the co-partnership of Geo. Borgfeldt & Co. in 1881. Borgfeldt conceived the idea of the sample showroom, where buyers from American department stores could view the best of the available European products and place orders, thus saving the stores the time and expense of sending their own buyers abroad. This novel approach to business proved so successful that within five years Borgfeldt had opened branch offices in England, France, Germany, Canada, and Bohemia. As early as 1895 Borgfeldt became involved in the manufacturing end of the business to the extent of registering doll trademark names and having his initials included in marks on dolls made for him by several German companies. In 1900 George Borgfeldt retired, and his partner, Marcell Kahle, became president of the company.

BONNIE BABE:
TRADEMARK 1926

Bisque head, painted hair, glass sleep eyes, open mouth with two lower teeth, dimples, cloth body, composition arms and legs; designed by Georgene Averill; heads made by Alt, Beck & Gottschalck

TYPICAL MARK:

Copr by
Georgene Averill
1005
Germany

15–16″ (38–41 cm)	**650–750**
22″ (56 cm)	**1100–1250**

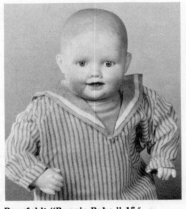

Borgfeldt "Bonnie Babe," 15″.
Courtesy of Christie's East.

CHILD DOLL

Bisque socket head, mohair wig, glass sleep eyes, open mouth, ball-jointed composition body; typical names: My Girlie (trademark 1912), Pansy (trademark 1921)

21″ (53 cm)	**300–350**
23–25″ (58–64 cm)	**400–500**

TYPICAL MARK:

NAME OF DOLL

CHARACTER BABY

Bisque socket head, wig, composition bent-limb baby body; heads by Armand Marseille

- Marked G. B. (open mouth)

18–19″ (46–48 cm)	**350–450**
23″ (58 cm)	**550–600**
25–26″ (64–66 cm)	**750–850**

- Mold 251 (open-closed mouth): GM 1912

10″ (25 cm)	**275–300**

TYPICAL MARK:

g B.

180

12″ (31 cm)	350–400

- Mold 329 (open mouth): GM 1913

14″ (36 cm)	300–350
20″ (51 cm)	450–500

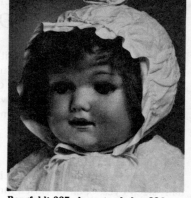

Borgfeldt 327 character baby, 22″.
Courtesy of Christie's South Kensington.

CHARACTER TODDLER

Bisque socket head, wig, glass sleep eyes, jointed composition toddler body; heads made by Armand Marseille

- Mold 251 (open/closed mouth): GM 1912

12–15″ (31–38 cm)	1100–1400

- Mold 327 (open mouth): GM 1912

24″ (61 cm)	650–700

JUST ME: TRADEMARK 1929

Bisque socket head, mohair or human hair wig, side-glancing glass sleep eyes, rosebud mouth, five-piece composition body; heads made by Armand Marseille

7–9″ (18–23 cm)	1000–1200
12″ (31 cm)	1300–1500
Painted bisque	650–750

TYPICAL MARK:

$G\ 327\ B$
Germany
A 12 M

TYPICAL MARK:

**Just Me
Registered
Germany**

CENTURY DOLL CO.

Founded in 1909 in New York City by Max Scheuer, Century Doll Co. made many composition mama and child dolls, but its most popular doll was a bisque-head infant designed to compete with the Bye-Lo in 1925.

INFANT: 1925+

Bisque head with flange neck, painted hair, sleep eyes, open or closed mouth, cloth body, composition arms and legs or celluloid hands; heads made by Kestner

14–15″ (36–38 cm)	500–600
18–20″ (46–51 cm)	800–900

TYPICAL MARK:

CENTURY D°LLC°

WITH THE KESTNER K IN A DIAMOND OR THE FULL KESTNER NAME BENEATH (ON HEAD)

Century bisque-head infant. *Private collection*.

HAMBURGER & CO.

A New York import firm with branch offices in Berlin and Nuremberg, Hamburger & Co. operated from 1889 until 1909. The company registered the following trademarks for the dolls it sold: Imperial, in 1898; Santa, in 1900; Old Glory and Marguerite, in 1902; Viola, in 1903; Dolly Dimple, in 1907.

DOLLY DIMPLE: TRADEMARK 1907

Bisque shoulderhead or socket head, mohair or human hair wig, glass sleep eyes, open mouth; shoulderhead model has kid body; socket-head model has jointed composition body; heads made by Gebrüder Heubach

- Shoulderhead version

19″ (48 cm)	**500–550**
22″ (56 cm)	**650–700**

TYPICAL MARK:

5777 DEP DOLLY DIMPLE H

WITH ONE OF GEBRÜDER HEUBACH'S SYMBOLS BENEATH

Hamburger "Dolly Dimple" shoulderhead, 22″. *Courtesy of Marvin Cohen Auctions.*

SANTA: TRADEMARK 1900

Bisque socket head, mohair or human hair wig, glass sleep eyes, pierced ears, open mouth, ball-jointed composition body; heads made by Simon & Halbig

12–13″ (31–33 cm)	450–500
16–19″ (41–48 cm)	650–750
22–24″ (56–61 cm)	800–950
27–29″ (69–74 cm)	1100–1400
37″ (94 cm)	1900–2200

TYPICAL MARK:

S & H
1249 DEP
SANTA

Hamburger "Santa" girl, 19″.
Courtesy of Christie's South Kensington.

VIOLA: TRADEMARK 1902

Bisque socket head, mohair or human hair wig, glass sleep eyes, open mouth, ball-jointed composition or composition and wood body; heads probably made by Schoenau & Hoffmeister

22–23″ (56–58 cm)	**300–350**
24–25″ (61–64 cm)	**400–500**
30″ (76 cm)	**850–900**

TYPICAL MARK:

Viola
H & CO.

Hamburger "Viola," 28″. *Courtesy of Christie's East.*

MOLDED-HAIR BISQUE

The molded-hair bisque category encompasses an enormous variety of dolls, from tiny white-bisque penny dolls to the high-quality aristocratic ladies of the third quarter of the 19th century. It is these latter dolls that most often come to mind when molded-hair bisques are mentioned. Collectors have traditionally called them "parians" after a type of silky white unpainted porcelain called "parian ware" used during the mid-19th century. This porcelain was made into miniature copies of classical statuary, to be placed on Victorian mantelpieces. As true parian ware bears little resemblance to any of the dolls in this category, the name is slowly being phased out.

After falling out of favor during the 1970s and early 1980s, the pale, elegant bisque ladies with their elaborate, ornamented coiffures are finding appreciation once again, as demonstrated by currently rising prices.

Originally, the shoulderheads were frequently purchased alone and given as trinkets to adult women, to be placed on a boudoir table or made into a doll. For this reason, very refined heads are often found on out-of-scale homemade cloth bodies, which only adds to their charm.

Also included in the molded-hair bisque category are the lovely flesh-tinted children of the late 19th century, as typified by the products of Alt, Beck & Gottschalck. Although not as expensive as the earlier lady dolls, the children are frequently of excellent quality, with short molded blond curls and painted or glass eyes.

Almost all molded-hair bisques were made in Germany, and aside from the small, coarse "sugar bisques" made for the bottom end of the market, you will find that the general quality is consistently high.

PRICE ADJUSTMENTS FOR CONDITION

Hairline crack in head, front	−50%
Hairline crack in head, back	−30%
Large crack or repair to head	−50 to −70%
Broken hair ornament	−30 to −50%
Body in poor condition	−25%
Replaced body	−30%
Wearing exceptional original clothing	+30 to +50%

LADY DOLLS

SHOULDERHEAD MODELS: 1860s–1880s

Untinted or pale tinted bisque shoulderhead, molded and painted hair (elaborately styled, sometimes with glazed or luster ornaments), occasionally with pierced ears, closed mouth, cloth body with kid or bisque arms

* Type I: painted eyes and blond hair

11–13 " (28–33 cm)	375–425
15–17 " (38–43 cm)	500–550
18–20 " (46–51 cm)	550–600
21–23 " (53–58 cm)	625–700
24–26 " (61–66 cm)	700–800

* Plain hairstyle and coarse bisque

14 " (36 cm)	200–250
21–24 " (53–61 cm)	300–400
26–27 " (66–69 cm)	450–500

Bisque lady with molded hair and painted eyes, 21 ". *Courtesy of Christie's East*.

* Type II: painted eyes, blond hair, and molded yoke

10 " (25 cm)	300–350
14–15 " (36–38 cm)	475–525
17 " (43 cm)	600–625
23–24 " (58–61 cm)	700–750

* Type III: painted eyes, brown hair

23 " (58 cm)	550–600

* Type IV: glass eyes

12–15 " (31–38 cm)	500–600
20 " (51 cm)	750–800+

Bisque lady with dark molded hair, molded hair ornament, and jewelry, 18 ½ ". *Courtesy of Richard W. Withington, Inc.*

SWIVEL-HEAD MODEL

Bisque swivel head on shoulderplate, molded and painted blond or brown hair, glass eyes, some with pierced ears, closed mouth, cloth body with kid or bisque arms

17–18" (43–46 cm)	**1200–1500**
22–26" (56–66 cm)	**1750–2000**

Swivel-head bisque lady with glass eyes and pierced ears, 15 1/2 ".
Courtesy of Richard W. Withington, Inc.

MALE DOLLS

Bisque shoulderhead with molded and painted blond hair, painted or glass eyes, exposed ears, closed mouth, cloth body with bisque or kid arms

- Type I: painted eyes

12" (31 cm)	**200–250**
23" (58 cm)	**500–600**

- Type II: glass eyes

16" (41 cm)	**1000–1200**

Bisque gentleman with molded hair, shirt yoke, and lustre tie, 16 1/2 ".
Courtesy of Richard W. Withington, Inc.

CELLULOID

Celluloid is a type of plastic made from nitrocellulose mixed with camphor, various fillers, and chemicals. It is laid into a mold in thin sheets and then given its desired form when hot air is forced into the mold.

Although it was introduced in the early 1870s as a doll-making material and has been used in many countries, celluloid dolls (with the exception of late European souvenir dolls) are relatively rare today. This is partly because the material was never as popular as bisque or composition and therefore wasn't used in great quantities. Also, celluloid becomes brittle with time and is easily broken. Because it is so thin, it is nearly impossible to repair. On the plus side, celluloid dolls are relatively inexpensive; they can be found in immensely appealing, imaginative forms; and if you find them in excellent condition, there is no reason why they shouldn't remain so if given proper care.

PRICE ADJUSTMENTS FOR CONDITION

Major crack or piece missing	−50 to −80%
Small crack	−30%
Mild discoloration	−30%
Extreme discoloration (orange)	−60 to −70%
Mint condition with original wig and clothing	+50%

ALL-CELLULOID

CHILD

All-celluloid, molded and painted hair, painted or glass eyes, closed mouth; unjointed, jointed at shoulders, or jointed at neck, shoulders, and hips

7–10″ (18–25 cm)	50–75
14″ (36 cm)	90–120
16–18″ (41–46 cm)	140–175
20″ (51 cm)	200–250

* Dressed souvenir doll: 1920s–1940s

7–10″ (18–25 cm)	30–40

* Frozen Charlotte type: 1900–1910

3–5″ (8–13 cm)	30–50

All-celluloid brown islander, 5 1/2″.
Courtesy of Christie's East.

BABY

All-celluloid, molded hair, painted or glass eyes, open or closed mouth, bent-limb baby body, jointed at shoulders and hips

3–4″ (8–10 cm)	25–35
11–14″ (28–36 cm)	75–125
15–18″ (38–46 cm)	125–175
21–24″ (53–61 cm)	175–225

Celluloid souvenir doll in regional costume, 7″. *Courtesy of Christie's East.*

PARSONS-JACKSON BABY
All-celluloid, socket head, molded hair, painted eyes, open/closed mouth, five-piece bent-limb baby body

12–14" (31–36 cm)   150–175

TYPICAL MARK:

THE PARSONS-JACKSON CO.
CLEVELAND, OHIO.

WITH STORK TRADEMARK

CELLULOID HEAD

SHOULDERHEAD MODEL: 1900–1920
Celluloid shoulderhead, usually mohair wig (sometimes molded hair), painted or glass eyes, open or closed mouth, oil cloth or kid body, celluloid or composition arms

- Child
10–11" (25–28 cm)	100–140
15–18" (38–46 cm)	225–275
23–27" (58–69 cm)	300–400

- Baby
16" (41 cm)	275–300

Kämmer & Reinhardt 225 celluloid shoulderheaded girl with glass eyes, 16". *Courtesy of Sotheby's, New York.*

SOCKET-HEAD MODEL: 1910+
Celluloid socket head, mohair wig, glass eyes, five-piece composition body

19–24" (48–61 cm)   250–400

KÄTHE KRUSE CHILD DOLL:
1955–1958
Celluloid socket head, human hair wig,
painted eyes, closed mouth, muslin
body

14–15″ (36–38 cm)	**300–350**
17″ (43 cm)	**375–400**

CHINA

Perhaps the most undervalued of all antique dolls, chinas represent a good buy for those who appreciate their serene beauty. Nearly all of them were made in Germany, and "china" is simply the collector's term for glazed porcelain. The vast majority of these dolls were produced with molded black hair and blue eyes. Wigs, unusual molded hair styles, brown eyes, or glass eyes are rare and greatly enhance the doll's value. Flesh tints, especially after 1860, are unusual as well. Blond or brown hair is also rare, although after about 1880 nearly one in three china dolls was produced with blond hair. During the mid-1800s, china heads were the most popular of all dolls, but with the arrival of the more realistic bisque heads in the last third of the century, china quickly became "second best."

During the 1880s, Alt, Beck and Gottschalck designed charming, high-grade china heads representing children. But aside from these, the quality of most china products deteriorated into the familiar "low brows" that flooded the market at the end of the 19th century. These inexpensive dolls with dull expressions continued to roll off the assembly lines until the late 1930s and beyond. Their large number and recent production is one reason many collectors shortsightedly shun all china dolls.

PRICE ADJUSTMENTS FOR CONDITION

Repaired head	− 60 to − 80%
Repaired shoulderplate	− 40 to − 50%
Cracked head	− 50 to − 70%
Cracked shoulderplate	− 30%
Chips in molded hair	− 20 to − 30%
Fading of painted features	− 20 to − 50%
Moderate kiln dirt (black specks) on head	− 30%
Worn body	− 30%
Replaced body	− 30 to − 40%
Original good clothing in fine condition	+ 30 to + 50%

ALT, BECK & GOTTSCHALCK

CHINA SHOULDERHEAD: CA. 1890+

Molded and painted black or blond hair in short curls with bangs and brush marks, painted or glass eyes, closed mouth, cloth body, china or kid arms and legs.

Mold numbers: 1000, 1008, 1028, 1030, and others

25–28″ (64–71 cm) **400–500**

TYPICAL MARK:

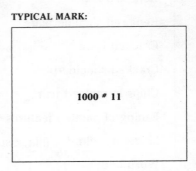

1000 # 11

HERTWIG & CO.

CHINA SHOULDERHEAD WITH NAME: REG. 1895

Molded and painted black or blond hair in rows of short, all-over curls; painted blue eyes, closed mouth, molded collar and bow with name in gold letters beneath, cloth body, china lower arms and legs; made for Butler Brothers; names: Agnes, Bertha, Dorothy, Edith, Esther, Florence, Helen, Mabel, Marion, Pauline, and Ruth

8″ (20 cm)	**40–60**
11–13″ (28–33 cm)	**80–110**
16–18″ (41–46 cm)	**120–150**
20–21″ (51–53 cm)	**175–225**
23–24″ (58–61 cm)	**250–300**

UNKNOWN
——— GERMAN ———
MANUFACTURERS

LONG CURLS: 1840s

White or flesh-tinted china shoulder-head with molded and painted black shoulder-length curls, painted brown or blue eyes, closed mouth, cloth body, often with leather arms

- Blue eyes
  14–16″ (36–41 cm) 1000–1500

- Brown eyes
  17″ (43 cm) 1400–1800

BUN: 1840s

China shoulderhead with molded and painted black hair (bun in back; some with exposed ears and/or brushmarks around face), cloth body

4–6″ (10–15 cm)	**350–450**
23″ (58 cm)	**1500–1750**

Brown-eyed 1840s china doll, 17″.
Courtesy of Christie's East.

China lady with 1840s-style braided bun, 24″. Courtesy of Richard W. Withington, Inc.

PEG-WOODEN BODY: 1840s–1850s

Flesh-tinted china shoulderhead, long molded and painted black curls, bun or "covered wagon" style hairdo, painted eyes, closed mouth, peg-jointed wood body, usually with china lower arms and legs

197

5–7" (13–18 cm)	850–1150
15" (38 cm)	2000–2100

"BERLIN-TYPE": CA. 1850

Flesh-tinted shoulderhead (coloring sometimes uneven) with very rosy cheeks, painted eyes, closed mouth, well-proportioned features, cloth body

18–20" (46–51 cm)	1200+

"Berlin-type" china doll representing a young girl, 20". *Courtesy of Christie's East.*

"COVERED WAGON": 1840s+

Pink-tint china shoulderhead with molded and painted black hair (center part, smooth to eye level, where row of vertical, chin-length corkscrew curls begins), painted blue or brown eyes, closed mouth; cloth body with cloth, kid, or china lower arms and legs

- Blue eyes

11–13" (28–33 cm)	300–350
17–19" (43–48 cm)	450–550
21–25" (53–64 cm)	700–850

- Brown eyes

13" (33 cm)	425–450
25" (64 cm)	1000–1200

"Covered Wagon" china, 21". *Courtesy of Christie's East.*

BALD: 1840s–1860s

White or pink-tint china shoulderhead (some with circular black-painted area on top of head), wig, blue painted eyes, closed mouth, kid or cloth body, some with china arms and legs

11–12 ″ (28–31 cm)	350–400
15 ″ (38 cm)	550–650
22 ″ (56 cm)	900–1000

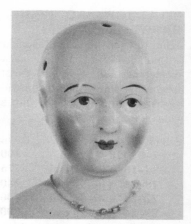

Bald china lady with painted brown eyes, four sew holes in her crown, 24 ″. *Courtesy of Christie's South Kensington.*

GLASS EYES: 1850s–1870s

White or pink-tint china shoulderhead with molded and painted black hair or open crown with wig, inset glass eyes, closed mouth, cloth body or kid body with china arms

- Molded black hair
  18 ″ (46 cm)   1800–2200

- Open crown with wig
  18 ″ (46 cm)   2500–3000

- Rohmer-type
  16–18 ″ (41–46 cm) 3500–5000

Bald china lady with blue, glass eyes, 25 ″. *Courtesy of Richard W. Withington, Inc.*

"FLAT TOP" AND "HIGH BROW": 1850s–1870s

White or pink-tint china shoulderhead with molded and painted black hair (center part, short vertical curls) high forehead, painted blue or brown eyes, closed mouth, cloth body with kid or china lower arms and legs

Flesh-tinted "high brow" china, 15".
Courtesy of Christie's East.

- Blue eyes

7–9" (18–23 cm)	100–140
13–16" (33–41 cm)	175–225
18–20" (46–51 cm)	240–280
22–24" (56–61 cm)	300–350
28–34" (71–86 cm)	500–750

- Brown eyes

14" (36 cm)	300–350
17–18" (43–46 cm)	425–475
20–22" (51–56 cm)	550–600
29" (74 cm)	750–800

ELABORATE HAIR STYLES: 1860s–1870s

White or pink-tint china shoulderhead, painted black hair (sometimes blond) molded with coiled braids, knots, wings, or other stylish elements, sometimes brush-stroked hairlines and/or molded accessories such as snoods, feathers, or flowers; cloth body with china or leather arms and legs

China lady with elaborate 1870s hairstyle, 18½". *Courtesy of Richard W. Withington, Inc.*

16–20" (41–51 cm)	600+

- Blond hair

17" (43 cm)	800–1200

- Pierced ears

16–18" (41–46 cm)	750+

"CURLY-TOP" 1870s

White china shoulderhead with molded and painted black, brown, or blond hair (large, evenly spaced horizontal curls on top of head, tapering at forehead), painted blue eyes, closed mouth, cloth body with china lower arms

12″ (31 cm)	350–400
16″ (41 cm)	550–600

"Curly-top" china, 17″. *Courtesy of Richard W. Withington, Inc.*

BANGS: 1880s

White or pink-tint china shoulderhead with molded and painted black or blond hair (all-over short curls with bangs and brush strokes where bangs meet face), painted blue eyes, closed mouth, cloth body, sometimes with china or kid lower arms and legs

15–17″ (38–43 cm)	300–400
20″ (51 cm)	450–500

CHILD: 1880s

White china shoulderhead with molded and painted black or blond hair (often with center part, short wavy or curly hair, and exposed ears), blue painted eyes, closed mouth, cloth or kid body with china arms and legs

8–10″ (20–25 cm)	100–150
16–17″ (41–43 cm)	225–275
19–21″ (48–53 cm)	300–350
22–24″ (56–61 cm)	375–425
26″ (66 cm)	450–500

Kling china-head child. *Private collection.*

201

COMMON: 1890s–1930s

White china shoulderhead with molded and painted black or blond hair (rows of all-over curls ending in scallops around the face), painted blue eyes, closed mouth, cloth body, some with china or bisque lower arms and legs

5–7″ (13–18 cm)	40–50
9–11″ (23–28 cm)	60–80
12–15″ (31–38 cm)	100–150
18–20″ (46–51 cm)	175–215
25″ (64 cm)	250–275

Late "low-brow" china doll, 23″. *Martie Cook*.

MAN: 1850s–1870s

White china shoulderhead with molded and painted black hair (very short, slightly wavy hair with brush strokes all around face), painted blue eyes, closed mouth, cloth or kid body

8″ (20 cm)	350–400
16–17″ (41–43 cm)	800–1200

Boy china shoulderhead, pink-tinted, ca. 1850, 3″. *Courtesy of Christie's East*.

FROZEN CHARLOTTE: 1850+

One-piece white or flesh-tinted girl or boy ("Charlie") china doll, molded and painted black or blond center-parted hair, painted blue or brown eyes, closed mouth, arms often extending forward from bent elbows

• Black hair and blue eyes

2–3″ (5–8 cm)	30–50
4–6″ (10–15 cm)	100–150
7–9″ (18–23 cm)	150–200
12–15″ (31–38 cm)	300–400

Flesh-tinted china "Frozen Charlotte," 5″. *Julie Collier*.

- Unusual hair style or decoration
  4–7″ (10–18 cm)   **200+**
- Blond hair or brown eyes
  4–6″ (10–15 cm)   **150–200**

Crib Note: *About 15 years ago, large flesh-colored Frozen "Charlies," once very rare, began to come on the market in relatively large numbers. They looked so good it was hard to believe they could be reproductions, but they were strangely without wear. Collectors speculated that these Frozen "Charlies" (or Badekinder) might have been from some long-forgotten stock, recently discovered in a basement or warehouse. The problem is that finds like that are welcome and usually make news. These dolls came without a story, and their origin is still a mystery.*

CLOTH

C loth dolls are currently enjoying immense popularity, with high-quality makers such as Käthe Kruse, Lenci, and Steiff rising in price faster than nearly any other category. Also finding favor and very sought after by collectors of folk art and Americana are early handmade cloth dolls and those of secondary quality, such as dolls manufactured by Chase and Rollinson. It's entirely possible that the turn-of-the-century homemade doll you spot in a thrift shop for $30—but reject because it has only one leg and its face is worn bare—will turn up at ten times the price in a classy Madison Avenue shop specializing in primitive sculpture.

PRICE ADJUSTMENTS FOR CONDITION

Face stained	−20 to −40%
Face faded	−30 to −60%
Small holes in face	−20 to −40%
Tears or large hole in face	−50 to −80%
Flattening of molded face	−40 to −60%
Clothes missing from a doll for which clothing is an intrinsic part, such as Lenci or Steiff	−40 to −60%
Pristine condition, wearing original clothes	+100 to +200%

ALABAMA
INDESTRUCTIBLE DOLL

Ella Smith of Roanoke, Alabama, produced cloth dolls from 1900 until 1925. Each of the dolls was handmade by Mrs. Smith or one of her assistants. During the production period, Mrs. Smith obtained several patents regarding the construction of her dolls.

DOLL: 1900–1925
All-cloth, molded head with oil-painted hair (occasionally wigged) and features, applied ears, oil-painted arms and legs sewn separately

12–14″ (31–36 cm)	1100–1250
18–19″ (46–48 cm)	1750–1900
21–22″ (53–56 cm)	2200–2350

TYPICAL MARK:

MRS. S.S. SMITH
MANUFACTURER
ROANOKE, ALA.

ON BODY

Alabama Baby, 13 ½″. *Courtesy of Richard W. Withington, Inc.*

205

ALEXANDER DOLL CO.

Madame Alexander's career in the doll business began in the late 1920s with cloth dolls that she and her three sisters made, painted, and dressed. The early clothing is tagged and the dolls are unmarked.

ALICE IN WONDERLAND: TRADEMARK 1930

All-cloth, yellow yarn hair, some with mask face, painted features

16–20 ″ (41–51 cm)	350–400

BOBBY Q AND SUSIE Q: 1940

All-cloth, yarn hair (Susie with braids and bangs), molded mask face, painted side-glancing eyes, brightly painted cheeks, rosebud mouth, striped stockings, shoes with spats

13 ″ (33 cm)	250–300
16 ″ (41 cm)	400–500

Alexander "Susie Q," 13 ″. *Courtesy of Christie's East.*

LITTLE SHAVER: 1937–1941

All-cloth, floss or fine yarn hair, molded mask face with painted features; stockinette body, arms, and legs

7 ″ (18 cm)	150–200
10–12 ″ (25–31 cm)	225–275
18–20 ″ (46–51 cm)	350–400

ART FABRIC MILLS

One of the largest producers of printed cloth dolls to be cut out, stuffed, and sewn, this New York company was in business from 1899 until 1910. The dolls continued to be produced into the 1920s by successors Selchow & Righter, who previously distributed them. Similar cut-out dolls were created by Arnold Print Works and other American firms, many as advertising premiums.

MARK:

PAT. FEB. 13, 1900

ON SOLE OF FOOT

TYPE I:
Child doll with printed undergarments, face, and hair: "Life Size Doll," "Dolly Dimple," "Merrie Marie," etc.

7″ (18 cm)	**60–90**
20″ (51 cm)	**150–200**
30″ (76 cm)	**200–250**

• Complete uncut doll
24–26″ (61–66 cm)	**300–400**

TYPE II:
Black children

20″ (51 cm)	**350–500**

TYPE III:
Character dolls: Punch and Judy, Buster Brown, Colonial Family, etc.; ca. 1900

20–24″ (51–61 cm)	**200–400**

Advertising premium doll for Richfield butter. *Courtesy of Marvin Cohen Auctions.*

BROWNIES

A writer and illustrator, Palmer Cox (1840–1924) developed the idea of the Brownies from childhood stories of the legends of Scotland's Grampian mountains. The first of the Brownies' adventures appeared in *St. Nicholas* magazine in 1883. Children were so captivated by these sprightly little creatures and their stories that nine years after the first story appeared, Cox designed twelve printed-cloth dolls so that the children could have their own Brownies to play with. The dolls were sold by the yard, ready to be cut out, stuffed, and sewn.

BROWNIE

Two-piece printed-cloth doll; characters included John Bull, Canadian, Chinaman, Dude, German, Highlander, Indian, Irishman, Policeman, Sailor, Soldier, and Uncle Sam; produced by the Arnold Print Works of North Adams, Massachusetts

7″ (18 cm)   100–125

TYPICAL MARK:

**Copyrighted 1892
by PALMER COX**

ON FOOT

BRUCKNER

Albert Bruckner of Jersey City, New Jersey, used his background in lithography to create a cloth doll with a molded and printed face. After patenting his idea in 1901, Bruckner produced the dolls for twenty-five years. Following his death in 1926, his sons continued the business into the 1930s. Some of his dolls were probably sold by E. I. Horsman.

BRUCKNER DOLL
All-cloth, molded mask face, printed features and hair

12″ (31 cm)	300–350
15″ (38 cm)	500–600

TYPICAL MARK:

PAT'D. JULY 8TH 1901

ON FRONT OF NECK

CHAD VALLEY

Originally a printing firm called Johnson Brothers, this English company first produced dolls around 1917 in its Chad Valley plant. Two of Chad Valley's best known designers of the 1920s were Norah Wellings and Mabel Lucie Atwell.

CHAD VALLEY DOLLS
All-cloth, felt face; usually velvet body, arms, and legs; mohair wig, glass or painted eyes; jointed at neck, shoulders, and hips

- Child with glass eyes

10–12″ (25–31 cm)	325–375
14–15″ (36–38 cm)	500–550

- Child with painted eyes

15″ (38 cm)	250–300

TYPICAL MARK:

HYGENIC TOYS
MADE IN ENGLAND BY
CHAD VALLEY CO. LTD.

LABEL USUALLY ON FOOT

- Royal Family
  15–20″ (38–51 cm)   1000–1250
- Snow White and Seven Dwarfs
  Set   1300–1500
  Dwarf 7″ (18 cm)   300–350

Chad Valley girl with painted eyes, 16″. *Julie Collier*.

CHASE

Martha Jenks Chase of Pawtucket, Rhode Island, produced painted stockinette dolls from about 1890 until her death in 1925. Other family members continued to produce the stockinette dolls for another ten years. Chase also produced sand-weighted babies and life-size adult dolls to be used as teaching aids in hospitals.

CHASE DOLLS
All-cloth; oil-painted head, forearms, and lower legs; soft cotton or pink sateen body

- Baby (applied ears, flexible at shoulders, elbows, hips, and knees)
  16–17″ (41–43 cm)   500–550
  20–24″ (51–61 cm)   600–750
  27–28″ (69–71 cm)   1000–1250

TYPICAL MARK:

- Child (molded bobbed hair)
   - 16–18" (41–46 cm)   550–650
   - 20–21" (51–53 cm)   650–700
   - 26" (66 cm)   1200–1500

- Hospital Baby
   - 21" (53 cm)   325–375

- Hospital Lady
   - 64" (163 cm)   1300–1500

Crib Note: Chase dolls usually show a moderate degree of wear; the hair is especially vulnerable to chipping. Deduct up to 50% for significant paint loss.

Chase baby, 12". *Courtesy of Christie's East.*

COLUMBIAN

Beginning in 1892, the Adams sisters of Oswego, New York, made and dressed cloth dolls in their home. The face of each doll made before 1900 was handpainted by Emma Adams. After Emma's death, Marietta Adams continued the business for another ten years, hiring artists to paint the dolls' faces.

211

COLUMBIAN DOLL

All-cloth; handpainted hair and features, lower arms, and legs; flexible at shoulders, hips, and knees

15–21″ (38–53 cm)   3400–3800

TYPICAL MARKS:
1892–1900

COLUMBIAN DOLL
EMMA E. ADAMS
OSWEGO CENTRE
NY

1906+

THE COLUMBIAN DOLL
MANUFACTURED BY
MARIETTA ADAMS RUTTAN
OSWEGO, N.Y.

STAMPED ON BACK

E. I. HORSMAN CO.

BABYLAND RAG: 1893–1920

All-cloth, painted or lithographed face and hair (sometimes human hair), jointed at shoulders and hips

- Painted face
  - 13–15″ (33–38 cm)   450–550
  - 22″ (56 cm)   600–700

- Printed face
  - 13–15″ (33–38 cm)   275–350

Horsman "Babyland" rag doll, 21″.
Courtesy of Christie's East.

EMBROIDERED WORSTED: 1893+

All-cloth, yarn hair, embroidered features and costumes; dressed as harlequins, clowns, etc.

17" (43 cm)   **250–300**

Embroidered worsted doll, probably Horsman, 17". *Courtesy of Marvin Cohen Auctions.*

KAMKINS

These difficult-to-find boy and girl dolls were made during the 1920s by Louise Kampes in Atlantic City, New Jersey, and were sold in her boardwalk shop there. A bit too "dolly-faced" to be considered a true art doll, Kamkins had great appeal nevertheless and sold originally for the relatively high price of $10 to $15.

KAMKINS: 1919+

All-cloth, mohair wig, molded mask face with painted features

18–20" (46–51 cm)   **800–1000**

TYPICAL MARK:

KAMKINS
A DOLLY MADE TO LOVE
PATENTED
FROM
L. R. KAMPES
STUDIOS
ATLANTIC CITY
N.J.

ON HEAD, CHEST, OR FOOT

KÄTHE KRUSE

German dollmaker Käthe Kruse was one of a number of talented early 20th-century painters who channeled their artistic energies into creating dolls. She made them first for her own children, then found success later by mass-marketing them. Kruse struggled for several years with various designs and potential manufacturers until 1911, when a well-received shipment to America started her fledgling company on the road to success.

Many collectors have been disconcerted to learn that Kruse's model for the first doll was not one of her children but a popular late Renaissance bust of a young child, and that she probably used a plaster copy of it to make the mold for her heads. As the Ciesliks point out, several other companies used the same model, including Armand Marseille for "Fany" and Kämmer & Reinhardt for their mold 115 characters. Because of the unique quality of construction and decoration, however, the Kruse dolls soon took on delightful characters of their own. As more models were added to the line, they achieved such a degree of popularity that Kruse's dolls are still being successfully produced today, nearly thirty years after her death.

DOLL I: 1910+

All muslin, oil-painted hair and features, pensive closed mouth, three vertical seams in back of head, chubby toddler body

- 1910–1930: wide hips, separately sewn thumb, deer or reindeer hair stuffing
- 1929+: some have wigs; after 1936, wigged version called IH

    17″ (43 cm)   **1800–2200**

TYPICAL MARK:
1911–1955

Käthe Kruse

STAMPED ON LEFT FOOT (WITH NUMBERS)

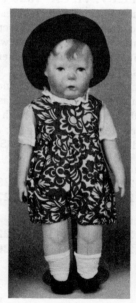

Käthe Kruse doll I, 17″. *Courtesy of Christie's East.*

BAMBINO: CA. 1915+

Used the Doll I face; very rare

8–9″ (20–23 cm) No price available

DOLL II: SCHLENKERCHEN: 1922–1930s

All-stockinette, oil-painted hair and features; painted upper eyelashes, smiling open-closed mouth; head, arms, and legs loosely sewn; one vertical seam in back of head

13" (33 cm)   **1300–1500**

Käthe Kruse "Schlenkerchen," 13".
Courtesy of Christie's East.

DOLLS V, VI: CA. 1925+

Roman numerals refer to sizes (V = 20" [51 cm] and VI = 24" [61 cm]) rather than faces; both V and VI were made with closed eyes (Traümerchen) or open eyes (DuMein).

All-cloth, oil-painted hair and features (Traümerchen has painted lashes; after 1930 DuMein also came with thin wig); closed, turned-down mouth; some had sand added for extra weight (Sand Baby)

- Traümerchen
  - **20" (51 cm)**   **2300–2500**
  - **24" (61 cm)**   **2700–2900**

- DuMein
  - **20" (51 cm)**   **2200–2400**
  - **24" 961 cm)**   **2600–2800**

Käthe Kruse "DuMein," model VI, 19 1/2". *Courtesy of Christie's East.*

DOLL VII: 1927+

- Type I: 1927–1930
  Used the DuMein face, painted hair
  (1927–1930), wigged (1929–1930)
- Type II: 1927–1950s
  Used the Doll I face; painted hair or,
  after 1929, wigged
  14″ (36 cm)   **1100–1400**

DOLL VIII, GERMAN
CHILD: 1929+

All-cloth, one vertical seam in back or
swivel head, human hair wig, painted
features, closed mouth

21″ (53 cm)   **900–1100**

**Small Käthe Kruse "DuMein," model
VII, 14″.** *Courtesy of Christie's East.*

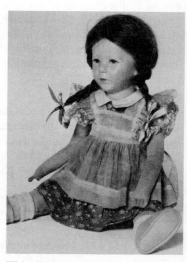

DOLL IX, SMALL GERMAN
CHILD: 1929+

Same as Doll VIII, only smaller

14″ (36 cm)   **750–800**

DOLL X: CA. 1935+

Used Doll I face, swivel head

14″ (36 cm)   **450–500**

Käthe Kruse doll VIII, 14″. *Courtesy
of Christie's East.*

LENCI

Few dolls have been imitated as much as the costly Lenci dolls created by Elena Konig Scavini. In 1918 Scavini and her brother began turning out pressed-felt dolls from her Turin apartment. Immediately successful, Scavini shrewdly hired artists to carry the creative end of the business further than she herself could, while she concentrated her own talents on concept and marketing. Their sophisticated designs and high quality of Scavini's product appealed to adults as well as to children, assuring even stronger sales. While Lenci dolls have a very distinctive look, it is often difficult to attribute untagged examples since so many models were produced and so many other companies copied them. True Lencis are only occasionally stamped on their feet.

DOLLS: 1919+

All-felt or felt with muslin body, molded head and features, mohair wig, painted (occasionally glass) side-glancing eyes, closed or open/closed mouth, swivel head, jointed at shoulders and hips

- Child:
  Model 100
  18″ (46 cm)   2400

  Models 109, 111, 300, and similar models

TYPICAL MARK:

218

12–13″ (31–33 cm)	575–625
14–15″ (36–38 cm)	650–750
16–18″ (41–46 cm)	850–1000
22–23″ (56–58 cm)	1300–1500

Model 110
17–18″ (43–46 cm)	1300–1500

Model 1500 (broad, frowning face)
17″ (43 cm)	1400–1700

• Glass eyes
19–20″ (48–51 cm)	2700–3000

• Lady
15″ (38 cm)	700–800

Lenci character child, probably from the III series, 13″. *Courtesy of Christie's South Kensington.*

Lenci girls 110 and 109, 17 and 22″. *Courtesy of Sotheby's New York.*

23–25″ (58–64 cm) 1350–1600
26–28″ (66–71 cm) 1500–1800
37″ (94 cm) 2100–2200

- Mascotte and miniature: surprised look, high eyebrows, open/closed mouth
  8–9″ (20–23 cm) 250–350

Crib Note: *"Lenci," Enrico Scavini's pet name for his wife, is pronounced Len-she, not Len-see, as many American collectors are inclined to say it.*

Lenci lady in regional costume, 26″. *Courtesy of Richard W. Withington, Inc.*

Lenci mascottes, 9″. *Courtesy of Marvin Cohen Auctions.*

MISSIONARY RAGBABIES

Julia Jones Beecher of Elmira, New York, began making cloth dolls in 1893 to raise missionary funds for the Park Congregational Church, where her husband was the minister. The dolls sold so well that Mrs. Beecher continued to make them for seventeen years.

DOLLS ARE UNMARKED

DOLL: 1893+
All-cloth (ribbed silk jersey), looped wool hair, facial features formed by stitches, painted eyes and mouth

21″ (53 cm) **2500–3000**

PHILADELPHIA BABY

These dolls were made by an unknown artist for the J. B. Sheppard department store in Philadelphia about 1900.

DOLLS ARE UNMARKED

DOLL: CA. 1900
All-cloth, molded head with oil-painted hair and features, some with applied ears, flexible at shoulders, hips, and knees

21–22″ (51–53 cm) **1750–2000**

"Philadelphia Baby," 28″. *Courtesy of Christie's South Kensington.*

RAGGEDY ANN

Johnny Gruelle's beloved books and dolls were inspired by a childhood doll of his mother's (Raggedy Ann) and a matching doll (Raggedy Andy) that belonged to his mother's closest childhood friend. Patented by Gruelle in 1915, Raggedy Anns have been made by Molleye's Doll Outfitters, Georgene Novelties, and Knickerbocker Toy Co., as well as by countless loving mothers.

RAGGEDY ANN: TO 1929

All-cloth, yarn hair, flat face, shoe-button eyes, triangular nose, wide smiling mouth, striped stockings

- Raggedy Ann or Andy
  16″ (41 cm)   **600–800**

- Molleye's: 1935+
  16″ (41 cm)   **100–150**

- Georgene Novelties: late 1930s–1964
  16–18″ (41–46 cm)   **60–85**

- Knickerbocker: 1964+
  24″ (61 cm)   **25–30**
  30″ (76 cm)   **35–45**
  36″ (91 cm)   **50–75**
  42″ (107 cm)   **100–120**

TYPICAL MARK (FOR RAGGEDY ANN OR ANDY ONLY):

> **PATENTED SEPT. 7, 1915**

STAMPED ON TORSO

Knickerbocker Raggedy Ann. *Private collection.*

ROLLINSON

Mrs. Gertrude Rollinson of Holyoke, Massachusetts, was the creator of charming dolls made originally as gifts for children in hospitals at Christmastime. The first commercial Rollinson dolls were manufactured by the Utley Company in 1916.

CHILD: 1916–1929

All-cloth, molded and oil-painted shoulderhead, wig or painted hair, painted eyes, open/closed or closed mouth

- Wigged
  18″ (46 cm)   **500–700**

- Painted hair
  20″ (51 cm)   **900–1100**

TYPICAL MARK:

ROLLINSON DOLL

HOLYOKE MASS.

ENCLOSED IN A DIAMOND STAMPED ON TORSO

Rollinson dolls, painted hair and wigged, 18″. *Courtesy of Margaret Woodbury Strong Museum.*

STEIFF

The company that has provided generations of children with beautifully crafted stuffed animals and dolls was founded in Württemberg, Germany, by Margarete Steiff in 1877. Toy production began in 1880, and dolls were introduced in 1893. By 1911, the Steiff doll line included international soldiers, policemen, farmers, and many other characters. Most of the early dolls have two typical Steiff characteristics: a seam down the center of the face and a button in the ear (by 1904).

DOLLS: 1893+

All-felt, mohair sewn to the head; button bead, or glass eyes; closed mouth, swivel head, jointed at shoulders and hips

- Characters: tend to have exaggerated or comical features, elongated limbs, and large feet

11–13 " (28–33 cm)	1200–1600
15–16 " (38–41 cm)	1800–2200
18–20 " (46–51 cm)	2600–3000

- Early children: 1913–1930
  All-felt, small nose, center seam down face

9–11 " (23–28 cm)	600–800

- Late children: 1930–1952
  Pressed felt head with no center seam, resemblance to Käthe Kruse dolls

14 " (36 cm)	400–500
17 " (43 cm)	600–800

Steiff polar explorer, ca. 1912, 16½", sold at auction for $5280. *Courtesy of Christie's East.*

IZANNAH WALKER

There is some debate as to the date Rhode Islander Izannah Walker first began to make cloth dolls, but she certainly was in business by 1873, when she patented her method of dollmaking. Although most are found in very worn states, these irresistible dolls are the most sought after and costliest of all cloth dolls.

DOLL

All-cloth, oil-painted head, painted hair, molded and painted features

18–20″ (46–51 cm)   8000–12,000

TYPICAL MARK:

Patented Nov 4th 1873

Izannah Walker doll, 18″. *Courtesy of Marvin Cohen Auctions.*

NORAH WELLINGS

Originally a designer for Chad Valley, Norah Wellings started her own English company with her brother Leonard in 1926. Most of her dolls were small cloth characters or regional dolls of the inexpensive, souvenir type, but her child dolls are quite lovely and command much higher prices.

CHILD DOLL

All-cloth (felt head, felt or velveteen arms and legs), human hair wig, molded head and features, painted side-glancing eyes, closed mouth

13–15″ (33–38 cm)	**325–275**
20″ (51 cm)	**550–600**

TYPICAL MARK:

> MADE IN ENGLAND
> BY
> NORAH WELLINGS

LABEL SEWN ON WRIST OR BOTTOM OF FOOT

CHARACTERS

All-cloth (felt, velvet, plush, and stockinette), molded head and features, painted side-glancing eyes (occasionally glass), smiling mouth (some with painted teeth); dressed as sailors, pixies, mounties, and regional characters

8–12″ (20–31 cm)	**45–60**
14–15″ (36–38 cm)	**80–90**

• Glass eyes
18″ (46 cm)	**300–400**

Norah Wellings sailor, 8″. *Courtesy of Christie's East.*

COMPOSITION AND PAPIER-MÂCHÉ

·

The first truly mass-produced dolls were the German composition shoulderheads (once known as "Milliner's Models") that were made during the first half of the 19th century. Although collectors usually refer to them as papier-mâché, they are not made of pasted layers of paper but of a paper pulp composition essentially the same as that used later in the century to make Greiners and similar German composition dolls. Each manufacturer had its own recipe, usually unknown, so it would be difficult to define the mixture precisely, even if we knew what it contained. At present collectors tend to separate the terms *composition* and *papier-mâché* by date, a practice that is traditional but inaccurate.

At any rate, composition was used as a mass-production doll-making material longer than any other. The basic difference from the 19th to the 20th century was a change from the cold-pressed to the hot-pressed method. Unfortunately, neither method was able to prevent the cracking, peeling, or flaking surfaces that have been the constant bane of the composition-doll collector's existence.

For this reason, perfect specimens are expensive and highly prized. The fact that they must be carefully preserved in temperature- and humidity-controlled environments does not seem to deter collectors from buying them, especially the American composition personality dolls from the 1930s and 1940s, which are among the most popular of all collectible dolls.

227

PRICE ADJUSTMENTS FOR CONDITION

Head:

Light crazing	−10 to −30%
Heavy crazing	−50 to −70%
One or two small cracks	−10 to −20%
Two or more large cracks	−50 to −70%
Minor chips or paint flakes	−10 to −30%
Heavy chipping or paint flaking	−60 to −80%
Hair cut short or matted	−30 to −40%
Eyes cloudy or cracked	−20 to −30%
Face repainted	−60 to −80%
Back of head or parts of body repainted	−20 to −35%

Body:

Minor cracks	−10 to −20%
Major cracks	−30 to −40%
Unclothed	−30%
Mint in box	+100%

EARLY
—— COMPOSITION/ ——
PAPIER-MÂCHÉ

EARLY GERMAN COMPOSITION WITH MOLDED HAIR: CA. 1820–1860

Papier-mâché shoulderhead with stylish molded black hair, painted (rarely glass) eyes, stiff leather body with wooden lower arms and lower legs, flat painted shoes, often wearing original gauze or net dress

1820–1840
- Painted eyes

8–11″ (20–28 cm)	350–400
12–14″ (31–36 cm)	500–750
15–19″ (38–48 cm)	800–1100
21–23″ (53–58 cm)	1200–1500

- Glass eyes

21″ (53 cm)	1800–2000

1850–1860
- Painted eyes

8″ (20 cm)	250–300
12–14″ (31–36 cm)	400–500
24″ (61 cm)	650–700

Composition lady doll, 1830s, 23″.
Courtesy of Marvin Cohen Auctions.

Composition man, 1850s, 24″.
Courtesy of Richard W. Withington, Inc.

229

• Glass eyes
   11–15″ (28–38 cm)   **275–375**
   20–23″ (51–58 cm)   **750–900**

Glass-eyed composition child, ca. 1850, 27″. *Courtesy of Richard W. Withington, Inc.*

"FRENCH-TYPE" COMPOSITION: MID-19TH CENTURY

Papier-mâché shoulderhead, short black brush-stroked hair with nailed-on wig covering, fixed pupil-less dark eyes, stiff pink leather body; German-made for the French market

17″ (43 cm)   **700–800**
20″ (51 cm)   **1000–1200**

GREINER

Ludwig Greiner was already producing toys in 1858, in Philadelphia, when he applied for the first known U.S. patent for making doll heads. Greiner's heads were made of an early type of composition consisting of beaten, cooked paper, Spanish whiting, rye flour, and glue. After these ingredients were mixed together, the dough was rolled out and cut into pieces for the mold. The inside of each head was

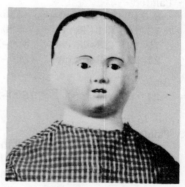

"French-type" composition doll, 26″. *Courtesy of Christie's East.*

reinforced with cloth, and the outside was covered with oil paint. The solid simplicity of these heads strongly reflects their German heritage and makes them a favorite of primitive-doll collectors. In 1872, Greiner's patent was extended; in 1874, his sons succeeded as heads of the business.

GREINER DOLL: 1858+

Composition shoulderhead, molded and painted hair, painted (rarely glass) eyes, exposed ears, closed mouth, cloth body with leather lower arms

- 1858 mark
  - **18–21″ (46–53 cm)**   **700–900**
  - **30–37″ (76–94 cm)**   **1200–1500**

- 1872 mark
  - **17–19″ (43–48 cm)**   **425–500**
  - **28–34″ (71–86 cm)**   **700–900**

- Glass eyes
  - **25–26″ (64–66 cm)**   **1500–1750**

TYPICAL MARK:

GREINER'S
PATENT DOLL HEADS.
No. 8
Pat. Mar. 30 '58 Ext. '72

Greiner composition doll with '58 label, 18″. *Courtesy of Christie's East.*

GERMAN COMPOSITION WITH MOLDED HAIR: LATE 19TH CENTURY

Composition shoulderhead, molded and painted blond or brunette hair (usually short curls corresponding with china dolls of the period), painted eyes, closed mouth, cloth body; produced by Fleischmann & Cramer, Muller & Strasburger, Dressel, and others

18–22″ (46–56 cm)	300–400
25–28″ (64–71 cm)	450–600
32″ (81 cm)	700–750

TYPICAL MARKS:

A F & C
Superior

M & S
Superior

GERMAN COMPOSITION: LATE 19TH CENTURY

Composition shoulderhead, mohair or skin wig, glass eyes, open or closed mouth, cloth body with composition lower arms and legs, sometimes with molded boots

- Fine quality (decoration comparable to good German bisque head of the same period, often paperweight-type eyes with feathered brows)

13–16″ (33–41 cm)	300–400
30″ (76 cm)	800–850

- Average quality (large head, bulging eyes, long limbs)

16–20″ (41–51 cm)	125–175
24–28″ (61–71 cm)	200–250

Two late 19th-century, glass-eyed composition girls, very good quality, 19 and 21″. *Courtesy of Marvin Cohen Auctions.*

20TH-CENTURY COMPOSITION

ALEXANDER DOLL COMPANY, INC.

The production of the Dionne Quintuplets in 1935 marked the beginning of the Alexander Doll Company's rise to the status of one of America's leading doll makers. For the next twelve years, Mme Alexander built her reputation by releasing one successful new doll after another.

BABY GENIUS: 1942–1946

Cloth body with composition head, arms, and legs; molded and painted hair or mohair wig, sleep eyes with inset lashes, closed mouth

18 " (46 cm)	150–200
20 " (51 cm)	175–225
24 " (61 cm)	250–300

MARK:

ALEXANDER

ON HEAD

233

DIONNE QUINTS: 1935–1939

Baby or toddler body, molded and painted hair or wig of mohair or human hair, painted or sleep eyes, open or closed mouth; all-composition dolls are jointed at neck, shoulders, and hips; composition and cloth dolls have composition swivel head and shoulderplate, cloth body, composition arms and legs; designed by Bernard Lipfert

7–8″ (18–20 cm)	
Set	1100–1300
Each	150–200
11″ (28 cm)	
Set	1700–1900
Each	235–285
14″ (36 cm)	
Set	1950–2100
Each	400–450
16″ (41 cm)	
Each	475–525
19–20″ (49–51 cm)	
Each	575–650

Crib Note: Original retail price at Wei-boldt's in 1936 was $1.98 each for the 7–8″ dolls.

TYPICAL MARKS:

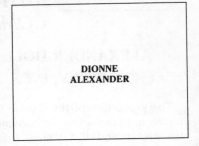

DIONNE
ALEXANDER

ON HEAD

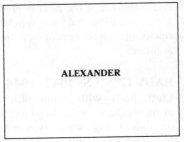

ALEXANDER

ON BACK

Alexander Dionne baby, 15″.
Courtesy of Christie's East.

JANE WITHERS: 1936–1937

All-composition, mohair wig, sleep eyes with inset lashes, open or closed mouth; jointed at neck, shoulders, and hips

13″ (33 cm)	475–525
15″ (38 cm)	550–600
20″ (51 cm)	750–800

Crib Note: Original retail price at Weiboldt's in December 1936 was $4.95 for the 20″ doll.

TYPICAL MARK:

> JANE WITHERS
> ALEXANDER DOLL CO.

ON HEAD

Alexander Jane Withers, 19″.
Courtesy of Marvin Cohen Auctions.

JEANNIE WALKER: 1939–1943

All-composition, mohair or human hair wig, brown sleep eyes with inset lashes, closed mouth; jointed at neck, shoulders, and hips; walking mechanism

14″ (36 cm)	325–375
18″ (46 cm)	450–500

MARK:

> ALEXANDER
> PAT. NO. 2171281

ON BACK

LITTLE BETTY: 1935–1942

All-composition, molded and painted hair or mohair wig, painted side-glancing eyes, closed mouth
8″: painted shoes and socks; jointed at shoulders and hips
9–11″: jointed at neck, shoulders, and hips; this model was used to portray many characters

- Little Betty characters
  - 9″ (23 cm)   **150–200**
  - 11″ (28 cm)   **225–250**

- Tiny Betty characters
  - 8″ (20 cm)   **140–170**

TYPICAL MARK:

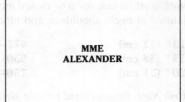

MME
ALEXANDER

ON BACK

MARGARET FACE: 1946–1947

All-composition, mohair wig, sleep eyes with inset lashes, closed mouth; jointed at neck, shoulders, and hips

- Alice in Wonderland
  - 18″ (46 cm)   **375–425**

- Margaret O'Brien
  - 14″ (36 cm)   **450–500**
  - 18″ (46 cm)   **600–650**
  - 21″ (53 cm)   **750–800**

TYPICAL MARK:

ALEXANDER

ON HEAD

PRINCESS ELIZABETH FACE: 1937–1944

All-composition, mohair or human hair wig, sleep eyes with inset lashes, open or closed mouth; jointed at neck, shoulders, and hips

- Princess Elizabeth: 1937–1938

13–14″ (33–36 cm)	200–250
16″ (41 cm)	275–300
18″ (46 cm)	350–400
20″ (51 cm)	425–450
24″ (61 cm)	475–525

- Flora McFlimsy: 1939, 1944

13″ (33 cm)	300–350
16″ (41 cm)	400–450

- Kate Greenaway: 1938–1942

20″ (51 cm)	450–500

- McGuffey Ana: 1937–1944

13″ (33 cm)	250–300
16″ (41 cm)	325–375
20″ (51 cm)	425–475
24″ (61 cm)	550–600

- Snow White: 1937–1939

13″ (33 cm)	275–325
16″ (41 cm)	375–425

Crib Note: *Original retail price at Weiboldt's in 1937 was $1.98 for the 16″ Princess Elizabeth doll. Original price for the 13″ McGuffey Ana with wardrobe and case was $4.98 at the same store in 1939.*

TYPICAL MARK:

> **PRINCESS ELIZABETH
> ALEXANDER DOLL CO.**

**Alexander "Princess Elizabeth," 16″.
Courtesy of Marvin Cohen Auctions.**

SONJA HENIE: 1939–1943

All-composition, mohair or human hair wig, sleep eyes with inset lashes, smiling open mouth with upper teeth and dimples; jointed at neck, shoulders, and hips; designed by Bernard Lipfert

13–14″ (33–36 cm)	275–325
15–16″ (38–41 cm)	350–400
18″ (46 cm)	500–600
21″ (53 cm)	700–750

TYPICAL MARK:

> MADAME ALEXANDER
> SONJA HENIE

ON HEAD

Alexander Sonja Henie, 18″. *Courtesy of Christie's South Kensington.*

WENDY-ANN FACE: 1936–1946

All-composition, mohair or human hair wig (occasionally with molded and painted hair), sleep eyes with inset lashes or painted eyes, closed mouth; jointed at neck, shoulders, and hips.

- Wendy-Ann: 1936

10″ (25 cm)	175–225
12–14″ (31–36 cm)	250–300
18″ (46 cm)	400–450
21″ (53 cm)	500–550

TYPICAL MARKS:

> MME. ALEXANDER

ON HEAD

- Carmen: 1937, 1942
  12″ (31 cm)   **225–275**

- Fairy Princess: 1942
  12″ (31 cm)   **250–300**

- Fairy Queen: 1940, 1946
  14″ (36 cm)   **300–325**

- Madeline: 1940
  21″ (53 cm)   **475–525**

- Military outfits: 1942–1943
  14″ (36 cm)   **300–350**

- Scarlett: 1937–1942
  11″ (28 cm)   **325–375**
  14–16″ (36–41 cm)   **400–500**
  18″ (46 cm)   **525–575**
  21″ (53 cm)   **600–650**

**WENDY-ANN
MME ALEXANDER
NEW YORK**

ON BACK

Alexander "Scarlett," 18″. *Julie Collier.*

LOUIS AMBERG AND SON

Although he imported his bisque heads from Germany, Amberg was one of the first American dollmakers to produce entire composition dolls in large quantity. Hundreds of new models were released every two or three years, not all of them memorable. Amberg's son Joshua became a partner of the firm in 1912 and directed it from 1915 (when the elder Amberg died) until 1927. The business was sold to the Horsman Company in 1930.

CHARLIE CHAPLIN: 1915

Composition head and arms, cloth body and legs; molded and painted hair, painted eyes, molded and painted mustache, open/closed mouth

15″ (38 cm)   **400–450**

TYPICAL MARK:

CHARLIE CHAPLIN DOLL/
WORLD'S GREATEST COMEDIAN/
MADE EXCLUSIVELY BY LOUIS
AMBERG & SON, NY/ BY
SPECIAL ARRANGEMENT WITH
ESSANAY FILM CO.

ON SLEEVE

EDWINA

All-composition, molded and painted hair, painted eyes, closed mouth, thoughtful expression; jointed at neck, shoulders, waist, and hips

14″ (36 cm)   **275–325**

TYPICAL MARK:

AMBERG
L.A. & S. 1928

ON HEAD

Amberg "Edwina," 14″. *Courtesy of Christie's East.*

VANTA BABY: 1927–1930

Cloth body with composition head, arms and legs; molded and painted hair, painted or sleep eyes, open mouth with upper teeth; this doll was used to advertise Vanta baby clothing

19" (48 cm)	200–250
25" (64 cm)	350–400

TYPICAL MARK:

Vanta Baby

ON HEAD

AMERICAN CHARACTER DOLL CO., INC.

Based in New York City, American Character Doll Company was in business by 1921, when the president was Samuel Block. The firm's most popular composition dolls were the Campbell Kids and Sally, a doll made to compete with Effanbee's Patsy.

CAMPBELL KID: 1928–1930

All-composition, molded and painted hair; painted, side-glancing eyes; round face with chubby cheeks, closed smiling mouth; jointed at neck, shoulders, and hips; designed by Grace Drayton

12" (31 cm)   400–450

MARK:

A
PETITE
DOLL

ON BACK

SALLY: 1930+

Type I: all-composition, molded and painted hair, painted eyes, closed mouth; jointed at neck, shoulders, and hips; Type II: cloth body with composition head, shoulderplate, arms, and legs; mohair wig, sleep eyes with inset lashes, closed mouth

12″ (31 cm)	140–165
16″ (41 cm)	200–225

TYPICAL MARK:

PETITE
SALLY

ON HEAD

ARRANBEE DOLL CO.

Born in Poland, William Rothstein came to America in 1909. He founded Arranbee in 1919 and was president of the company until his death on November 23, 1957. Three of Arranbee's most popular composition dolls were Nancy (a Patsy type), Nancy Lee, and Debuteen.

DEBU TEEN: 1938+

All-composition or cloth body with composition swivel head, shoulderplate, arms, and legs; human hair or mohair wig, sleep eyes with lashes, closed mouth; all-composition doll is jointed at neck, shoulders, and hips

20″ (51 cm)　　　　**150–200**

Crib Note: Original retail price at Weiboldt's in 1938 was $2.98.

MARK:

R & B

ON HEAD

Arranbee "Debuteen," 18″. *Private collection.*

NANCY: 1930+

All-composition, jointed at neck, shoulders, and hips

- Type I: molded and painted hair, painted eyes
　　12″ (30 cm)　　**175–200**

- Type II: wig, sleep eyes with inset lashes
　　16″ (41 cm)　　**225–275**

TYPICAL MARK:

ARRANBEE

DOLL CO.

ON BACK

NANCY LEE: 1940+

All-composition, mohair or human hair wig, sleep eyes with inset lashes, closed mouth; jointed at neck, shoulders, and hips

21″ (53 cm)   200–250

TYPICAL MARK:

R & B

ON HEAD

AVERILL MANUFACTURING COMPANY

A profusion of trade names, including "Madame Georgene," "Madame Hendron," and "Georgene Novelties," are associated with the Averill Manufacturing Company, run by Paul Averill. His wife Georgene was chief designer. The company was in operation by 1915, and though the Averills departed in 1923 (taking the names "Mme. Georgene" and "Georgene Novelties" with them), the firm continued production until 1964.

LITTLE BROTHER OR SISTER: 1927

Cloth body with composition shoulderhead, arms, and legs; molded and painted hair, painted eyes, smiling mouth, designed by Grace Corry

14″ (36 cm)   350–400

MADAME HENDREN DOLLS: 1915+

Composition head or shoulderhead, cloth body, composition arms, cloth or composition legs; molded and painted hair or wig, painted or tin sleep eyes, open or closed mouth

22″ (56 cm)   250-300

TYPICAL MARK:

> GENUINE
> "MADAME HENDREN"
> DOLL
> (Various numbers)
> MADE IN U.S.A.

ON SHOULDERPLATE OR STAMPED ON BODY

GEO. BORGFELDT AND CO.

The Borgfeldt company started as an import firm in 1881. By the time the company began distributing composition dolls in the 1920s, they had opened a division called K&K Toy Co. to manufacture doll bodies. The heads for the Gladdie dolls were made in Germany; the composition heads for the Baby Bo Kaye dolls were made by Cameo.

BABY BO KAYE: 1926-1928

Composition head with flange neck, cloth body, composition arms and legs; molded and painted hair, sleep eyes, open/closed mouth; designed by Joseph Kallus

500-600

GLADDIE: 1928+

Biscaloid (composition imitating bisque) head with flange neck, cloth body, composition arms and legs; molded and painted hair, painted or glass eyes, smiling open/closed mouth with painted teeth; designed by Helen Jensen

18–19″ (46–48 cm)	850–1000
24–27″ (61–69 cm)	1150–1300

MARK:

> Gladdie
> Copyright [sic] By
> Helen W. Jensen
> Germany

IN SCRIPT ON HEAD

Borgfeldt "Gladdie," 18″. *Courtesy of Christie's East.*

CAMEO DOLL COMPANY

Joseph L. Kallus was a man of many talents. While still in art school, he was hired by the Borgfeldt Company to do the rough modeling for Rose O'Neill's Kewpie doll. Later, he sculpted the head for Borgfeldt's Baby Bo Kaye. In 1922, he founded the Cameo Doll Company in Port Alleghany, Pennsylvania. Through the years, he designed most of the dolls his firm produced. He is best known for his happy, comic-type characters. After heading Cameo for nearly fifty years, Mr. Kallus retired in 1970.

BETTY BOOP: 1932+

Composition head; typical body has molded swimsuit, segmented wooden arms and legs, molded and painted hair, painted side-glancing eyes, closed mouth; designed by Joseph Kallus

12″ (30 cm)   **475–525**

MARK:

> **"BETTY BOOP"**
> **DES. & COPYRIGHT**
> **BY FLEISCHER**
> **STUDIOS**

IN STYLIZED HEART LABEL ON CHEST

GIGGLES: CA. 1946

All-composition, molded and painted hair with bangs, painted side-glancing eyes, closed smiling mouth; jointed at neck, shoulders, and hips

11″ (28 cm)   **450–500**

> **UNMARKED**

JOY: 1932+

Composition head, wood or composition body, segmented wooden arms and legs, molded and painted hair with molded loop for ribbon, painted eyes, closed smiling mouth; designed by Joseph Kallus

10″ (25 cm)   **300–350**

MARK:

DES. & COPY
JOY
J.L. KALLUS

IN CIRCULAR LABEL ON CHEST

Cameo "Joy," 10″. *Julie Collier*.

1. Carved, wooden doll in original clothing, ca. 1750, 16″. *(Courtesy of Christie's Scotland)*

2.

2. Group of French automata by
Leopold Lambert and by Vichy.
(Courtesy of Sotheby's, New York)

3. Two "Tête Jumeau"-marked bébés,
17″ and 19″. *(Courtesy of Marvin
Cohen Auctions)*

3.

4.

5.

4. Huret lady doll with painted
eyes, 17 1/2 ". *(Courtesy of
Richard W. Withington, Inc.)*

5. Bru "Bébé Brevété," incised
O, 14 ". *(Courtesy of Richard W.
Withington, Inc.)*

6. Schneider porcelain
pincushion figure, 4 ". *(Private
collection)*

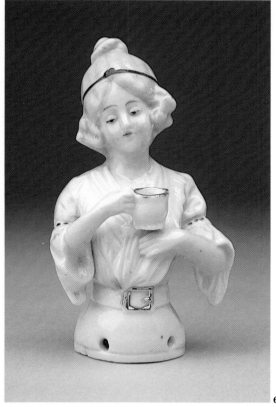

6.

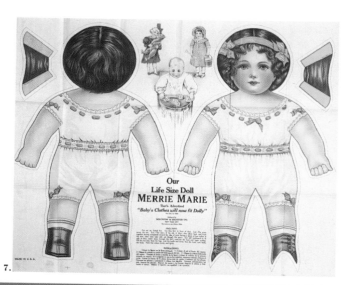

7.

9.

7. Selchow and Righter uncut
cloth doll, "Merrie Marie," 24".
(Courtesy of Julie Collier)

8. A. T. bébé, 25". *(Courtesy of
Christie's East)*

9. Rare Kestner baby with
molded bonnet, incised JDK
12, 15". *(Courtesy of Christie's
South Kensington)*

10. Steiff soldier doll and
accessories, ca. 1915, 20½".
(Courtesy of Christie's East)

10.

11.

12.

13.

11. Kämmer & Reinhardt 126 character baby, 18″ (left); Handwerck doll, incised 79, 34″ (right). *(Courtesy of Christie's East)*

12. C series Steiner, 21″; "Tête Jumeau," 26″. *(Courtesy of Marvin Cohen Auctions)*

13. Late 19th century, French bisque-headed doll with candy box torso, 16½″. *(Courtesy of Richard W. Withington, Inc.)*

14. Pair of Kewpie salt and pepper shakers, 2¼″. *(Private collection)*

15. Francois Gaultier bébé, cartouche mark, 25″. *(Courtesy of Christie's South Kensington)*

15.

16. Jumeau "long-faced" bébé, 19 1/2″
(left); Bru Jeune bébé, 18 1/2″ (right).
*(Courtesy of Christie's South
Kensington)*

17. Three Madame Alexander
"Alexanderkins," 8″, ca. 1953.
(Courtesy of Julie Collier)

16.

17.

MARGIE: 1928+

Composition head, wood or composition body, segmented wooden arms and legs, molded and painted hair, painted eyes, smiling mouth; designed by Joseph Kallus

10″ (25 cm)   **200–250**

MARK:

"MARGIE"
DES. & COPYRIGHT
BY JOS. KALLUS

IN STYLIZED HEART LABEL ON CHEST

Cameo "Margie," *10″. Private collection.*

PINKIE: 1930+

Composition head, hands and legs; wooden torso and segmented arms, molded and painted hair, painted side-glancing eyes, closed smiling mouth; the parts made of wood or composition varied; designed by Joseph Kallus

10½″ (27 cm)   **275–325**

TYPICAL MARK:

PINKIE
DES. & COPYRIGHT
BY JOS. KALLUS

IN STYLIZED HEART LABEL ON CHEST

SCOOTLES: 1925 +

All-composition, molded and painted hair; painted, usually side-glancing eyes; closed smiling mouth; toddler body jointed at neck, shoulders, and hips; designed by Rose O'Neill

12" (31 cm)	325–375
15" (38 cm)	425–475

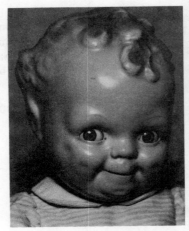

Rare, sleep-eyed composition "Scootles." *Private collection.*

EFFANBEE DOLL CORPORATION

The trademark name Effanbee was created from the initials of the company founders, Fleishacker and Baum. They headed the New York firm from its inception in 1910 until 1940, when Hugo Baum died and Bernard Fleishacker moved to California. Effanbee's early success was a result of effective marketing techniques combined with the owners' ability to choose doll designs with wide public appeal.

AMERICAN CHILDREN: 1936–1939

All-composition, human hair wig, sleep eyes with inset lashes or painted eyes, open or closed mouth; jointed at neck, shoulders, and hips; designed by Dewees Cochran

• Boy (closed mouth, painted eyes)
   17" (43 cm)   1100–1300

TYPICAL MARK:

EFFANBEE
AMERICAN
CHILDREN

ON HEAD

- Barbara Joan (open mouth, sleep eyes)
  15″ (38 cm)   **500–600**
- Barbara Lou (open mouth, sleep eyes)
  21″ (53 cm)   **650–750**
- Gloria Ann (closed mouth, sleep eyes)
  20″ (51 cm)   **900–1100**
- Peggy Lou (closed mouth, painted eyes)
  20″ (51 cm)   **1100–1300**

TYPICAL MARK:

> **EFFANBEE**
> **ANNE SHIRLEY**

ON BODY

Effanbee "Peggy Lou," 20″. *Julie Collier.*

ANNE SHIRLEY: 1935+

All-composition, human hair wig, sleep eyes with inset lashes, closed mouth; jointed at neck, shoulders, and hips

15" (38 cm)	175–225
18" (46 cm)	250–300
21" (53 cm)	325–375
27" (69 cm)	400–450

MARK:

> EFFANBEE
> ANNE SHIRLEY

ON BACK

Effanbee "Anne Shirley," 18".
Private collection.

BABY DAINTY: 1912–1925

Composition shoulderhead and arms, cloth body, composition or cloth legs, molded and painted hair or mohair wig, painted or tin sleep eyes, open or closed mouth

13–15" (33–38 cm)	150–200

TYPICAL MARKS:

EFFANBEE
BABY DAINTY

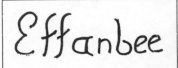

Effanbee

ON SHOULDER

BABY GRUMPY: 1913–1939

Cloth body with composition shoulder-head, arms, and legs; molded and painted hair, painted eyes, closed mouth, frowning

12″ (31 cm)   **175–225**

TYPICAL MARK:

EFFANBEE
BABY GRUMPY
COPYRIGHT

ON SHOULDER

TYPICAL MARK:

BUBBLES: 1924+

Composition shoulderhead and arms, cloth body, composition or cloth legs; molded and painted hair, sleep eyes with inset lashes, dimples, smiling open mouth with two upper teeth or open/closed mouth with two molded and painted upper teeth; designed by Bernard Lipfert

EFFANBEE
BUBBLES
COPYR. 1924
MADE IN U.S.A.

ON SHOULDER

16″ (41 cm)	**150–175**
18″ (46 cm)	**200–225**
20″ (51 cm)	**250–275**
22″ (56 cm)	**275–300**
25″ (64 cm)	**350–400**

Crib Note: Bubbles was an extremely popular doll that sparked many imitations, the best known of which was Horsman's "Dimples." The original retail price for an 18″ Bubbles was $4.79 in 1927.

Effanbee "Bubbles." *Private collection.*

CANDY KID: 1946-1947

All-composition, molded and painted hair, sleep eyes with inset lashes, closed mouth; toddler body jointed at neck, shoulders, and hips

13" (33 cm)   **175-225**

MARK:

EFFANBEE

ON HEAD

HISTORICAL DOLLS: 1939

Effanbee made three exhibition sets of 30 dolls each to promote a new series of dolls. The 20" exhibition dolls were dressed in velvet, satin, and lace costumes representing, American fashion 1492-1939; the 14" dolls in the new series were dressed in cotton replicas of the exhibition dolls' gowns

Replicas: All-composition, human hair wig; painted eyes with very short, painted lashes and feathered eyebrows; closed mouth; jointed at neck, shoulders, and hips

14" (36 cm)   **300-400**

MARK:

EFFANBEE
ANNE SHIRLEY

ON BACK

LAMKIN: CA. 1930

Cloth body with composition head, arms, and legs; molded and painted hair, sleep eyes, open mouth with tongue

16" (41 cm)   **250-300**

LITTLE LADY: 1939–1949
All-composition, human hair or mohair or yarn wig, sleep eyes with inset lashes, closed mouth; jointed at neck, shoulders, and hips

14″ (36 cm)	175–200
17″ (43 cm)	225–250
20″ (51 cm)	275–325

TYPICAL MARK:

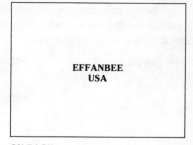

EFFANBEE
USA

ON BACK

LOVUMS: 1928–1939
Cloth body with composition swivel head, shoulderplate, arms, and legs; molded and painted hair or caracul wig, sleep eyes with inset lashes, open mouth with teeth or closed mouth

16″ (41 cm)	200–250

TYPICAL MARK:

EFFANBEE
LOVUMS
©
PAT. NO 1,283,558

ON SHOULDER

MAE STARR: 1928
Cloth body with composition shoulderhead, arms, and legs; human hair wig, sleep eyes with inset lashes, open or open/closed mouth; talking mechanism

29″ (74 cm)	400–500

MARK:

MAE
STARR
DOLL

ON SHOULDER

MARILEE: 1924

Cloth body, composition shoulderhead, arms, and legs; mohair wig, sleep eyes, open mouth with upper teeth

24″ (56 cm)   **200–300**

MARK:

ON SHOULDER

PATSY SERIES: 1927+

All-composition (sometimes Patsy Ruth has a cloth body), closed mouth; jointed at neck, shoulders, and hips (except Wee Patsy who has a one-piece body and head); designed by Bernard Lipfert

• Baby or Patsy Tinyette (molded and painted hair, painted eyes)
  7″ (18 cm)   **150–200**

• Patricia (molded and painted hair or wig, sleep eyes with inset lashes)
  14″ (36 cm)   **250–300**

TYPICAL MARKS:

- Patsy (molded and painted hair or wig, sleep eyes with inset lashes or painted eyes)
  14″ (36 cm)   **275–325**
- Patsy Ann (molded and painted hair or wig, sleep eyes with inset lashes)
  19″ (48 cm)   **300–350**
- Patsy Baby (molded and painted hair or wig, sleep eyes with inset lashes)
  11″ (28 cm)   **185–210**
- Patsy Babyette (molded and painted hair or wig, painted eyes)
  9″ (23 cm)   **150–200**
- Patsy Joan (molded and painted hair or wig, sleep eyes with inset lashes)
  16″ (41 cm)   **200–300**

- Patsy Jr. (molded and painted hair, painted eyes)
  11″ (28 cm)   **225–275**
- Patsy Lou (molded and painted hair or wig, sleep eyes with inset lashes)
  22″ (56 cm)   **350–400**
- Patsy Mae (wig, sleep eyes with inset lashes)
  30″ (76 cm)   **500–600**
- Patsy Ruth (wig, sleep eyes with inset lashes)
  26″ (66 cm)   **550–600**
- Wee Patsy (molded and painted hair, painted eyes, painted shoes and socks)
  6″ (15 cm)   **250–300**

Members of the "Patsy" family. *Courtesy of Marvin Cohen Auctions.*

Crib Note: Original retail prices: Patsy, $4.50 in 1929; Patsy Ann, $7.50 in 1929; $5.95 in 1934; Patsy Jr., $3.95 in 1934; Patsy Lou, $7.95 in 1934; Tinyette, $.85 in 1934.

ROSEMARY: 1925+

Cloth body with composition shoulder-head, arms, and legs; mohair or human hair wig, tin sleep eyes with inset lashes, open mouth (some with upper teeth)

22″ (56 cm)　　　　**200–250**

SKIPPY: 1928+

All-composition or cloth body with composition head, arms, and legs; molded and painted hair, painted side-glancing eyes, chubby cheeks, tiny closed mouth; used the Patsy body

14″ (36 cm)　　　　**300–400**

Crib Note: Original retail price at Rosenberg's, in 1929, was $3.00.

MARK:

> EFFANBEE
> ROSEMARY
> WALK-TALK-SLEEP

ENCLOSED IN A CIRCLE ON SHOULDER

MARK:

> EFFANBEE
> SKIPPY
> ©
> P. L. Crosby

ON HEAD

Effanbee "Skippy." *Private collection.*

SUZANNE

All-composition, mohair or human hair wig, sleep eyes with inset lashes, closed mouth; jointed at neck, shoulders, and hips

14" (36 cm)   **200–250**

MARKS:

```
SUZANNE
EFFANBEE
```

ON HEAD

```
SUZANNE
EFFANBEE
MADE IN U.S.A.
```

ON BACK

FREUNDLICH NOVELTY CORPORATION

Founded in 1929 by Ralph Freundlich, the New York company made composition dolls from its inception until the mid-1940s.

AMERICAN MILITARY DOLLS: CA. 1942

All-composition, molded and painted hair and hat, painted eyes, closed mouth; jointed at shoulders and hips, wearing original army or navy uniform

15" (38 cm)   **140–175**

```
UNMARKED
```

BABY SANDY: 1939+

All-composition, molded and painted hair or wig, sleep eyes with inset lashes or painted eyes, open mouth; toddler body jointed at neck, shoulders, and hips

12″ (31 cm)	200–250
14–16″ (36–41 cm)	275–325

MARK:

BABY SANDY

ON HEAD

GENERAL DOUGLAS
MacARTHUR: 1942

All-composition, molded and painted hair and hat, painted eyes, closed mouth; jointed at shoulders and hips, wearing original uniform

17″ (38 cm)	200–250

THE MARY HOYER DOLL MFG. CO.

From 1937 until 1946, Mrs. Hoyer sold undressed composition dolls along with patterns, kits, and instruction books so that her customers could dress the dolls themselves.

MARY HOYER DOLL

All-composition, mohair wig, sleep eyes
with inset lashes, closed mouth; jointed
at neck, shoulders, and hips; designed
by Bernard Lipfert

14″ (36 cm)   **275–325**

TYPICAL MARK:

THE
MARY HOYER
DOLL

ON BACK

E. I. HORSMAN COMPANY

Founded by Edward Imeson Horsman (1843–1927), the New York City–
based company was a leader in the field
of composition dolls. Beginning in the
early 1900s, the firm produced one popular composition doll after another. The
company is known for happy-faced babies and children. Fortunately for collectors, the heads of Horsman dolls tend
to have come through the years with
less crazing and cracking than other
composition dolls of the period.

BABY DIMPLES: 1928+

Cloth body with composition head, arms, and legs; molded and painted hair, tin sleep eyes, open mouth (some with upper teeth)

14″ (36 cm)	125–175
21–23″ (53–58 cm)	225–275
27″ (69 cm)	325–350

TYPICAL MARK:

©

E.I.H. CO. INC.

ON HEAD

Horsman "Dimples," 16″. *Julie Collier.*

BILLIKEN: 1909–1912

Composition head with cloth body, arms, and legs; molded and painted hair, narrow painted eyes, closed mouth with wide smile

11″ (28 cm)	325–375

Crib Note: *Billiken, "the god of things as they ought to be," was the creation of Florence Pretz.*

TYPICAL MARK:

LICENSED STAMP
COPYRIGHT 1909 BY
THE BILLIKEN
COMPANY

LABEL ON CHEST OR FOOT

262

CAMPBELL KIDS

1910: composition head with flange neck or composition shoulderhead, composition arms, cloth body and legs, molded and painted hair or mohair wig, painted side-glancing eyes, closed smiling mouth
1948: all-composition, molded and painted hair, painted side-glancing eyes with heart-shaped pupils, closed smiling mouth, painted shoes and socks; jointed at neck, shoulders, and hips; designed by Grace Drayton

- 1910+
    10″ (25 cm)   150–200
- 1948
    12″ (31 cm)   200–300

TYPICAL MARK:

1910
E.I.H. © 1910

ON HEAD

1948 VERSION IS UNMARKED

Horsman "Campbell Kid," 1948 version, 12″. *Julie Collier.*

HEbee-SHEbee: 1925+

All-composition, painted eyes, button nose, upside-down "U"-shaped mouth, molded and painted clothes and booties; jointed at neck, shoulders, and hips; HEbee wears blue shoes, SHEbee pink; designed from drawings by Charles Twelvetrees

11″ (28 cm)   450–500

Horsman "HEbee," 11″. *Courtesy of Christie's East.*

JEANNE: 1937

Cloth body with composition head, arms, and legs; molded and painted hair with peak, sleep eyes with inset lashes, tiny closed mouth; jointed at neck, shoulders, and hips

16″ (41 cm)   **125–175**

MARK:

```
JEANNE
HORSMAN
```

ON HEAD

JO-JO: 1937

All-composition, molded and painted hair or wig, sleep eyes with inset lashes, closed mouth; jointed at neck, shoulders, and hips

13″ (33 cm)   **150–200**

MARK:

```
JO-JO
© 1937 HORSMAN
```

ON HEAD

ROSEBUD: 1914–1929

Cloth body with composition swivel shoulderhead, arms, and legs; mohair wig, tin sleep eyes with inset lashes, dimples, smiling open mouth with teeth

20″ (51 cm)   **225–275**

MARK:

ROSEBUD

ON SHOULDER

Horsman "Rosebud," 16″. *Julie Collier*.

TYNIE BABY: 1924+

Composition head and arms, cloth body and legs, molded and painted hair, painted or sleep eyes, closed mouth, fretful expression

15″ (38 cm)   **250–300**

TYPICAL MARK:

© 1924
E.I. HORSMAN
CO. INC.

ON HEAD

IDEAL NOVELTY AND TOY COMPANY

Morris Michtum's career in the toy business began with a pair of stuffed teddy bears (said to have been America's first) made by his wife in 1903 and placed in the window of his Brooklyn stationery store. The bears were such an immediate hit that Michtum was soon manufacturing them in quantity, and the Ideal Toy Company was born. Today, Ideal is best known for its dolls, particularly the composition celebrity dolls such as Shirley Temple, Deanna Durbin, and Judy Garland, produced during the 1930s and 1940s.

DEANNA DURBIN: 1939

All-composition, human hair or mohair wig, sleep eyes with inset lashes, smiling open mouth with upper teeth and felt tongue; jointed at neck, shoulders, and hips

21″ (53 cm)	450–550
25″ (64 cm)	600–650

TYPICAL MARKS:

**DEANNA DURBIN
IDEAL DOLL**

ON HEAD

266

IDEAL DOLL

ON BODY

Ideal Deanna Durbin, 21″. *Private collection.*

FLEXY DOLLS

Composition head, hands, and feet; wire body, arms, and legs; molded and painted hair, painted eyes, open/closed mouth

- Fannie Brice (Baby Snooks), designed by Joseph Kallus
  12″ (31 cm)   **200–250**

- Mortimer Snerd
  12″ (31 cm)   **200–250**

TYPICAL MARK:

IDEAL DOLL
U.S.A.

ON HEAD

JUDY GARLAND

All-composition, human hair wig, brown sleep eyes with inset lashes, open mouth with upper teeth; jointed at neck, shoulders, and hips; designed by Bernard Lipfert

18″ (46 cm)   **750–1000**

TYPICAL MARKS:

IDEAL DOLL

ON HEAD

18
IDEAL DOLL
MADE IN U.S.A.

ON BACK

SNOW WHITE: 1930s

Cloth body with composition shoulder-head, arms, and legs; molded and painted black hair, painted eyes, closed mouth

20″ (51 cm)   **450–500**

TYPICAL MARK:

IDEAL DOLL

ON HEAD

SHIRLEY TEMPLE: 1934–1939

All-composition, mohair or human hair wig, sleep eyes with inset lashes, dimples, open mouth with upper teeth and tongue; jointed at neck, shoulders, and hips; designed by Bernard Lipfert; clothes designed by Mollye Goldman

11″ (28 cm)   **550–600**
13″ (33 cm)   **450–500**
15–16″ (38–41 cm)   **500–550**

TYPICAL MARKS:

SHIRLEY TEMPLE

ON HEAD

SHIRLEY TEMPLE
(size number)

ON BACK

18″ (46 cm)	550–600
22″ (56 cm)	600–650
25″ (64 cm)	750–800
27″ (69 cm)	900–1100

• Hawaiian
    13″ (33 cm)   550–600

Crib Note: Original retail price at Wei-boldt's in 1934 and 1935 for the 18″ doll was $4.95.

Ideal Shirley Temple, 15″. *Courtesy of Christie's East*.

Ideal Shirley Temple baby. *Private collection*.

UNEEDA KID: 1914–1919

Muslin body with composition head and arms, molded and painted composition rain boots; painted hair and eyes, closed mouth

15″ (38 cm)   **300–400**

MARK:

> **Uneeda Kid**
> **Patented Dec. 8, 1914**
> **IDEAL TOY and NOVELTY CO.**
> **BROOKLYN, N.Y.**

LABEL ON SLEEVE OF RAINCOAT

MONICA STUDIOS

Designed by Hansi Share, the dolls produced by the Monica Studios were the only composition dolls to have rooted hair.

"MONICA": 1941+

All-composition, rooted human hair, painted eyes, closed mouth; jointed at neck, shoulders, and hips

20″ (51 cm)   **250–350**

Crib Note: *Although "Monica" is the name widely identified with these dolls, their actual names were Veronica, Rosalind, Joan, Fairy Tale Princess, The Doll She Dreams About, etc. In 1946, the original retail price for a 20″ doll was $22.95.*

> **DOLLS ARE UNMARKED**

"Monica," 20″. *Courtesy of Christie's East.*

DORA PETZOLD
ART DOLLS

The dolls designed by Dora K. Petzold were produced in her Berlin factory.

DORA PETZOLD DOLL: 1919+

Composition head with cloth body, arms, and legs; wig, realistic face, painted features

18″ (46 cm)	300–400
24–26″ (61–66 cm)	700–850

TYPICAL MARK:

DORA PETZOLD

STAMP ON BACK

RALEIGH DOLLS

When World War I halted the importation of German dolls, Jessie McCutcheon Raleigh decided to help fill the void with a line of composition dolls. She hired Emory Seidel and other sculptors to design a series of dolls that looked like real American children. The doll parts were held together with steel springs connected to hardwood plugs inserted into the composition. Mrs. Raleigh's early dolls were distributed exclusively by Butler Brothers.

RALEIGH DOLL: 1917–1920

All-composition (sometimes with cloth body), painted hair, or mohair or human hair wig; sleep or painted eyes, open or closed mouth.

- Baby
  14″ (36 cm)   350–400
- Child
  18″ (46 cm)   475–550

VOGUE DOLLS, INC.

The Toddles dolls, also known as composition Ginnys, came in various outfits representing storybook characters and children from many lands. The clothes were all designed by Mrs. Jennie Graves, owner of the company.

TOODLES: 1937–1947

All-composition, molded and painted hair or mohair wig, painted blue side-glancing eyes, closed mouth; jointed at neck, shoulders, and hips: designed by Bernard Lipfert

8″ (20 cm)   200–250

MARK:

VOGUE

ON HEAD AND BACK

UNKNOWN AMERICAN MANUFACTURERS

BABY: 1915+

All-composition (some with cloth bodies), molded and painted hair, painted or sleep eyes, open or closed mouth, bent-limb baby body

9–13″ (23–33 cm)   25–50
16–18″ (41–46 cm)   75–125
21–25″ (53–64 cm)   150–200

Unmarked composition baby, 22″.
Courtesy of Grace Young.

CHILD: 1920s–1940s

All-composition, molded and painted hair or mohair wig, painted or metal sleep eyes, open or closed mouth, five-piece body jointed at neck, shoulders, and hips

8–10″ (20–25 cm)	**40–60**
14–16″ (36–38 cm)	**75–125**

Unmarked composition baby, 9″.
Courtesy of Dorothy Balz.

MAMA DOLL: 1920+

Cloth body with composition head, arms, and legs; mohair wig, sleep eyes with inset lashes, open mouth, crier

16–18″ (41–46 cm)	**75–100**
20–24″ (51–61 cm)	**125–175**

METAL

T he most common type of metal-head doll is the familiar "tin head," dating from the turn of the century. Inexpensive, with pleasant but rather banal expressions, their painted surfaces have the disadvantage of being easily chipped, so they are difficult to find in excellent condition. All-metal dolls were produced periodically between the mid-19th and mid-20th centuries. They are rarely seen, but their prices remain low because they are not avidly collected.

The most interesting of the metal dolls is the small Swiss Bucherer of the 1920s, which has an intricate ball-jointed metal body with painted composition head and hands. These dolls are popular, not only because they are fun to play with but because they can be found with a wide variety of standard and character heads.

PRICE ADJUSTMENTS FOR CONDITION

Lightly chipped head	−30 to −50%
Badly chipped head	−50 to −80%
Dented head	−20 to −30%
Dented face	−30 to −50%
Rust on head	−50 to −60%
Minor chips or cracks on Bucherer head	−20 to −30%
Minor damage to Bucherer body	−20 to −30%

A. BUCHERER

A. Bucherer & Cie. was a Swiss company that produced diminutive dolls with posable ball-jointed metal bodies during the 1920s. These dolls came with molded composition heads representing comic characters and celebrities, as well as standard "civilian" types. They are sewn into their original clothes, making an examination of their unique bodies difficult.

CHARACTER: CA. 1920+

Composition head with molded and painted hair and features; metal body with ball joints at neck, shoulders, elbows, wrists, hips, knees, and ankles; composition hands and feet

- Standard head
  7 ½ " (18.5 cm)   **125–175**

- Comic character or celebrity head
  6 ½–7 ½ " (16–18.5 cm)
                      200–300

TYPICAL MARK:

MADE IN
SWITZERLAND
PATENTS
APPLIED FOR

STAMPED ON FRONT OF TORSO

Bucherer "Mutt and Jeff," 6 and
7 ½ ". *Courtesy of Christie's East.*

BUSCHOW & BECK

Buschow & Beck took over a metal doll-making firm in 1890, and for the next forty years produced various types of metal, celluloid, and celluloid-covered metal dolls. Their "Minerva" trademark is so well known that it became the generic name for metal-head dolls, even though there were other German manufacturers of similar dolls during the same period, such as Karl Standfuss (trademark Juno) and Alfred Heller (trademark Diana).

MINERVA: 1891+

Metal shoulderhead, molded and painted hair or mohair wig, glass sleep or inset eyes or painted eyes, open or closed mouth, cloth body with wooden lower arms and legs or kid body with celluloid lower arms; heads also sold separately

- Molded hair, painted eyes
10–13″ (25–33 cm)	100–125
15–17″ (38–43 cm)	140–160

- Molded hair, glass eyes
12–14″ (31–36 cm)	140–180

- Mohair wig, glass eyes
17–20″ (43–51 cm)	225–275

Crib Note: *Prices for Juno and Diana heads can be calculated at the Minerva rates.*

TYPICAL MARK:

ON FRONT OF SHOULDER

"Minerva" shoulderhead with painted eyes, 10″. *Courtesy of Christie's East.*

PLASTIC

The amazing prices being paid today for hard plastic and vinyl dolls would have been unbelievable to collectors thirty years ago. Although it is possible that adults began collecting modern mass-produced dolls as an inexpensive substitute for antique dolls, the practice became so widespread that many Mme Alexander models were soon outpricing German bisques. Mme Alexanders are by far the most expensive of the plastic dolls, and the quality of their design makes them well worthy of that status.

As the Alexanders rose steeply in price and became more difficult to find, collectors bought similar dolls made by other companies. For example, the Arranbee "Nanette" and American Character "Sweet Sue" are substitutes for the Alexander "Margaret" face; Vogue "Ginnies" are now almost as pricey as the eight-inch Alexanderkins, with Nancy Ann "Muffies" on the rise. Investors should keep these trends in mind.

The most important thing for new collectors of plastic dolls to realize is that condition is everything. Because they are still relatively abundant, only perfect dolls command full price. Then too, a beautifully set Saran wig is like no other; once it has been combed out, many collectors feel that the doll has been ruined. This would never be the case with the wig of a bisque doll.

PRICE ADJUSTMENTS FOR CONDITION

Discoloration of plastic	−50 to −70%
Crack in hard plastic head	−40 to −60%
Crack in hard plastic body	−30 to −50%
Hair combed out	−40 to −50%
"Shelf dirt" on doll and clothing	−30 to −50%
Missing small item of clothing	−20 to −30%
Missing major item of clothing, or redressed	−40 to −60%
1950s doll, mint in box	+100% or more
1960s doll, mint in box	+30 to +50% and up
1970s doll and later, mint in box	+0% (list price assumed MIB)

ALEXANDER DOLL CO., INC.

Mme Alexander has produced high-quality, beautifully costumed plastic dolls since 1948. The dolls come in a wide variety of outfits representing regional, fictional, or historical characters as well as fashionable young ladies. Each doll's original clothing has a tag, usually imprinted with the name of the doll or the character the doll represents.

ALEXANDER-KINS: 1953 TO DATE

All-hard plastic, saran wig, sleep eyes with molded lashes, rosebud or smiling (for Maggie Mixup) closed mouth; jointed at neck, shoulders, and hips

- Identification by date:
  1953: Straight legs
  1954–1955: straight legs, walks
  1956–1965: jointed knees, walks
  1966–1972: jointed knees
  1973–1976: straight legs; dark, arched eyebrows
  1977: new mark

Prices are all for mint condition, except where noted; size: 7½–8″ (19–20 cm).

Wendy Ann / Wendy / Wendy-Kins, 1953–1965, in outfits
                                    350–450

- Characters*
  Africa, 1966–1971   300–350
  Alice in Wonderland, 1972–
      1977, mint in box   375–425
  American Girl, 1962–1964
                            525–575

* See also Sound of Music.

MARKS:
1953–1976

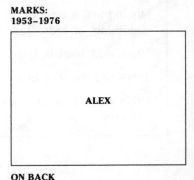

ALEX

ON BACK

1977 ON

ALEXANDER

ON BACK

280

Amish Boy or Girl, 1966–1969
475–525
Argentine Boy, 1965–1966
450–500
Bolivia, 1963–1966   425–475
Colonial Girl, 1962–1970
300–350
Cowboy or Cowgirl, 1966–1970
450–500
Easter Doll, 1968   1400–1500
Ecuador, 1963–1966   350–400
Enchanted Doll, 1980–1981, mint
in box   300–325
English Guard, 1966–1968
375–425
Eskimo, 1966–1969   400–450
Greek Boy, 1965–1968 375–425
Hawaiian, 1966–1969   400–435
Indian Boy or Girl, 1966–1970
475–525
Korea, 1968–1970   375–415
Maggie Mixup, 1960–1961
375–425
Miss U.S.A., 1966–1968
450–500
Morocco, 1968–1970   360–400
Nurse, 1956, 1960, 1963
575–625
Peruvian Boy, 1965–1966
475–525
Prince Charles, 1957   600–650
Queen, 1954–1955   900–1000
Quiz-kin, 1953–1954   475–525
Romeo and Juliet, 1955
2500–3000
Snow White, 1972–1977, mint in
box   450–500
Southern Belle, 1954–1956, 1963
750–800
Spanish Boy, 1964–1968
350–380
Vietnam, 1968–1969   400–435

Alexander-kins bendable knee
walker, 8″. *Martie Cook.*

Alexander-kins International
"Turkey," 8″. *Private collection.*

281

CAROLINE: 1961–1962

Vinyl and plastic, rooted saran hair with side part, sleep eyes with inset lashes, smiling open/closed mouth; toddler body jointed at neck, shoulders, and hips

15″ (38 cm) (mint)   **300–350**

MARK:

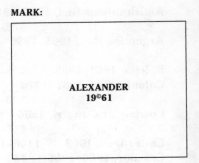

**ALEXANDER
19©61**

ON HEAD

CISSETTE FACE: 1957 TO DATE

All-hard plastic, saran wig, sleep eyes with molded lashes, pierced ears, rosebud closed mouth, high-heel feet; jointed at neck, shoulders, hips, and knees

Prices all mint; size: 10″ (25 cm).

- Cissette: 1957–1963
Ballerina	**275–300**
Basic, in chemise	**100–150**
Bride	**225–260**
Dresses	**200–250**
Evening gowns	**300–350**

- Characters:*
Agatha, 1968	**425–475**
Denmark, 1962	**700–750**
Gibson Girl, 1962	**775–825**
Godey, 1968–1970	**450–500**
Gold Rush, 1963	**1500–1600**
Jacqueline, 1962	**450–500**
Jenny Lind, 1969–1970	
	550–580

* See also Peter Pan and Sound of Music.

MARK:

**MME
ALEXANDER**

ON BACK

Klondike Kate, 1963	**1500–1600**
Margot, 1961	**400–450**
Melinda, 1968–1969	**300–350**
Queen, 1957–1963, 1972–1973	
	325–365
Renoir, 1968–1970	**325–375**
Scarlett, 1968–1973	**375–415**
Sleeping Beauty, 1960	**275–315**
Southern Belle, 1968–1973	
	275–315

Crib Note: After a lapse of 14 years, the company resumed production of the Portrettes in 1987. The mark is the same. The names of the 1987 dolls are Rosette, Daisy, Jasmin, Lily, Iris, and Violetta.

CISSY FACE: 1953–1962

Common Characteristics: Hard plastic, saran wig, sleep eyes with inset lashes, closed mouth; jointed at neck, shoulders, and hips

- Binnie, 1954–1955: Rooted hair in vinyl skullcap (vinyl over-sleeve arms and extra joints at elbows and knees in 1955) (prices are for excellent condition)

- Winnie Walker: 1953 (prices are for excellent condition)

Alexander "Cissette," 10″. *Private collection.*

MARK:

ALEXANDER

ON HEAD

15″ (38 cm)	200–250
18″ (46 cm)	275–325
25″ (64 cm)	350–400

• Cissy: Pierced ears, vinyl over-sleeve arms, high-heel feet, extra joints at elbows and knees (prices are for mint condition; size: 20″ [57 cm])

Dresses 1955–1959	**350–400**
Formals 1955–1959	**500–600**
Melanie 1961	**800–900**
Queen 1955–1959, 1961–1962	
	450–550
Scarlett 1961	**650–800**

• Sweet Violet, 1954: Rooted hair in vinyl skullcap; extra joints at elbows, wrists, and knees

18″ (46 cm), excellent condition
275–325

Alexander "Cissy" as "Queen," 20″. *Martie Cook.*

COCO: 1966

Vinyl and plastic, rooted hair, sleep eyes with inset lashes, closed smiling mouth; jointed at neck, shoulders, and waist

• Coco or 1966 Portraits
20″ (51 cm), mint in box
2000–2200

MARK:

ALEXANDER
1966

ON HEAD

ELISE: 1957 TO DATE

Saran hair, sleep eyes with inset lashes, closed mouth; jointed at neck, shoulders, and hips*

- Identification by date
  1957–1960: 16½″ (42 cm), hard plastic with vinyl arms, wig; extra joints at elbows, knees, and ankles.
  1961–1962: 17″ (43 cm), vinyl head, wig, same body, some with Kelly face
  1963–1964: 18″ (46 cm)
  1966 on: 17″ (43 cm), rooted hair, change to present vinyl and plastic body

All prices for mint condition.

1957–1960

Basic	**225–250**
Bride	**250–300**
Dresses	**300–400**
Formals	**400–500**

1961–1964

Ballerina or bride	**300–350**

1966+	**175–225**

1967

Marlo character	**550–650**

* See also Sound of Music.

TYPICAL MARKS:

ALEXANDER

ON HARD PLASTIC HEAD

**ALEXANDER
19©66**

ON VINYL HEAD

Alexander "Elise" as "Maria" from *Sound of Music* set, 17″. *Private collection.*

FIRST LADIES

Vinyl and plastic, sleep eyes with inset lashes, rooted hair, closed mouth; jointed at neck, shoulders, and hips. Mary Ann and Martha face.

Each set consists of six dolls, with each doll representing one of the First Ladies. The series begins with Martha Washington and continues in chronological order.

• Set I (1976–1978): Martha Washington, Abigail Adams, Martha Randolph, Dolley Madison, Elizabeth Monroe, Louisa Adams

• Set II (1979–1981): Sarah Jackson, Angelica Van Buren, Jane Findlay, Julia Tyler, Sarah Polk, Betty Taylor Bliss

• Set III (1982–1984): Abigail Fillmore, Jane Pierce, Harriet Lane, Mary Todd Lincoln, Martha Johnson Patterson, Julia Grant.

Prices are for mint in box; size: 14″ (36 cm).

Set I	**1100–1200**
Set II	**650–700**
Set III	**550–600**

Group of Alexander First Ladies. *Courtesy of Marvin Cohen Auctions.*

JACQUELINE FACE: 1961 TO DATE

Vinyl and plastic, rooted hair, sleep eyes with inset lashes, smiling closed mouth, high-heel feet; jointed at neck, shoulders, and hips; 21″ (53 cm)

• Jacqueline, 1961–1962
  Mint   **700–750**

• Portrait series (mint in box)
  Agatha, 1974–1976,

MARK:

ALEXANDER
19©61

ON HEAD

1979–1981	350–400
Cornelia, 1972–1976, 1978	
	350–400
Gainsborough, 1968,	
1972, 1973, 1978	400–500
Godey, 1965, 1967,	
1969–1971, 1977	450–550
Lady Hamilton, 1968	550–600
Magnolia, 1977	450–500
Melanie, 1966–1971,	
1974, 1979–1981	400–450
Mimi, 1971	650–700
Renoir, 1965, 1967,	
1969–1971, 1977	550–600

JANIE FACE: 1964–1970

Vinyl and plastic, rooted hair, sleep eyes
with inset lashes, smiling closed mouth;
toddler body jointed at neck, shoulders,
and hips; 12″ (31 cm)

- Janie, 1964–1966
  Excellent condition   225–275

- Characters* (mint in box)
Lucinda, 1969–1970	375–425
Rozy, 1969	350–400
Suzy, 1970	375–425

* See also Sound of Music and Peter Pan.

MARK:

ALEXANDER
19©64

ON HEAD

Alexander "Janie" as "Gretl" from
Sound of Music, 12″. *Courtesy of
Nancy Spore*.

KELLY FACE: 1958–1965
Vinyl and plastic, rooted hair, sleep eyes with inset lashes, open/closed mouth; jointed at neck, shoulders, waist, and hips

All prices for mint condition.

- Kelly, 1958–1959
  16" (41 cm)   300–350
  22" (65 cm)   375–400

- Characters
  Edith, 1958–1959, 16"
    (41 cm)   250–300
  Marybel, 1959–1965,
    16" (41 cm)   250–300
  Pollyanna, 1960–1961
    16" (41 cm)   250–300
    22" (65 cm)   325–375

LISSY FACE: 1956–1967
All-hard plastic, saran wig, sleep eyes with molded lashes, rosebud closed mouth, medium-high-heel feet; jointed at neck, shoulders, elbows, hips, and knees (Lissy face characters have straight arms and legs and flat feet)

All prices for mint condition; size: 12" (31 cm).

- Lissy
  1956–1958   275–350

- Characters
  Cinderella, 1966   850–950
  Katie or Tommie, 1962
                     1000–1200
  Kelly, 1959   400–450
  Laurie   350–400
  Little Women, 1957–
    1967, each   200–250

TYPICAL MARK:

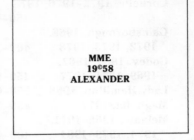

MME
19©58
ALEXANDER

IN A CIRCLE ON HEAD OR BACK

DOLLS ARE UNMARKED

Alexander "Lissy" as "Beth" from *Little Women*, 12". *Martie Cook.*

McGuffey-Ana, 1963	**800–900**
Pamela, 1962–1963	**450–500**
Scarlett, 1963	**850–900**
Southern Belle, 1963	
	1000–1200

LITTLE GENIUS: 1956–1962

Vinyl with hard plastic head, Saran wig, sleep eyes with molded lashes, nurser mouth; bent-limb baby body jointed at neck, shoulders, and hips

8″ (20 cm), mint in box   250–300

MARK:

ALEX

ON BACK

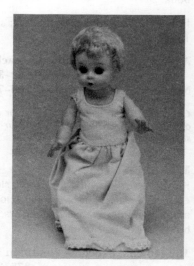

Alexander "Little Genius," 8″.
Courtesy of Christie's East.

289

Alexander "Little Women," Lissy-face. *Courtesy of Christie's East.*

LITTLE WOMEN: 1948–1956

This series used both the Maggie- and Margaret-face dolls dressed as characters from Louisa May Alcott's popular book.

Prices are for excellent condition; size: 14–15″ (36–38 cm).

Amy, Beth, Jo, Meg, Marmie, each
250–300
Nat, 1952   **700–750**

Crib Note: The original retail price for one of these dolls was $9.95 in 1951 at Marshall Fields.

MADELINE: 1952–1953

Hard plastic with vinyl head, wig, sleep eyes with inset lashes, open/closed mouth; jointed at neck, shoulders, elbows, wrists, hips, and knees

18″ (46 cm), excellent condition
275–325

Crib Note: Original retail price for Basic Madeline (in slip, panties, shoes, and socks) was $12.95 in 1952.

MARK (Madeline):

ALEXANDER

ON HEAD

Alexander "Madeline," 18″. *Courtesy of Christie's East.*

290

MAGGIE FACE: 1948–1956

All-hard plastic, saran or mohair wig, sleep eyes with inset lashes, closed mouth; jointed at neck, shoulders, and hips

Prices are for excellent condition.

- Maggie, 1948–1953

14–15 ″ (36–38 cm)	250–300
18 ″ (46 cm)	325–350
21–23 ″ (53–58 cm)	375–400

- Characters*

Alice in Wonderland, 1950–1951

14 ″ (36 cm)	300–350
18 ″ (46 cm)	375–400

Annabelle, 1952

18 ″ (46 cm)	350–400

Godey Man, 1949

14 ″ (36cm)	600–650

Kathy, 1951

15 ″ (38 cm)	350–400
18 ″ (46 cm)	425–450

Polly Pigtails, 1949

14 ″ (36 cm)	250–300

Rosamund Bridesmaid, 1953

18 ″ (46 cm)	275–325

Treena Ballerina, 1951

14 ″ (36 cm)	300–325

* See also Little Women.

TYPICAL MARK:

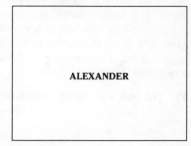

ALEXANDER

ON HEAD

Alexander "Maggie" as "Annabelle," 20 ″. *Courtesy of Christie's East.*

MAGGIE MIXUP: 1960–1961

Vinyl and plastic, saran wig (straight red-orange hair with bangs), green sleep eyes with inset lashes, freckles, closed mouth; jointed at neck, shoulders, elbows, hips, knees, and ankles

17″ (43 cm), excellent condition
250–300

MARK:

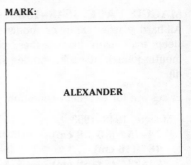

ALEXANDER

ON HEAD

MARGARET FACE: 1948–1956

All-hard plastic; saran, mohair, or floss wig; sleep eyes with inset lashes, closed mouth; jointed at neck, shoulders, and hips

Prices are for excellent condition.

TYPICAL MARK:

ALEXANDER

ON HEAD

- Characters*
  Babs Skater 1948–1950
  - **14″ (36 cm)**   **300–350**
  - **18″ (46 cm)**   **350–400**
  Blue Danube, 1953–1954
  - **18″ (46 cm)**   **450–500**
  Bride, 1948–1954
  - **15″ (38 cm)**   **200–250**
  - **18″ (46 cm)**   **300–350**
  Cinderella, 1950
  - **14″ (36 cm)**   **500–550**
  - **18″ (46 cm)**   **600–650**
  Fairy Queen, 1948–1949
  - **14″ (36 cm)**   **325–375**
  - **18″ (46 cm)**   **425–475**
  Godey Lady, 1950
  - **14″ (36 cm)**   **600–650**
  Lucy Bride, 1948
  - **14″ (36 cm)**   **350–400**
  Margaret O'Brien, 1948
  - **18″ (46 cm)**   **500–550**

* See also Little Women.

Margaret Rose, 1953
21″ (53 cm)   250–300
Margot Ballerina, 1951–1955
14″ (36 cm)   350–400
Mary Martin, 1949–1950
14″ (36 cm)   550–600
18″ (46 cm)   650–700
Nina Ballerina, 1949–1951
14″ (36 cm)   350–400
Prince Charming, 1950
14″ (36 cm)   500–550
18″ (46 cm)   600–650
Prince Philip, 1953
14″ (36 cm)   500–550
Queen Elizabeth II, 1953
18″ (46 cm)   600–650
Snow White, 1952
14″ (36 cm)   450–500
18″ (46 cm)   550–600
Wendy Bride, 1951–1955
18″ (46 cm)   300–350

Alexander "Margaret" as "Queen Elizabeth," 18″. *Courtesy of Christie's East.*

MARY ANN FACE: 1965 TO DATE

Vinyl and plastic, rooted hair, sleep eyes with inset lashes, closed mouth; jointed at neck, shoulders, and hips; 14″ (36 cm)

- Mary Ann
  1965   250–300

- Characters*
  Easter Doll, 1968, excellent condition   850–950

* See also First Ladies, Peter Pan, and Sound of Music.

MARK:

> ALEXANDER
> 19©65

ON HEAD

Gidget, 1966   225–275
Goldilocks, 1978–1983, mint in
  box   75–100
Grandma Jane, 1970–1972, mint
  in box   225–275
Jennie Lind, 1970, mint in box
                              425–475
Jennie Lind & Cat, 1969–1971,
  mint   350–400
Little Granny, 1966, mint
                              250–300
Madame, 1967–1975, mint in box
                              250–300
Orphan Annie, 1965–1966, mint
                              250–300
Riley's Little Annie, 1967
                              250–300

Alexander "Mary Ann" as "Poor Cinderella," 14". *Private collection*.

MARY ELLEN: 1954–1955

Vinyl and hard plastic, rooted hair, sleep eyes with inset lashes, smiling open/closed mouth; jointed at neck, shoulders, hips, and knees; walks

31″ (79 cm), excellent condition
350–400

MARK:

> MME
> ALEXANDER

ON HEAD

Alexander "Mary Ellen," 29″.
Courtesy of Christie's East.

NANCY DREW FACE: 1967 TO DATE

Vinyl and plastic, rooted hair, sleep eyes with inset lashes, closed mouth; jointed at neck, shoulders, and hips; 12″ (31 cm)

- Nancy Drew, 1967
  mint   **250–300**

- Characters*
  Lord Fauntleroy, 1981–1983,
  mint in box   **75–100**
  Renoir Child, 1967, mint in box
  275–300

* See also Sound of Music.

MARK:

> ALEXANDER

ON HEAD

PETER PAN SET: 1969
This set used Mary Ann–face dolls for Peter Pan and Wendy, a Janie-face doll for Michael, and a Cissette-face doll for Tinkerbelle.

Prices are for mint condition.

Alexander "Nancy Drew" as "Lord Fauntleroy," 12". *Courtesy of Nancy Spore.*

Michael, 12″ (31 cm)	**350–400**
Peter Pan, 14″ (36 cm)	**250–300**
Tinkerbelle, 11″ (28 cm)	**350–400**
Wendy, 14″ (36 cm)	**250–300**

POLLY: 1965
Vinyl, rooted hair, sleep eyes with inset lashes, smiling closed mouth; jointed at neck, shoulders, and hips

17″ (43 cm), mint   **250–300**

MARK:

ALEXANDER DOLL CO., INC.
1965

ON HEAD

296

SHARI LEWIS: 1959

All-hard plastic with vinyl arms, saran wig, sleep eyes with inset lashes, pierced ears, closed mouth, high-heel feet; jointed at neck, shoulders, and hips

14″ (36 cm), mint	**300–350**
21″ (53 cm), mint	**425–475**

MARK:

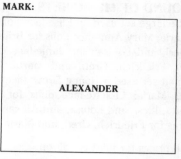

ON HEAD

SLEEPING BEAUTY: 1959

Hard plastic with vinyl arms, blond saran wig, blue sleep eyes with inset lashes, slightly smiling closed mouth, high-heel feet; jointed at neck, shoulders, elbows, hips, and knees

17″ (43 cm), excellent condition
425–475
21″ (53 cm), excellent condition
500–550

MARK:

ALEXANDER

ON HEAD

SMARTY: 1962–1963

Vinyl and plastic, rooted hair, sleep eyes with inset lashes, smiling open/closed mouth; toddler body; jointed at neck, shoulders, and hips

12″ (31 cm), excellent condition
200–250

SOUND OF MUSIC SETS

The large set used an Elise-face doll for Maria; Mary Ann–face dolls for Brigitta, Liesl, and Louisa; and Janie-face dolls for Friedrich, Gretl, and Marta. The small set used a Nancy Drew–face doll for Maria; Cissette-face dolls for Brigitta, Liesl, and Louisa; and Alexanderkins for Friedrich, Gretl, and Marta.

All prices for mint condition.

- Large set, 1965–1970

Brigitta, 14″ (36 cm)		**225–250**
Friedrich, 11″ (28 cm)		**250–275**
Gretl, 11″ (28 cm)		**175–200**
Liesl, 14″ (36 cm)		**225–250**
Louisa, 14″ (36 cm)		**250–275**
Maria, 17″ (43 cm)		**300–325**
Marta, 11″ (28 cm)		**225–250**

- Small set, 1971–1973

Brigitta, 10″ (25 cm)		**200–225**
Friedrich, 8″ (20 cm)		**275–300**
Gretl, 8″ (20 cm)		**175–200**
Liesl, 10″ (25 cm)		**250–275**
Louisa, 10″ (25 cm)		**300–325**
Maria, 12″ (31 cm)		**275–300**
Marta, 8″ (20 cm)		**200–225**

Crib Note: *Mme Alexander also produced doll furniture, accessories, and extra outfits for many of her dolls. These accessories, in good condition, are much sought after by collectors.*

Alexander "Sound of Music," small set. *Courtesy of Christie's East.*

AMERICAN CHARACTER DOLL CO., INC.

American Character produced popular, well-designed plastic dolls from the late 1940s until the company closed in 1968.

BETSY McCALL: CA. 1957–1961

1957–1958: 8″ (20 cm); hard plastic with vinyl arms, saran wig or rooted hair in vinyl skullcap, sleep eyes with molded lashes, closed mouth; jointed at neck, shoulders, and hips

1958–1961 (all other sizes):

all vinyl, rooted hair, sleep eyes with inset lashes, closed mouth; jointed at neck, shoulders, and hips

Prices are for excellent condition.

8″ (20 cm)	100–115
14″ (36 cm)	125–150
20″ (51 cm)	150–175
30″ (76 cm)	225–250

• Sandy
36″ (91 cm)	275–325

TYPICAL MARK:

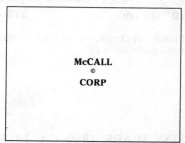

McCALL
©
CORP

ENCLOSED IN A CIRCLE ON BACK

SWEET SUE: CA. 1949–1958

Sleep eyes with inset lashes, closed mouth; jointed at neck, shoulders, and hips; walkers and nonwalkers

• Type I: all-hard plastic, saran wig

• Type II: rooted saran hair in vinyl skullcap; some with vinyl over-sleeve arms and extra joints at elbows; some with extra joints at knees

• Type III: rooted saran hair, extra joints at waist and ankles

TYPICAL MARK:

AME. CHAR.

ON HEAD

Prices are for excellent condition.

14″ (36 cm)	140–165
18–21″ (46–53 cm)	175–200
22–25″ (56–64 cm)	200–250
30″ (76 cm)	275–300

Crib Note: *Original retail price for the 14″
doll was $8.98 in 1951.*

TINY TEARS: 1950–CA. 1955

Hard plastic head with rubber or vinyl
baby body; molded and painted hair,
caracul wig or rooted saran hair in vinyl skullcap; sleep eyes with inset
lashes, "tear ducts," pierced nostrils,
nurser mouth; jointed at neck, shoulders, and hips

Prices are for excellent condition.

12″ (31 cm)	50–65
15″ (38 cm)	70–80
20″ (51 cm)	100–115

American character, "Sweet Sue,"
18″. *Courtesy of Alison Cook.*

TYPICAL MARK:

> PAT. NO. 2,675,644
> AME. CHARACTER

ON HEAD

American character, "Tiny Tears,"
12″. *Private collection.*

ARRANBEE DOLL COMPANY

Under the leadership of William Rothstein, Arranbee made plastic dolls from the late 1940s until Rothstein's death in November 1957. Shortly thereafter, the company was sold to Vogue Dolls, Inc. Vogue continued the R & B line of dolls until 1960.

NANETTE: CA. 1948–1956

All-hard plastic; mohair, saran or dynel wig; sleep eyes with inset lashes, closed mouth; jointed at neck, shoulders, and hips

Prices are for excellent condition.

14″ (36 cm)	**150–200**
18″ (46 cm)	**225–250**
21″ (53 cm)	**275–300**

Crib Note: Original retail price for the 14″ doll in 1951 was $9.98.

MARK:

R&B

ON HEAD (MARK MAY BE RATHER FAINT)

Arranbee "Nanette," 22″. *Martie Cook.*

301

COLECO
—————— INDUSTRIES, ——————
INC.

When Maurice Greenberg founded the Connecticut Leather Company in 1932, he could not have imagined the phenomenal success his company would have, fifty years later, selling a peculiar-looking cloth baby doll. The incredible story began in August 1982, when Arnold Greenberg, president of Coleco and son of the founder, secured the licensing rights to the "Little People," hand-made, all-cloth dolls created by Xavier Roberts in 1977. Coleco introduced its versions of Roberts's dolls, renamed "Cabbage Patch Kids," to the public in June 1983 and hoped to sell about a million of them by Christmas. The company was not prepared for the maniacal buying and media hype that ensued. By the end of the year, they had sold 2.5 million dolls and had hundreds of thousands of unfilled back-orders. Despite turning out well over a million Cabbage Patch Kids a month the following year, Coleco still couldn't keep up with the public demand. The mania began to subside in the spring of 1986 after sales in excess of $1.2 billion. No wonder. There wasn't a household left in America that wasn't knee deep in Cabbage Patch Kids.

CABBAGE PATCH KID: 1983 +

Vinyl head, rooted yarn hair, decal eyes, closed or open/closed mouth (some with 1 or 2 dimples), receding chin; cloth body, arms, and legs.

Prices are for mint in box; size: 16" (41 cm).

1983	100–175
1984	50–85
1985	35–50

TYPICAL MARKS:

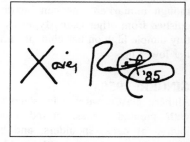

© COPY R. 1978 1982
ORIGINAL APPALACHIAN ART WORKS INC.
MANUFACTURED BY COLECO IND. INC.

ON HEAD

ON SEAT

Coleco "Cabbage Patch Kid," 16".
Private collection.

COSMOPOLITAN DOLL & TOY CORP.

For collectors who didn't get Ginny dolls before prices skyrocketed, there is a less expensive but attractive and well-constructed alternative. She is a sweet-faced little doll named Ginger, made by Cosmopolitan Doll & Toy Corp. Although unmarked, she can be distinguished from other Ginny types by the tiny dimple high on her chin, just under her lower lip.

GINGER: 1950s

All-hard plastic, saran wig, sleep eyes with molded lashes, closed mouth; jointed at neck, shoulders, and hips; walker; later ones came with vinyl head and jointed knees

7–8″ (18–20 cm), mint   75–100

Crib Note: *Extra outfits for Ginger were also available.*

TYPICAL MARK:

> **DOLLS ARE UNMARKED**

CLOTHING TAG:

> **Fashions for "Ginger"**
> **Cosmopolitan Doll & Toy Corp.**
> **JAMAICA, N.Y.**
> **®TRADEMARK**

Cosmopolitan, "Ginger," 8″. *Martie Cook.*

EFFANBEE
DOLL
CORPORATION

Noma Electric Corporation owned Effanbee from 1946 until 1953, when Bernard Baum and his partners bought the company. In 1971 Leroy Fadem and Roy R. Raizen became the new owners of Effanbee. Currently, Fadem is chairman of the board and Raizen is president of the firm.

DY-DEE BABY: 1950–1958

Hard plastic head, molded and painted hair or caracul wig, sleep eyes with inset lashes, applied ears, nurser mouth; baby body jointed at neck, shoulders, and hips

- Identification by date
  1950–1954: rubber body, rubber ears
  1955–1958: vinyl body, rubber or vinyl ears
    **15″ (38 cm), excellent
    condition   125–150**
    **20″ (51 cm), excellent condition
                        175–200**

MARK:

> EFF-AN-BEE
> DY-DEE BABY
> US PAT.-1-857-485
> ENGLAND-880-060
> FRANCE-723-980
> GERMANY-585-647
> OTHER PAT PENDING

ON BACK

HONEY: 1949–1957

Hard plastic, saran wig, sleep eyes with inset lashes, closed mouth; jointed at neck, shoulders, and hips

- Identification by date
  1949–1951: nonwalker
  1952–1955: walker
  1956: walker, extra joints at knees and ankles

MARK:

> EFFANBEE

ON HEAD AND BACK

1957: same as 1956 except change to vinyl arms, some jointed at elbows.
14" (36 cm), excellent condition
150–200
18" (46 cm), excellent condition
225–250

Crib Note: *In 1951 a Honey type called "Tintair" was introduced. This doll came with coloring lotion and had a Dynel wig.*

Effanbee "Honey," 14". *Martie Cook.*

THE LEGEND SERIES
Introduced in 1980; each doll was made for one year

Prices are for mint in box.

- W. C. Fields Centennial Doll, 1980
  15½" (39 cm)   175–200

- John Wayne (American Symbol of the West), 1981
  17" (43 cm)   75–100

- Mae West, 1982
  18" (46 cm)   70–85

- John Wayne (American Guardian of the West), 1982
  18" (46 cm)   70–85

- Groucho Marx, 1983
  17" (43 cm)   60–75

LIMITED EDITIONS
Beginning in 1975, Effanbee made a new Limited Edition doll each year. The dolls were sold only to members of the Effanbee Limited Edition Doll Club. Prices are for mint in box.

- Precious Baby, 1975
  25" (64 cm)   **350–400**

- Patsy, 1976
  16" (41 cm)   **250–300**

- Dewees Cochran, 1977
  16½" (42 cm)   **150–200**

- Crowning Glory, 1978
  16" (41 cm)   **150–200**

- Skippy, 1979
  14" (36 cm)   **250–275**

- Susan B. Anthony, 1980
  15" (38 cm)   **125–150**

- Girl with a Watering Can, 1981
  16" (41 cm)   **100–150**

- Diana, Princess of Wales, 1982
  18" (46 cm)   **135–165**

- Sherlock Holmes, 1983
  18" (46 cm)   **110–140**

SUZIE SUNSHINE: 1961–1979

All vinyl, rooted hair, sleep eyes with inset lashes, freckles, closed mouth; toddler body jointed at neck, shoulders, and hips; designed by Eugenia Dukas

18" (46 cm), mint in box   **40–65**

MARK:

EFFANBEE

ON HEAD

HASBRO, INC.

Founded in 1925, this Pawtucket, Rhode Island, company is still directed

by members of the Hassenfeld family.
Alan Hassenfeld, president, and Ste-
phen Hassenfeld, chairman of the board,
are sons of Sylvia Hassenfeld, vice-
president, and the late Merrill Hassenfeld, the former chief executive officer.
Hasbro manufactures dolls and action
figures, Playskool toys, and Milton
Bradley games.

G.I. JOE: 1964-1969

Vinyl and plastic; molded and painted
black, brown, or blond hair; painted
blue or brown eyes, closed mouth;
jointed at neck, shoulders, upper arms,
elbows, wrists, waist, hips, knees, and
ankles

• Identification by date
  1964: original mark
  1965: change in mark; black soldier
  added to group

MARKS: 1964

> G.I.JOE ©
> COPYRIGHT 1964
> BY HASBRO ®
> PATENT PENDING
> MADE IN USA

**ON BACK OF RIGHT HIP; 1965-1966:
SAME EXCEPT © CHANGED TO ®**

BEGUN IN 1967

> G.I.JOE ®
> COPYRIGHT 1964
> BY HASBRO ®
> PAT.NO.3,277,602
>
> MADE IN USA

ON BACK OF RIGHT HIP

1966: six international soldiers added: French, German, Japanese, British, Australian, Russian
1967: change in mark; talking commander added to group
1970: flocked hair added

Prices are for mint in box; size: 11 1/2" (29 cm).

Painted hair	**100–150**
Talking commander	**150–200**
Flocked hair	**50–75**
Black	**200–250**
Foreign	**250+**

Crib Note: G.I. Joe has developed a cult following among male collectors over the past several years. This has resulted in a steady price increase for the early dolls. According to a 1966 Time *magazine article, the G.I. Joe face is "a composite of 20 Congressional Medal of Honor winners."*

Hasbro G.I. Joe #1, 11 1/2". *Courtesy of David Cook*.

THE MARY
——— HOYER DOLL ———
MFG. CO.

After making composition dolls for more than ten years, Mary Hoyer switched to hard plastic in 1948. Most of these dolls were sold undressed because Mrs. Hoyer also sold doll clothing kits, patterns, and instruction books.

MARY HOYER DOLL:
1948–1950s

All-hard plastic, saran wig, sleep eyes with inset lashes, closed mouth; jointed at neck, shoulders, and hips; designed by Bernard Lipfert

14″ (36 cm), excellent condition
300–350

MARK:

ORIGINAL
Mary Hoyer.
DOLL

ON BACK

IDEAL TOY CORPORATION

By the time Ideal began producing plastic dolls in 1948, Ben Michtum was directing the company. His father and company founder, Morris Michtum, died in 1938. Ideal made the most popular girl doll of the early 1950s, Toni. Sold with a pretend permanent wave set and curlers, Toni was an instant hit with little girls and has become a very popular doll with collectors. In addition to making their own dolls, Ideal produced unmarked dolls for small companies to market under their own labels.

BETSY McCALL: 1952–1954

Hard plastic with vinyl head, wig, sleep eyes with inset lashes, closed mouth; jointed at neck, shoulders, and hips; used the Toni body

14 ″ (36 cm), excellent condition
125–175

Crib Note: In 1952 the retail price for a Betsy McCall doll was $8.50 at Marshall Field.

COOS FAMILY: 1948–1952

Baby Coos, Brother Coos, and Sister Coos—hard plastic head, cloth body with composition arms and legs or "Magic Skin" body, molded and painted hair or wig, sleep eyes with inset lashes, closed mouth; designed by Bernard Lipfert

Prices are for excellent condition.

15 ″ (38 cm)	100–125
20 ″ (51 cm)	140–165
25 ″ (64 cm)	175–200

MARK:

McCALL CORP.

ON HEAD

MARK:

IDEAL DOLL
MADE IN U.S.A.

ON HEAD

311

CRISSY: 1969–1970

Vinyl and plastic, rooted auburn hair (with portion that "grows" when knob in center of back is turned), dark brown sleep eyes with inset lashes, smiling open/closed mouth with painted teeth; jointed at neck, shoulders, and hips

18″ (46 cm), mint in box   50–65

MARKS:

© 1968
IDEAL TOY CORP.
GH-17-H129

ON HEAD

1969
IDEAL TOY CORP.
GH-18
U.S. PAT.#3,162,976

ON BACK OF RIGHT HIP

Ideal "Crissy," 18″. *Private collection.*

CUDDLY KISSY: 1963 +

Cloth body with vinyl head, arms, and legs; rooted saran hair, sleep eyes with inset lashes, open mouth; kissing mechanism: arms close and lips move when stomach is pressed

15 ″ (38 cm), excellent condition
60–75

MARK:

© IDEAL TOY CORP.
KB-17-E

ON HEAD

Ideal "Cuddly Kissy," 15 ″. *Martie Cook*.

HARRIET HUBBARD AYER: 1953–1954

Vinyl head and arms, hard plastic body and legs, saran wig, sleep eyes with inset lashes, closed mouth; jointed at neck, shoulders, and hips; used the Toni body; came with makeup kit

Prices are for excellent condition.

14 ″ (36 cm)	100–125
16 ″ (41 cm)	125–140
19 ″ (48 cm)	150–175
21 ″ (53 cm)	200–225

MARK:

MK-14
IDEAL DOLL

ON HEAD

MISS IDEAL: 1960–1962

Vinyl and plastic, rooted hair, sleep eyes with inset lashes, closed smiling mouth; jointed at neck, shoulders, wrists, waist, hips, and ankles

Prices are for excellent condition.

25″ (64 cm)	125–150
30″ (76 cm)	150–175

MARK:

> IDEAL TOY CORP.
> SP-25-S

ON HEAD

MISS REVLON: 1956–1958

Vinyl and plastic, rooted saran hair, sleep eyes with inset lashes, closed mouth, high-heel feet; jointed at neck, shoulders, waist, hips, and knees

Prices are for excellent condition.

- Little Miss Revlon
  - 10 ½″ (27 cm) — 45–65

- Miss Revlon
  - 18″ (46 cm) — 75–90

Crib Note: Original retail price for a Little Miss Revlon basic doll in bra, girdle, and high heels was $2.98 in 1957. Extra outfits cost from $1.00 for a nightie to $3.98 for a formal outfit. Original retail price for Miss Revlon in 1958 was $11.95.

MARK:

> IDEAL DOLL
> VT-(18)

ON HEAD
NUMBER FOLLOWING VT-
CORRESPONDS TO DOLL'S HEIGHT

Ideal "Miss Revlon," 18″. *Courtesy of Christie's East.*

PLAYPAL FAMILY: 1960

All-vinyl, sleep eyes with inset lashes, closed mouth; jointed at neck, shoulders, and hips; probably designed by Bernard Lipfert

Prices are for excellent condition.

* Patty
  35″ (89 cm)   **175–200**

* Penny
  32″ (81 cm)   **175–200**

* Peter
  38″ (97 cm)   **450–500**

* Suzy
  28″ (71 cm)   **175–200**

TYPICAL MARK:

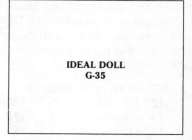

IDEAL DOLL
G-35

ON HEAD
NUMBERS CORRESPOND TO DOLL'S HEIGHT

SAUCY WALKER: 1951–1955

All-hard plastic, saran wig, sleep eyes with inset lashes, open mouth with tongue and two teeth; jointed at neck, shoulders, and hips; 1955 version has vinyl head, rooted hair, closed mouth

Prices are for excellent condition.

14″ (36 cm)	**75–100**
16–17″ (41–43 cm)	**130–160**
22–23″ (56–58 cm)	**170–185**

MARK:

IDEAL DOLL

ON HEAD

SHIRLEY TEMPLE: 1957, 1972

Vinyl and plastic, rooted saran hair, sleep eyes with inset lashes (1957) or inset eyes and lashes (1972), smiling mouth with teeth; jointed at neck, shoulders, and hips

• 1957, excellent condition

12″ (31 cm)	125–150
15″ (38 cm)	175–200
17″ (43 cm)	225–250
19″ (48 cm)	275–300
36″ (91 cm)	1150–1300

MARKS: 1957

```
                    IDEAL DOLL
                    ST-(17)
```

ON HEAD
THE NUMBER FOLLOWING ST-
CORRESPONDS TO DOLL'S HEIGHT

1972

```
                    © 1972

                IDEAL TOY CORP.
                  ST-14-H-213
                  HONG KONG
```

ON HEAD

- 1972, mint in box
  17″ (43 cm)   **75–100**

Ideal 1957 Shirley Temple, 36″.
Courtesy of Marvin Cohen Auctions.

Ideal 1957 Shirley Temple, 12″.
Private collection.

TAMMY: 1962–1965

All vinyl, rooted saran hair, painted side-glancing eyes, closed mouth; jointed at neck, shoulders, and hips

12″ (31 cm), mint in box   35–50

Crib Note: *Original retail price for Tammy was $3.00 in 1963. Extra clothes were priced from $.80 (for a skirt) to $5.00 (for a ski outfit).*

MARK:

© IDEAL TOY CORP.
BS-12

ON HEAD AND BACK

Ideal "Tammy," 12″. *Martie Cook*.

TONI: 1949–1955

All-hard plastic, nylon wig, sleep eyes with lashes, closed mouth; jointed at neck, shoulders, and hips; walkers and nonwalkers; designed by Bernard Lipfert

Prices are for excellent condition.

• Toni

P-90, 14″ (36 cm)	140–160
P-91, 16″ (41 cm)	175–190
P-92, 19″ (48 cm)	200–225
P-93, 21″ (53 cm)	250–275

TYPICAL MARK:

P-(90-93)
IDEAL DOLL
MADE IN U.S.A.

ON HEAD

318

- Miss Curity, 1952
  - **14″ (36 cm)**   **150–175**
  - **16″ (41 cm)**   **185–200**

- Mary Hartline, 1953
  - **14″ (36 cm)**   **150–175**
  - **16″ (41 cm)**   **185–200**

Crib Note: *Original retail price for Toni (P-90) in 1949 was $9.95.*

TYPICAL MARK:

> **IDEAL DOLL**
> **P-(90-93)**

ON BACK

Ideal "Toni" P91, 16″. *Martie Cook.*

KENNER
PARKER TOYS,
INC.

Once a subsidiary of General Mills, Kenner Parker Toys became an independent company in 1985. Presently there are two divisions, Parker Brothers and Kenner Products.

319

STAR WARS, "LARGE SET": 1978–1980

Following the success of the movie *Star Wars*, Kenner began manufacturing a series of action figures representing characters from the film and its sequel. The dolls, with human faces, are all-vinyl with molded and painted hair (except Leia, who has rooted hair), painted features; jointed at neck, shoulders, and hips. The other figures are fully jointed and made of styrene.

The set consists of Princess Leia Organa, No. 38070, 11″ (29 cm); Luke Skywalker, No. 38080, 11″ (30 cm); Chewbacca, No. 38600, 15″ (38 cm); Darth Vader, No. 38610, 15″ (38 cm); C-3PO, No. 38620, 12″ (30 cm); R2-D2, No. 38630, 7″ (19 cm); Boba Fett, No. 39140, 13″ (34 cm); Han Solo, No. 39170, 12″ (30 cm); Stormtrooper, No. 39180, 12″ (30 cm); Ben (Obi-Wan) Kenobi, No. 39340, 12″ (30 cm); Jawa, No. 39350, 8″ (21 cm); IG-88, No. 39960, 15″ (38 cm)

Each, mint in box   75–100

TYPICAL MARKS:

© GMFGI 1978

ON HEAD

©GMFGI 1978 KENNER PROD
CINCINNATI, OHIO 45202
MADE IN HONG KONG

ON BACK

— *MATTEL, INC.* —

This California-based company was founded in 1945 by Harold Matson and Elliot Handler. Mr. Handler's wife, Ruth, conceived the idea of having the company produce a teenage doll. The Mattel Barbie doll was the result. The present chairman and chief executive officer of the company is Arthur S. Spear.

BARBIE

All-vinyl, rooted hair, painted eyes, pierced ears, closed mouth, high-heel feet; jointed at neck, shoulders, and hips

- Identification by date
  #1 (1959): soft blond or brunette ponytail and bangs, blue eyeliner, colorless irises, arched eyebrows, holes in bottom of feet; skin tone fades to pale color
  #2 (1959): same as #1 except no holes in bottom of feet
  #3 (1960): same as #2 except blue irises and curved eyebrows; some have brown eyeliner
  #4 (1960–1961): same as #3 except skin tone doesn't fade
  #5 (1961): same as #4 except coarse, curly bangs and hollow torso
  1961–1962: red-haired doll added; "bubble-cut" hairdo introduced
  1963: uses the same body and mark as Midge; Fashion Queen introduced (molded hair, came with three wigs)
  1964: "swirl ponytail" (no bangs), and version with sleep eyes introduced; mark same, with addition of "PATENTED."
  1965: bendable knees; same mark as Midge
  1967: new face, jointed waist

Prices are for mint in box; size 11½″ (29 cm).

#1	1500–2000
#2	1500–1800
#3	350–400
#4	200–250
#5	100–150
"Bubble-cut"	100–150

MARK: 1959–1962

> Barbie (in script)
> PATS. PEND.
> © MCMLVIII
> BY
> MATTEL
> INC.

ON BACK OF RIGHT HIP

Mattel "Barbie," ca. 1960, 11½″. *Private collection.*

Mattel "Bubble-cut Barbie," ca. 1962, 11½″. *Private collection.*

Crib Note: *Original retail price for Basic Barbie (in swimsuit) was $3.00 in 1962. Clothing was priced from $.80 (for a blouse) to $5.00 (for a wedding gown).*

KEN

All-vinyl, painted features; jointed at neck, shoulders, and hips

• Identification by date:
  1961: flocked hair
  1962: painted hair
  1963: new mark
  1964: new mark
  1965: some with bendable knees
  1969: new face

Prices are for mint in box; size: 12 ″ (31 cm).

Flocked hair	**125–175**
Painted hair	**70–85**

Crib Note: *Original retail price for Basic Ken (in swim trunks) was $3.50 in 1962. His clothing cost from $.80 (for a vest) to $5.00 (for a tuxedo).*

MARKS: 1961–1962

```
KEN (in script)
PATS. PEND.
© MCMLX
BY
MATTEL
INC.
```

ON BACK OF RIGHT HIP

1963

```
Ken (in script)
© 1960
BY
MATTEL, INC.
HAWTHORNE
CALIF., U.S.A.
```

ON BACK OF RIGHT HIP

1964

```
©
1960
BY
MATTEL, INC.
HAWTHORNE
CALIF., U.S.A.
```

ON BACK OF RIGHT HIP

MIDGE

All-vinyl; rooted blond, brunette, or red hair; painted blue eyes, freckles, closed mouth, high-heel feet; jointed at neck, shoulders, and hips; bendable knees introduced in 1965

11 ½ ″ (29 cm), mint   **100–125**

MARKS: 1963

Midge (in script)
© 1962
Barbie (in script)
© 1958
BY
MATTEL, INC.

ON BACK OF RIGHT HIP; 1964 MARK SAME, WITH ADDITION OF *PATENTED*

1965

© 1958
MATTEL, INC.
U.S.PATENTED
U.S. PAT. PEND.

Mattel "Midge," Barbie's best friend, 11 ½ ″. *Private collection.*

SKIPPER:

All-vinyl; rooted, waist-length hair with bangs (blond, brunette, and redhead); painted blue eyes, closed mouth; jointed at neck, shoulders, and hips; bendable knees introduced in 1965

9″ (23 cm), mint in box   70–85

MARK: 1964

> SKIPPER
> © 1963
> MATTEL, INC.

**ON BACK OF RIGHT HIP;
1965–1967 MARK SAME EXCEPT
"SKIPPER" OMITTED**

Mattel "Skipper," Barbie's little sister, 9″. *Private collection.*

SKOOTER

All-vinyl; rooted blond, brunette, or red hair; brown eyes, freckles, smiling closed mouth; jointed at neck, shoulders, and hips; bendable knees introduced in 1966

9″ (23 cm), mint in box   80–100

MARK: 1965–1967

> © 1963
> MATTEL, INC.

ON BACK OF RIGHT HIP

MONICA STUDIOS

Hansi Share designed the only hard plastic doll to have hair rooted directly into the head. The expense involved in this process may account for the very short period of time Monica Studio dolls were produced.

MARION: 1949–1950

All-hard plastic, rooted hair, sleep eyes with inset lashes; jointed at neck, shoulders, and hips

18″ (46 cm), excellent condition
275–325

> **UNMARKED**

NANCY ANN DRESSED DOLLS

All of Nancy Ann's hard plastic dolls were well made and carefully costumed. Although the Storybook dolls have always been the most popular set, collectors are showing a growing interest in the Style Show series, Nancy Ann's most expensive line of dolls

MUFFIE: CA. 1952–1957

All-hard plastic; blond, brunette, or red dynel wig; sleep eyes, closed mouth; jointed at neck, shoulders, and hips

- Type I: painted lashes, nonwalker.
- Type II: molded lashes, walks
  8″ (20 cm), excellent condition
  80–130

MARK:

> **STORYBOOK DOLLS CALIFORNIA**

ON BACK

Crib Note: Muffie came dressed (in panties, shoes, and socks) or undressed. Also available were accessories and extra outfits. Original prices ranged from $.25 (for a plastic doll stand) to $17.95 (for a metal trunk containing Muffie, five outfits, and numerous accessories).

Nancy Ann "Muffie," 8″. *Martie Cook*.

STORYBOOK DOLLS: 1949–LATE 1950s

All-hard plastic, mohair wig, painted "O"-shaped mouth, painted shoes; jointed at neck (except some small ones), shoulders, and hips; panties attached to body with masking-type tape

- Type I: painted eyes

- Type II: black sleep eyes

- Type III: blue sleep eyes with molded lashes
  3 ½–7″ (9–18 cm), mint in box
  40–50

Crib Note: Original retail prices for one doll ranged from $1.25 to $4.00.

MARK:

> STORYBOOK
> DOLLS
> USA
> TRADEMARK
> REG

ON BACK

Nancy Ann "Storybook Doll," 6″. *Private collection*.

STYLE SHOW: 1952–1955

All-hard plastic (some had vinyl heads with rooted hair in 1955), saran wig, sleep eyes with inset lashes, closed mouth; jointed at neck, shoulders, and hips; beautifully dressed in long, elaborate gowns; only identification is on the wrist tag

17–18″ (43–46 cm), excellent condition   300–350

UNMARKED

SASHA DOLLS LIMITED

Sasha Morganthaler (1893–1975), a talented painter and sculptor, began making dolls and toys for her children during the 1920s and progressed to a limited commercial output by the early 1940s. It wasn't until the mid-1960s that she was finally able to mass-produce a line of dolls that met her artistic specifications and high standards of quality. The "Sasha" dolls, with their wistful, serious expressions and dark-toned skin, represent all children of the world and are stylistically related to the earlier "art dolls" of Marion Kaulitz and Käthe Kruse. They were produced in Stockport, Cheshire, England, from 1969 until 1986.

BABY DOLLS

All-vinyl, rooted hair, painted eyes, closed mouth; baby body jointed at neck, shoulders, and hips

12″ (30 cm), mint in box   125–175

LIMITED EDITIONS: 1981–1986

Sashas or Gregors in special outfits, each model produced for only one year. The company closed before the production of the 1986 edition was complete; therefore, the price of the last edition is much higher than the rest.

Sasha baby, 12″. Private collection.

Prices are for mint-in-box condition.

Velvet, 1981	**375–425**
Pintucks, 1982	**225–250**
Kiltie, 1983	**325–350**
Harlequin, 1984	**225–250**
Prince Gregor, 1985	**250–275**
20th Anniversary, 1985 (reproduction of the first Sasha doll produced by Trendon Ltd in 1965)	
	200–250
Princess, 1986	**1300–1500**

SASHA OR GREGOR

All-vinyl, rooted hair, painted eyes, closed mouth; jointed at neck, shoulders, and hips

16″ (41 cm), mint in box   125–175

Crib Note: The dolls are unmarked, but they came with circular wrist tags. "Sasha" is printed on one side of the tag, and "MADE IN/SERIE/ENGLAND" on the other. Extra clothing and accessories were also available.

Sasha girl, 16″. Private collection.

STORYBOOK TYPE

Produced by many small companies during the 1950s, the dolls were intended to compete with the highly successful Nancy Ann Storybook dolls. However, it is not difficult to distinguish between Nancy Ann's dolls and the imitations. The imitations are usually unmarked, with one-piece bodies and legs. The clothing, which is stapled to the doll's body, is often poorly constructed, with unfinished hems and underwear.

6–9″ (15–23 cm), mint in box 10–15

Storybook-type doll, 7 ½″. *Private collection*.

TERRI LEE

Mrs. Violet Gradwohl began making these very distinctive dolls in 1946. The dolls were produced at a plant in Lincoln, Nebraska, until 1952, when Mrs. Gradwohl moved the company to Apple Valley, California.

CONNIE LYNN: 1955
All-hard plastic, wig, sleep eyes with inset lashes, open/closed mouth; jointed at neck, shoulders, and hips

18″ (46 cm), excellent condition
300–350

JERRI LEE: 1950

All-hard plastic; caracul wig, painted features; jointed at neck, shoulders, and hips; same mark as Terri Lee

16″ (41 cm), excellent condition
200–250

LINDA BABY: 1951

All-vinyl, molded and painted hair, painted eyes and mouth; jointed at neck, shoulders, and hips

10″ (25 cm), excellent condition
150–200

TERRI LEE

All-hard plastic (by 1949), wig, painted features; jointed at neck, shoulders, and hips

16″ (41 cm), excellent condition
225–275

MARK:

TERRI LEE

ON BACK
USED FOR BOTH TERRI LEE AND
JERRI LEE

Terri Lee dolls, 16″. *Courtesy of Marvin Cohen Auctions.*

TINY TERRI LEE OR TINY JERRI LEE: CA. 1951–1956

All-hard plastic, wig (caracul for Jerri), sleep eyes with inset lashes, closed mouth; jointed at neck, shoulders, and hips; walker

10″ (25 cm), excellent condition
Tiny Jerri Lee	170–190
Tiny Terri Lee	125–150

UNEEDA DOLL CO., INC.

Founded in 1917 by Benjamin Sklarsky, Uneeda has remained a family company. Currently, Samuel Sklarsky is the president/treasurer, and Bob Sklarsky is the vice-president/secretary.

DOLLIKIN: 1957

All-hard plastic with vinyl head, rooted hair, sleep eyes with inset lashes, pierced ears, closed mouth; jointed at neck, shoulders, upper arms, elbows, wrists, waist, hips, knees, and ankles

MARK:

UNEEDA
2S

ON HEAD

19″ (48 cm), mint   **65–85**

**Uneeda "Dollikin" in original box,
19″.** *Courtesy of Christie's East.*

VOGUE DOLLS, INC.

In 1948, Jennie Adler Graves introduced her most popular plastic doll, Ginny. The first of the eight-inch plastic play dolls, Ginny had an extensive wardrobe and numerous accessories. Her clothing was designed by Mrs. Graves's daughter, Virginia Graves Carlson. After a long and successful career, Mrs. Graves retired in 1960.

GINNY: 1948–1962

All-hard plastic, wig, closed mouth; jointed at neck, shoulders, and hips; designed by Bernard Lipfert; 8″ (20 cm)

- Identification by dates:
  1948–1950: painted eyes, molded hair, with attached wig
  1950–1953: sleep eyes, painted lashes, Dynel or caracul wig

MARKS: 1948–1953

VOGUE DOLL

ON BACK

1954: Dynel wig; walks; new mark
1955–1956: molded lashes, new mark
1957–1962: jointed at knees

1948–1950, excellent condition
                                    250–300
1950–1953, all mint   225–275
1954, all mint   225–275
1955–1956, all mint   175–200
1957–1962, all mint   150–175

• Crib Crowd (caracul wig and bent-limb baby body)
   excellent condition   300–350

Crib Note: *Original retail price for a basic Ginny (in panties, shoes, and socks) was $2.00 in 1958. Extra outfits and accessories retailed from $.25 (for shoes and socks) to $29.45 (for Ginny Bride in wood chest with five extra outfits) in 1956.*

1954

> GINNY
> VOGUE DOLLS
> INC.
> PAT. PEND.
> MADE IN U.S.A.

ON BACK

Vogue "Ginny" in Coronation costume, 8″. *Courtesy of Marvin Cohen Auctions.*

1955–1962

> GINNY
> VOGUE DOLLS
> INC.
> PAT.NO.2687594
> MADE IN U.S.A.

ON BACK

JILL: 1957–1960

All-hard plastic, saran wig, sleep eyes with molded lashes, pierced ears, closed mouth; jointed at neck, shoulders, hips, and knees

10 ½″ (27 cm), mint   75–85

Crib Note: Original retail price for a basic Jill in leotard and high heels was $3.00 in 1958. At the same time, Jill dressed as a bride sold for $7.00.

MARK:

JILL
VOGUE DOLLS
MADE IN U.S.A.
© 1957

ON BACK

JEFF: 1958–1960

All-vinyl, molded and painted hair, sleep eyes with molded lashes, closed mouth; jointed at neck, shoulders, and hips

11″ (28 cm), mint   50–60

Vogue "Jill," 10 ½″. *Private collection.*

WAX

Some of the most beautiful of all dolls have been fashioned in wax, and although many have survived admirably for more than a century, collectors continue to be intimidated by them. They do need to be maintained in temperature- and humidity-controlled environments; however, so do other varieties of dolls, such as painted composition.

While small 18th-century poured-wax figures are sometimes discovered by collectors, the earliest wax dolls to be found in any number are the delightful English wax-over-composition dolls from the 1830s to 1850s. Their small mouths are turned up in smiles, and a large proportion of them still wear their original clothes.

The most costly waxes are the poured English examples made by the Pierotti and Montanari families during the second half of the 19th century. Because their beautifully modeled, realistic heads are of thick poured wax rather than a separate material dipped in wax, they do not crack as easily and so are valued even more highly by collectors.

Though the quality of wax dolls began to decline toward the end of the 19th century, some of the German examples with molded hair or hats are charming in their simplicity and sense of period. Many of them tend to turn up in original clothes as well.

Beware of rewaxed dolls. The process is rarely successful and is never as desirable as a network of fine cracks in an original surface.

PRICE ADJUSTMENTS FOR CONDITION

Minor cracks in head	−30 to −40%
Major cracks in head	−50 to −80%
Minor warped head	−20 to −40%
Major warped head	−50 to −80%
Warped limbs	−30 to −50%
Softening of features	−20 to −40%
Discoloration (depending on degree of)	−30 to −70%
Rewaxed well	−40 to −50%
Rewaxed badly	−70%
Original coiffure	+40%
Original clothes	+50%
Original coiffure and clothes, sharp features, good color	+100 to +200%

ENGLISH MANUFACTURERS

POURED-WAX DOLL

Poured-wax shoulderhead, inset human hair or mohair, naturalistic features, fixed glass eyes, cloth body with wax lower arms and legs; made by Montanari, Pierotti, Marsh, Peck, and others

- Child

8–10″ (20–25 cm)	400–500
15–17″ (38–43 cm)	800–1100
18–20″ (46–51 cm)	1200–1500

- Lady

17–19″ (43–48 cm)	1000–1200
22–25″ (56–64 cm)	2000–2250
28″ (71 cm)	2500–2600

Poured-wax child, 1850s, 24″.
Courtesy of Christie's South
Kensington.

WAX-OVER-COMPOSITION: 1840s–1850s

Round-faced shoulderhead, hair wig inserted into a slit in top of head, fixed glass eyes or sleep eyes operated by a wire lever, closed smiling mouth, cloth body with leather arms

16–18″ (41–46 cm)   450–600

Crib Note: These charming dolls are frequently found in original clothing but nearly always, unfortunately, have cracked faces.

Wax-over-composition doll, 1840s, 25″. Courtesy of Christie's East.

GERMAN MANUFACTURERS

WAX-OVER-COMPOSITION DOLL WITH MOLDED HAIR: 1850s–1890s

Waxed shoulderhead with molded blond hair (usually in a late 1860s–early 1870s style with "pompadour" front), bulging glass eyes, cloth body with waxed or plain composition lower arms and legs (frequently with molded boots)

14–17″ (36–43 cm)   **250–300**

• Taufling type (composition lower torso and upper leg section)
    24–26″ (61–66 cm)   **450–600**

• Molded hat
    14–17″ (36–43 cm)   **900–1200**

WAX-OVER-COMPOSITION WITH WIG: LATE 19TH–EARLY 20TH CENTURY

Waxed shoulderhead, mohair or human hair wig, sleep or fixed eyes, open or closed mouth, cloth body with waxed or plain composition lower arms and legs

• Fine quality, 1880s–1890s
    13–17″ (33–43 cm)   **250–300**
    25″ (64 cm)   **450–500**

• Average quality, early 20th century
    13–17″ (33–43 cm)   **125–175**
    25″ (64 cm)   **250–300**

Wax-over-composition child with taufling-type body, ca. 1860, 24″. *Courtesy of Marvin Cohen Auctions.*

WOOD

One of the oldest materials used in doll making is wood. The most sought-after all-wood examples date from the late 17th century to the very early 19th century. They are called "Queen Annes" by collectors, even though the reign of that English queen lasted for only a tiny portion of the dolls' period of manufacture. Fine, unrestored examples of these early wooden dolls come on the market only occasionally, and when they do, their prices are far beyond the means of the average collector.

The cheap, crudely made late "peg-wooden" doll bears little resemblance to its sophisticated ancestor's delicately carved and painted pear-shaped head and fine mortise-and-tenon joints. The loveliest of these German dolls were produced between 1800 and 1820, and as an added bonus to collectors, a large proportion of them are found dressed in their original Empire-style costumes.

Although wooden dolls continued to be home-carved during the 19th century, very few were mass-produced until late in the century, when several Vermont firms took out patents on similar-looking jointed wood dolls. The "Springfield" dolls have an austere, primitive look that is most appealing; unfortunately, few are found with their paint intact.

Early in this century another wooden doll, the "Bébé Tout en Bois" made its appearance. This doll, distributed by various French and German companies, is not particularly attractive but is of historical interest to some collectors and museums. More sought after by far are the American wooden dolls made by Albert Schoenhut, beginning about 1911. Although Schoenhut designed some very ordinary dolly faces, the company also produced several excellent character types; the most desirable had lovely carved hair.

One of the most frustrating problems with wooden dolls is the tendency of their painted surfaces to chip—a malady for which apparently no remedy was found between the manufacture of the Queen Annes and the Schoenhuts two hundred years later.

PRICE ADJUSTMENTS FOR CONDITION

Splits, minor to moderate	−30 to −50%
Wormholes, moderate	−20 to −50%
Missing wig	−10 to −30%
No clothes	−20 to −30%
Paint worn or chipped, minor	−10 to −30%
Paint worn or chipped, major	−50 to −80%
Repainted head	−40 to −70%
Original clothing on an 18th-century doll	+100% or more

EARLY WOOD
(UNKNOWN MAKERS)

QUEEN ANNE TYPE: LATE 1600s–1800

All-wood, gesso finish on head and shoulders, human hair wig nailed to head, "stitched" or one-stroke eyebrows, inset pupil-less eyes or painted eyes, closed mouth, fork-type hands, jointed at shoulders and hips

15–18″ (38–46 cm)	2350–2850
22–24″ (56–61 cm)	3800–4200
Fine quality and condition	10,000+

Peg-wooden "tuck comb," ca. 1820. *Courtesy of Christie's South Kensington.*

TUCK COMB: CA. 1800–1825

All-wood; pear-shaped head with carved and painted hair, comb, and features; pierced ears; jointed at shoulders, elbows, hips, and knees

6″ (15 cm)	400–500
9–10″ (23–25 cm)	800–1000
25″ (64 cm)	2200–2600

Late 18th-century, "Queen Anne"-type wooden doll, 15 1/2″. *Courtesy of Richard W. Withington, Inc.*

SPRINGFIELD, VERMONT

At least three different types of wooden dolls were produced in Springfield, Vermont, in the third quarter of the 19th century. Joel A. H. Ellis, F. D.

341

Martin, and Henry H. Mason (with Luke W. Taylor) obtained patents for different kinds of doll construction. Ellis's doll, patented in 1873, was jointed at the shoulders, elbows, hips, and knees, with slot-and-tenon joints held together with pins. Martin's patent of 1879 called for joints in the same places as in Ellis's doll but used ball-and-socket joints with the arms held in position by a spring that went through the body from shoulder to shoulder. The other joints were held together by screws or rivets. Mason and Taylor's patent of 1881 dealt with the doll's head (made of composition), which was attached to the wooden body by a pin and groove, allowing the head to turn.

VERMONT DOLL: 1873+

All-wood, molded and painted hair, painted features, some with metal hands and feet; dolls will show wear

11–12 ″ (28–31 cm)	375–425
15 ″ (38 cm)	450–550

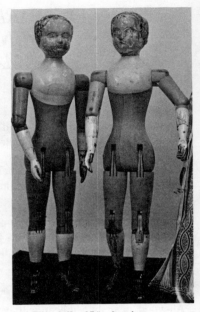

Joel Ellis dolls, 15 ″, showing common degree of paint loss.
Courtesy of Marvin Cohen Auctions.

———— SCHOENHUT ————

Albert Schoenhut, a native of Germany, immigrated to America about 1865. Seven years later, he established a toy company that eventually manufactured, among other playthings, the Schoenhut circus and the Schoenhut doll. The doll, patented in 1911, was all wood with metal joints and springs that compressed rather than stretched when pulled. The spring compression added to the durability of Schoenhut dolls. When the elder Schoenhut died in 1912, his son, Albert F., became president of the company. Another of the founder's sons, Harry E., sculpted the models for the heads of the later dolls.

CHARACTER CHILD: 1911+

All-wood, painted eyes (closed or open/closed), pensive or smiling mouth; jointed at neck, shoulders, elbows, wrists, hips, knees, and ankles

- Type I (with mohair wig)
  16–19″ (41–48 cm)   1100–1300

- Type II (with carved and molded hair)
  14–16″ (36–41 cm)   1500–1800

TYPICAL MARK:

Schoenhut character girl with mohair wig, 19″. *Courtesy of Richard W. Withington, Inc.*

343

CHILD: 1915+

All-wood, mohair wig, painted or decal eyes, open mouth with teeth or open/closed mouth with painted teeth; jointed at neck, shoulders, elbows, wrists, hips, knees, and ankles

17–19″ (43–48 cm)	**450–550**
20–22″ (51–56 cm)	**750–800**

• Sleep eyes

19–20″ (48–51 cm)	**700–750**
21–22″ (53–56 cm)	**825–875**

TODDLER: 1913+

All-wood, mohair wig, painted eyes, closed mouth; jointed at neck, shoulders, elbows, wrists, hips, knees, and ankles

14–15″ (36–38 cm)	**600–650**

BABY: 1913+

All-wood, wig or painted hair, painted eyes, open or closed mouth, bent-limb baby body

12–13″ (31–33 cm)	**500–550**
15–16″ (38–41 cm)	**600–650**

Schoenhut dolly face, 20″. *Courtesy of Marvin Cohen Auctions.*

Schoenhut toddler and baby, 15 and 14″. *Courtesy of Marvin Cohen Auctions.*

344

PART 2

DOLLS AND PRICES · BY TYPE

"BELTON TYPE"

"Belton" refers to a type of French or German doll with a slightly flattened, solid-dome bisque head and two or three small holes in the top (probably used originally for stringing the doll or attaching the wig). Most of the makers are unknown, and although there is no evidence that the Belton firm manufactured any of these dolls, the name has stuck, probably because no one has come up with a simple descriptive alternative (somehow "pierced solid-dome flattened-head" doesn't have the proper ring to it).

CHILD DOLL

Bisque solid-dome socket head, wig, paperweight eyes, pierced ears, closed mouth, jointed composition body with straight wrists and cupped hands; usually marked with only a size number

"Belton-type" doll, incised *10*, 18″.
Courtesy of Richard W. Withington, Inc.

- French type

9–11″ (23–28 cm)	650–700
12–14″ (31–36 cm)	1100–1300
15–17″ (38–43 cm)	1500–1800
18–22″ (46–56 cm)	1900–2400
23–25″ (58–64 cm)	2500–3000

- German type

9–11″ (23–28 cm)	425–475
12–14″ (31–36 cm)	700–800
15–17″ (38–43 cm)	850–950
18–22″ (46–56 cm)	1000–1500

BLACK DOLLS

Black dolls can be found in practically every type and material produced during the past 150 years of doll making. They range from plastic storybook dolls to elegant bisque ladies of the 1870s expensively dressed in the latest Paris fashions. Contemporary records indicate that until recently the market for black dolls was among white children rather than black, even when price was not a factor. Those most sought-after by grown-up collectors are good bisque examples with negroid features, black versions of already popular dolls like Chase Stockinette and Hilda babies, and early homemade cloth dolls.

———— BISQUE ————

FRENCH COMPANIES
Bru Jeune & Cie

BÉBÉ

Bisque socket head, skin or mohair wig, glass eyes, pierced ears, open/closed mouth, gusseted kid body with bisque lower arms

15–17″ (38–43 cm)   17,000–19,000

TYPICAL MARK:

BRU JNE

Jumeau

BÉBÉ

Bisque socket head, cork pate, mohair wig, paperweight eyes, pierced ears, open mouth, jointed composition body

13″ (33 cm)	**800–1000**
16–18″ (41–46 cm)	**1900–2300**

Gaultier

BÉBÉ

Bisque socket head, skin wig, glass eyes, closed mouth, ball-jointed composition body

11-14″ (28-35 cm)   **1800-2200**

TYPICAL MARK:

F.G.

S.F.B.J.

CHILD DOLL

Bisque socket head, mohair wig, glass sleep eyes, pierced ears, open mouth, jointed composition body.
Mold number: 60

14″ (36 cm)   **350-400**

TYPICAL MARK:

S.F.B.J.

60

PARIS

Jules Steiner

BÉBÉ

Bisque socket head, mohair wig, glass eyes, pierced ears, open mouth, jointed composition or composition and wood body

10-11″ (25-28 cm)   **1300-1500**
16-17″ (41-43 cm)   **2000-2200**

TYPICAL MARK:

A-9
PARIS

GERMAN COMPANIES
Ernst Heubach

CHARACTER BABY
Bisque solid-dome socket head, glass sleep eyes, composition bent-limb baby body

- Mold 399 (pierced ears, pierced nose, closed mouth)

6–8″ (15–20 cm)	300–350
9–10″ (23–25 cm)	325–375
13–14″ (33–36 cm)	400–450

- Mold 418 (molded and painted hair, pierced ears, open laughing mouth)

10″ (25 cm)	400–450
13″ (33 cm)	550–600

TYPICAL MARK:

Heubach Koppelsdorf

WITH MOLD NUMBER BENEATH

Ernst Heubach black baby, incised *399, 14″. Courtesy of Marvin Cohen Auctions.*

Kämmer & Reinhardt

CHILD DOLL
Bisque socket head, mohair wig, glass sleep eyes, open mouth, jointed composition body; size number only

19″ (48 cm)	1200–1500

CHARACTER BABY
Bisque socket head, composition bent-limb baby body

- Mold 100: GM 1909 (molded and painted hair, painted eyes, closed mouth)
  11″ (28 cm)   **650–700**

- Mold 119 (wig, glass eyes, open/closed mouth)
  24″ (61 cm)   **5500–6000**

- Mold 126: GM 1914 (wig, glass sleep eyes, open mouth)
  10″ (25 cm)   **450–500**

CHARACTER CHILD: GM 1909
Bisque socket head, mohair wig, painted eyes, closed mouth, jointed composition or composition and wood body.
Mold number: 101

12″ (31 cm)   **2400–2600**

Kestner

HILDA BABY: GM 1914
Bisque socket head, wig, glass sleep eyes, open mouth, composition bent-limb baby body.
Mold number: 245

12–13″ (31–33 cm)   **2500–3000**
17–19″ (43–48 cm)   **4500–6000**

TYPICAL MARK:

TYPICAL MARK:

245
J.D.K.Jr.
Hilda

Armand Marseille

CHILD DOLL

Bisque socket head, mohair wig, glass eyes, open mouth, jointed composition body.
Mold number: 390

13″ (33 cm)	**300–350**
24″ (61 cm)	**550–600**

TYPICAL MARK:

Armand Marseille
390

CHARACTER BABY

Bisque socket head, open mouth, composition bent-limb baby body

• Mold 351 (solid dome head, glass sleep eyes)
   11–12″ (28–31 cm)   **300–400**
   17–18″ (43–46 cm)   **600–700**

• Mold 362 (molded and painted hair, glass eyes)
   15″ (38 cm)   **800–900**

TYPICAL MARK:

A.M.
Germany
351 2½K

Armand Marseille 341 black baby, dressed as an Indian, 20″. *Courtesy of Christie's East.*

Theodor Recknagel

CHILD DOLL

Bisque socket head, wig, set glass eyes, pierced nose, open mouth, jointed composition body.
Mold number: 34 (GM 1914)

6–9" (15–23 cm)   **350–450**

TYPICAL MARK:

34–15

Franz Schmidt

CHARACTER BABY

Bisque socket head, molded and painted hair, glass sleep eyes, pierced nostrils, open mouth, composition bent-limb baby body.
Mold number: 1297

10" (25 cm)   **450–500**

TYPICAL MARK:

FS&C
SIMON & HALBIG
1297
Germany

Schoenau & Hoffmeister

CHARACTER TODDLER: HANNA

Bisque socket head, mohair wig, glass eyes, open mouth, jointed composition toddler body

8–9" (20–23 cm)   **250–300**

TYPICAL MARK:

CHILD DOLL

Bisque socket head, wig, brown glass eyes, open mouth, jointed composition body.

Mold number: 5000 (GM 1903)

12″ (31 cm)   **200–250**

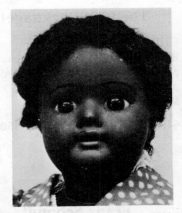

Schoenau & Hoffmeister black 5000 child, 12 ½″. *Courtesy of Marvin Cohen Auctions.*

Simon & Halbig

CHILD DOLL

Bisque socket head, mohair or human hair wig, glass sleep or fixed eyes, pierced ears, open mouth, ball-jointed or jointed composition or composition and wood body

- Mold 719
  22″ (56 cm)   **1800–2100**

- Mold 739
  17–18″ (43–46 cm)   **1200–1500**

- Mold 949
  11″ (28 cm)   **700–750**
  15–17″ (38–43 cm)   **1000–1200**

- Mold 1009: GM 1889
  Prices not available

- Mold 1078 or 1079: GM 1892
  8″ (20 cm)   **300–350**
  16″ (41 cm)   **550–600**
  22″ (56 cm)   **900–1100**

- Mold 1249: GM 1898
  21″ (53 cm)   **1350–1500**

TYPICAL MARKS:

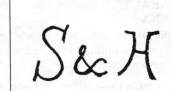

• Mold 1358
   20″ (51 cm)   **4400–4750**

**Simon & Halbig 1358 black character
girl, 21 1/2″. *Courtesy of Christie's
South Kensington*.**

CHARACTER TODDLER
Bisque socket head, mohair or human
hair wig, glass sleep or fixed eyes, open
mouth, ball-jointed composition toddler
body

• Mold 1294
   21″ (53 cm)   **1400–1500**

• Mold 1489
   22″ (56 cm)   **4200–4300**

**Simon & Halbig black 1009 girl,
14 1/2″. *Courtesy of Christie's South
Kensington*.**

——— CLOTH ———

MAMMY: 1900–1930
Homemade with painted or embroidered features, wig or kerchief, original clothes

16–24″ (41–61 cm)   **150+**

Cloth "Mammy" doll, ca. 1920, 22″.
Courtesy of Christie's East.

CHILD: LATE 19TH–EARLY 20TH CENTURY
Stockinette or painted stockinette, short curly black wig, embroidered or painted features, well modeled and proportioned, original clothes

18–22″ (46–56 cm)   **1500–2000**

LATE CHILD: 1930s–1940s
Cotton, rayon, or stockinette, yarn or floss wig, printed or embroidered features, flat face and simple body with little overall detail

12–16″ (31–41 cm)   **150–250**

——— COMPOSITION ———

LOUIS AMBERG & SON

CHARLESTON TODDLER: 1926+
All-composition, black wig, painted

eyes, pierced ears; jointed at neck, shoulders, and hips

11″ (28 cm)   400–450

TYPICAL MARK:

**CHARLESTON
AN
AMBERG
SPECIALTY
TRADEMARKED 1926
GERMANY
TODDLER**

ENCLOSED IN A CIRCLE

CAMEO

SCOOTLES

All-composition, molded and painted hair, painted eyes, closed smiling mouth; toddler body jointed at neck, shoulders, and hips

12–13″ (31–33 cm)   400–500

Tony Sarg composition Mammy, 18″, $400–$500 when in fine condition. *Courtesy of Christie's East.*

EFFANBEE

PATSY FAMILY

All-composition, molded and painted hair with three yarn braids, painted eyes, closed mouth; jointed at neck, shoulders, and hips

Patsy	600–650
Patsy Jr	525–575
Wee Patsy	625–675

TYPICAL MARK:

EFFANBEE
PATSY
DOLL

• Bubbles
16–18″ (41–46 cm)   **500–600**

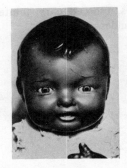

Effanbee "Black Bubbles." *Private collection*.

—— *PLASTIC* ——

ALEXANDER DOLL CO., INC.

CYNTHIA: 1952–1953
All-hard plastic, black saran wig, brown sleep eyes with inset lashes, closed mouth; jointed at neck, shoulders, and hips

Prices are for excellent condition.

15″ (38 cm)	**425–475**
18″ (46 cm)	**550–600**
22–23″ (56–58 cm)	**750–1000**

TYPICAL MARK:

> ALEXANDER

ON HEAD

LESLIE (POLLY FACE): 1965–1971

Plastic and vinyl, rooted black hair, brown sleep eyes with inset lashes, closed mouth; jointed at neck, shoulders, and hips

17″ (43 cm), mint   **300–350**

TYPICAL MARK:

ALEXANDER DOLL CO, INC.
1965

ON HEAD

Alexander "Leslie," 18″. *Private collection*.

SASHA

BABY

All-vinyl, rooted curly black hair, brown painted eyes, closed mouth, baby body jointed at neck, shoulder, and hips

Cara, 12″ (31 cm), mint in box
150–200

DOLLS ARE UNMARKED

CHILD

All-vinyl, rooted curly black hair, painted brown eyes, closed mouth; jointed at neck, shoulders, and hips

Prices are for mint in box; size: 16″ (41 cm).

Cora	**175–225**
Caleb	**150–200**

DOLLS ARE UNMARKED

— *WOOD* —

SCHOENHUT

CHARACTER CHILD: CA. 1915

All-wood, black molded and painted hair, brown intaglio eyes, closed pouty mouth, jointed body (painted brown)

16″ (41 cm)   **2000–2400**

Schoenhut black boy, 16″. *Courtesy of Christie's East.*

BOUDOIR DOLLS

Grown-up dolls for adults, these chic, long-limbed creatures reached the height of their popularity during the 1920s. They most often represent sultry, sophisticated flappers; movie stars; suave, pretty boys; harlequins; or elegant ladies in period costume. They were usually made of cloth but can also be found in composition, wax, bisque, and china. Quality ranges from the high of Lenci's exquisitely haughty ladies in period costumes to the low of late composition examples with garishly painted faces.

FINE QUALITY CLOTH: 1920s

Cloth head, fine painted features, strong expression, silk or mohair wig, beautifully dressed, sometimes hand made, sometimes representing movie stars or other personalities.

200+

LENCI

Felt head and body, mohair wig, painted features, elaborate period or fashionable 1920s costume.

24–28″ (61–71 cm)   **1500–2500**

Lenci lady, "Mimi," 26″. *Courtesy of Christie's East.*

STANDARD-QUALITY CLOTH: 1920s–1930s

Cloth head, sometimes with stiffened mask-type face, mohair wig, painted or printed features, original costume.

75–125

COMPOSITION: LATE 1930s +

Composition head, painted hair or mohair wig, cloth or composition body.

50–80

Boudoir group: bride, groom, and mother-in-law. *Courtesy of Richard W. Withington, Inc.*

BYE-LO BABIES

A true character doll, the Bye-Lo Baby was designed in 1922 by Grace Storey Putnam to represent a three-day-old infant. After acquiring the licensing rights from Mrs. Putnam in 1923, the Geo. Borgfeldt Company began to produce the dolls, with bisque heads made in Germany by Alt, Beck & Gottschalck; Hertel & Schwab; J. D. Kestner; and Kling. The cloth bodies were made by Borgfeldt's K&K Toy Company. The popularity of the Bye-Los inspired a number of imitations, including Armand Marseille's Dream Baby. Amberg's New Born Babe was not an imitation, as it was first produced in 1914, but the success of the Bye-Lo prompted the company to start producing the New Born Babe again in 1926.

BISQUE HEAD WITH FLANGE NECK: 1923+

Painted hair, sleep eyes, closed mouth, cloth body with celluloid or composition hands

8–9″ (20–23 cm)	275–325
10–11″ (25–28 cm)	325–375
12–13″ (31–33 cm)	400–450
14–15″ (36–38 cm)	475–525
16–17″ (41–43 cm)	600–700
18–19″ (46–48 cm)	1000–1250

- Smiling with open mouth

13″ (33 cm)	1100–1200

- Black

9″ (23 cm)	1300–1500
11–13″ (28–33 cm)	2400–2600

TYPICAL MARK:

Copr. by
Grace S Putnam

Bye-Lo baby, bisque head with flange neck, 12″. *Courtesy of Christie's East.*

BISQUE SOCKET HEAD: 1923+

Painted hair, sleep eyes, closed mouth, composition bent-limb baby body

- ABG Mold 1369
  - 12–13″ (31–33 cm)   1000–1100
  - 14–15″ (36–38 cm)   1200–1300

Bye-Lo baby, Alt, Beck & Gottschalck, #1369 mold, 13 1/2″. *Courtesy of Christie's East.*

ALL-BISQUE: CA. 1925

- Type I: swivel head, painted hair, sleep eyes, closed mouth, jointed at shoulders and hips
  - 4–5″ (10–13 cm)   325–375
  - 6–7″ (15–18 cm)   450–500

- Type II: wig, sleep eyes, closed mouth, jointed at shoulders and hips
  - 4″ (10 cm)   400–450
  - 7–8″ (18–20 cm)   800–1000

- Type III: painted hair, painted eyes, closed mouth, jointed at shoulders and hips
  - 4–6″ (10–15 cm)   275–325
  - 7–8″ (18–20 cm)   425–475

All-bisque Bye-Lo with wig, 5″. *Courtesy of Christie's East.*

CELLULOID

Socket head with flange neck, painted hair, painted eyes, closed mouth, muslin body with celluloid hands; heads made by Karl Standfuss

10″ (25 cm)　　　　　**375–425**

COMPOSITION: LATE 1920s

Socket head with flange neck, painted hair, sleep eyes, closed mouth, muslin body with composition or celluloid hands; heads made by Cameo

12–13″ (31–33 cm)　　　　**325–375**

Composition Bye-Lo baby, 14″.
Private collection.

VINYL: CA. 1948

Vinyl head with painted features, cloth body with vinyl arms and legs; this particular vinyl becomes sticky with age

16″ (41 cm)　　　　　**100–150**

Vinyl Bye-Lo baby, 16″. *Courtesy of Christie's East.*

WAX

Socket head with flange neck, molded
hair and features, cloth body, celluloid
hands

16″ (41 cm)   **2500–2750**

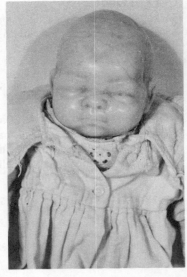

Wax Bye-Lo baby, 20″. *Courtesy of
Richard W. Withington, Inc.*

GOOGLY-EYED DOLLS

These cute little imps were popular as novelty dolls during the 1910s and 1920s and are even more popular with today's collectors, as their astronomical prices will attest. Heads can be found in composition as well as bisque; and although the composition bodies are often cheaply made, their bisque heads are usually of excellent quality. Googly eyes are also known by the trade name "Rougish Eyes."

— BISQUE —

BAEHR & PROESCHILD

CHARACTER TODDLER

Bisque socket head, wig, glass sleep eyes, closed mouth, ball-jointed composition or composition and wood toddler body.
Typical mold number: 686

TYPICAL MARK:

12″ (31 cm)	**2200–2500**

DEMALCOL

CHARACTER BABY

Bisque socket head, wig, glass sleep eyes, slightly smiling closed mouth, composition bent-limb baby body

TYPICAL MARK:

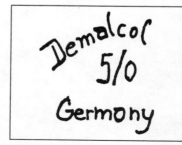

9–10″ (23–25 cm)	**650–750**

MAX HANDWERCK

ELITE: GM 1915

A series of four models representing German, English, American, and Turk/Austrian (a double-face doll) characters; bisque socket head with molded hat and hair, glass eyes, watermelon smile, ball-jointed composition and wood body

12–13″ (31–33 cm)   1400–1600

TYPICAL MARK:

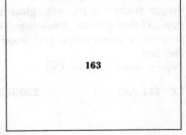

Dep.
Elite

HERTEL & SCHWAB

JUBILEE DOLL SERIES: CA. 1914

Made for Strobel and Wilken; all with bisque socket heads

- Mold 163 (molded and painted hair, glass sleep eyes, open/closed watermelon smile, jointed composition toddler body or composition bent-limb baby body)

    12″ (31 cm)   1900–2100
    15″ (38 cm)   2700–2900

TYPICAL MARK:

163

ON HEAD

Hertel & Schwab 163 googly toddler, 15″. *Courtesy of Marvin Cohen Auctions.*

- Mold 165 (wig, glass sleep eyes, open/closed watermelon smile, jointed composition toddler body or composition bent-limb baby body)
  10–12" (25–31 cm)   2500–2750
  16–18" (41–46 cm)   3200–3500

- Mold 172 (molded and painted hair, glass eyes, watermelon smile, jointed composition toddler body)
  22" (56 cm)   6500–7000

Hertel & Schwab 165 and 172 googlies, 16 and 22". *Courtesy of Marvin Cohen Auctions.*

GEBRÜDER HEUBACH

CHARACTER TODDLER

Bisque socket head, molded and painted hair, painted eyes, closed mouth with pursed lips, jointed composition toddler body

7" (18 cm)   550–600

TYPICAL MARK:

KÄMMER & REINHARDT

ALL-BISQUE TODDLER

Socket head, mohair wig, glass sleep, side-glancing eyes; closed smiling mouth, five-piece body.

Mold number: 131

9–10″ (23–25 cm)   2750–3000

TYPICAL MARK:

> **K * R**
> **SIMON & HALBIG**
> **131**

KESTNER

CHARACTER TODDLER

Bisque socket head, wig, glass sleep eyes, watermelon smile, jointed composition or composition and wood toddler body.

Typical mold number: 221

12″ (31 cm)	3500–3800
15″ (38 cm)	4000–4500
17″ (43 cm)	5000–5500

TYPICAL MARK:

> **J.D.K.**
> **Ges. Gesch**

ALL-BISQUE TODDLER

Wig, closed mouth, swivel head on five-piece body.

Mold number: 189

6″ (15 cm)   1200–1500

KLEY & HAHN

CHARACTER CHILD

Bisque socket head, wig, glass eyes, open/closed laughing mouth, jointed composition body; heads made by Hertel & Schwab.

Mold number: 180
16" (41 cm)   **3050 (1)**

TYPICAL MARK:

K & H
180

ARMAND MARSEILLE

CHARACTER BABY OR TODDLER

Bisque socket head, jointed composition toddler body or composition bent-limb baby body

- Mold 200: GM 1911 (wig, glass eyes, closed smiling mouth)
  6" (15 cm)   **900–1100**
  11" (28 cm)   **1500–1800**

- Mold 210: GM 1910 (molded and painted hair, painted eyes, closed smiling mouth)
  7" (18 cm)   **300–350**

- Mold 252: GM 1912 (molded and painted hair, painted eyes, watermelon smile)
  14" (36 cm)   **1500–1750**

- Mold 253 "Nobbi Kid" (wig, glass sleep eyes, closed smiling mouth)
  7" (18 cm)   **600–650**
  10" (25 cm)   **900–1100**

TYPICAL MARK:

Germany
323
A. 6/0. M.

Armand Marseille 253 googly toddler, 10". *Courtesy of Christie's South Kensington.*

- Mold 254 (painted eyes, closed mouth)

  6″ (15 cm)   **275–325**

- Mold 320: GM 1913 (molded and painted hair, painted eyes, watermelon smile)

  6″ (15 cm)   **350–400**

- Mold 323 (wig, fixed or sleep glass eyes, closed smiling mouth)

7–9″ (18–23 cm)	**550–650**
10–12″ (25–31 cm)	**1100–1250**
13–14″ (33–36 cm)	**1400–1500**

- Mold 325 (wig, fixed glass eyes, closed smiling mouth)

  8–9″ (20–23 cm)   **500–600**

ALL-BISQUE TODDLER

Molded and painted hair, painted side-glancing eyes, closed smiling mouth, painted shoes and socks, five-piece body.
Mold number: 322

7″ (18 cm)   **250–300**

Armand Marseille 323 googly, 7″.
Courtesy of Christie's East.

HERMANN STEINER

BISQUE SOCKET HEAD

Molded and painted hair, glass eyes, open/closed mouth or watermelon smile, cloth body with celluloid hands

12″ (31 cm)   **1500–1750**

TYPICAL MARK:

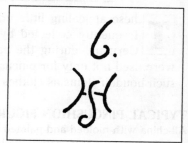

Hermann Steiner googly, incised *2 HS*, 12″. *Courtesy of Christie's East.*

COMPOSITION

"MASK FACE"

Round, pale composition face, plush or mohair wig, glass eyes, small closed smiling mouth, cloth body; known by various trade names, such as "Hug Me Kiddies" (distributed by Samstag & Hilder)

10–12″ (25–31 cm)   **600–800**

Composition "mask-face" googlies, 10 and 12½″. *Courtesy of Christie's South Kensington.*

PINCUSHION FIGURES

These appealing little ornaments are not true dolls but are frequently collected by doll fanciers. Most were made in Germany during the early years of the 20th century and were used not only for pincushions and tea cozies but as tops for such boudoir items as clothes brushes, powder puffs, and lamps.

TYPICAL PINCUSHION FIGURE

All-china with molded and painted hair and features, many half-dolls have molded and painted blouses and bonnets. The quality of the modeling and decoration increases with the complexity of the mold.

- Arms against body
  2–3 " (5–8 cm)   25–40

Crib Note: Japanese versions of this type should be about one-half the German price.

- Hands touching body but space between arms and body
  2–3 " (5–8 cm)   35–45
  4 " (10 cm)   50–60
  5 " (13 cm)   65–75

- Arms extended
  2–3 " (5–8 cm)   55–65
  4 " (10 cm)   75–95
  5 " (13 cm)   100–150
  6 " (15 cm)   175–225
  10 " (25 cm)   250–350

- Jointed arms
  4 " (10 cm)   125–150

- Legs only
  2–4 " (5–10 cm)   20–30

TYPICAL MARKS:

> NUMBERS AND/OR
> ("MADE IN) GERMANY"
> OR UNMARKED

Flapper pincushion figure, 12 " with feet. *Courtesy of Christie's South Kensington.*

374

FANCY

Ladies with elaborate molded and painted hairdos (blond, brunette, or gray), sometimes molded and painted bonnets and/or bodices, accessories; fine painting and modeling

2" (5 cm)	100–150
4" (10 cm)	250–300
5" (13 cm)	375–450
7" (18 cm)	800–1100

• Children

2–3" (5–8 cm)	100–150

Eighteenth-century-style pincushion figure holding mirror, 8", with skirt. *Courtesy of Sotheby's, New York.*

Googly-eyed child pincushion figure, 2 1/4". *Julie Collier.*

DRESSEL & KISTER

2–3" (5–8 cm)	175–225
4–5" (10–13 cm)	300–350
10" (25 cm)	1000–1200

TYPICAL MARK:

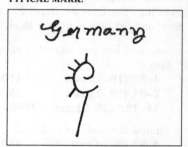

Dressel & Kister pincushion figure, 4 1/2". *Courtesy of Christie's East.*

KEWPIES

Rose O'Neill first drew Kewpies as decorations around the edges of her letters. When she began to have her work published, she always found a way to include a few of the little characters in each drawing or story. In 1909, the editor of *Ladies' Home Journal* suggested that she develop a series of illustrated Kewpie adventures for the magazine's children's page. The Kewpies proved to be so popular that two years later O'Neill was working with the Geo. Borgfeldt Company to design a doll that looked like her illustrations. The company hired Joseph Kallus, still a young art student at that time, to do the rough modeling. After Rose O'Neill finished the sculpting, the firm sent her to Germany to choose the companies to produce the bisque versions of the doll. The first soft Kewpies, called Kuddle Kewpies, were made of silk. They were designed by O'Neill and sewn by her sister for the Christmas season of 1925.

ALL-BISQUE: 1912+

Molded and painted hair, painted side-glancing eyes, closed watermelon smile, tiny, molded blue wings on shoulders

- Standard Kewpie, jointed at shoulders

4–5″ (10–13 cm)	110–140
7–9″ (18–23 cm)	250–325
11–12″ (28–31 cm)	1000–1250

- Jointed at shoulders and hips

4–5″ (8–10 cm)	350–400

TYPICAL MARK:

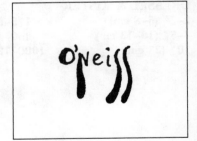

ON SOLE OF FOOT

• Character and action Kewpies

Bride or groom
 4–5″ (10–13 cm) 200–225
Buttonhole
 2″ (5 cm) 125–175
Farmer
 4″ (10 cm) 500–550
Holding book
 2″ (5 cm) 325–375
 4″ (10 cm) 600–650
Holding broom
 4″ (10 cm) 450–500
Holding pen
 2″ (5 cm) 375–425
Huggers
 4″ (10 cm) 150–200
Huggers with books
 4″ (10 cm) 200–250
On chair
 3″ (8 cm) 225–250
Shoulderhead only
 2″ (5 cm) 275–325
Thinker
 4–6″ (10–15 cm) 200–250
Traveller
 3–4″ (8–10 cm) 200–225

Bisque Kewpie, 5″. *Courtesy of Christie's East.*

With cat
 3″ (8 cm) 350–400
With Doodledog on bench
 3″ (8 cm) 1200–1500
With spider
 3″ (8 cm) 325–375
With turkey
 2″ (5 cm) 250–300

Group of bisque action Kewpies. *Courtesy of Christie's East.*

BISQUE HEAD
Molded and painted hair, glass eyes, watermelon mouth, composition toddler body

10–12″ (25–31 cm)   **3500–3750**

Bisque-headed Kewpie with composition body, incised *O'Neill, J.D.K., 10, 10″. Courtesy of Sotheby's, New York.*

CELLULOID: 1912+
All-celluloid, painted features, standing position with legs together, jointed at shoulders; most made by Karl Standfuss

5″ (13 cm)   **50–75**
8″ (20 cm)   **100–125**

Early celluloid Kewpie, embossed *Design Patent, 2¼″. Julie Collier.*

CLOTH: 1929+
All-cloth with pointed "kwip" on top of head, flat face with printed or painted features; made by King Innovations and Richard G. Krueger, Inc.

12–14″ (31–36 cm)   **125–175**
17–22″ (43–56 cm)   **225–275**

Satin Cuddle Kewpie, 12″. *Courtesy of Christie's East.*

COMPOSITION

All-composition, molded and painted hair, painted side-glancing eyes, closed watermelon smile, jointed at shoulders and hips; made by Cameo

11–12″ (28–31 cm)   **150–200**

TYPICAL MARK:

> **KEWPIE**
> **DES. & COPYRIGHT**
> **ROSE O'NEILL**

ENCLOSED IN HEART-SHAPED LABEL ON CHEST

Composition Kewpie, 11″. *Private collection.*

VINYL

All-vinyl, molded and painted hair, painted side-glancing eyes, watermelon smile, jointed at neck and shoulders or shoulders and hips

9–10″ (23–25 cm)   **50–75**

Vinyl Kewpie, 10″. *Courtesy of Christie's East.*

379

MECHANICAL DOLLS

There are many categories of mechanical dolls, from simple hand-held walking dolls to hand-cranked specimens to sophisticated adult amusements with complex clockwork mechanisms and movements. The finest mass-produced mechanical dolls were made in France during the late 19th and early 20th centuries. Because their bisque heads (supplied by firms such as Simon & Halbig, F. G., and Jumeau) are often the only part of the automata that are marked, beginning collectors frequently attribute the pieces to these companies in error. Correct attributions can usually be made by learning to recognize characteristics in their construction.

Unfortunately, space does not permit a detailed listing of the products of all mechanical doll firms. The following entries give a general overview of the most common "doll-like" specimens (hence, the exclusion of Vichy and Phalibois) collectors are likely to come across as they hunt for other dolls.

LEOPOLD LAMBERT

Lambert, apparently an apprentice to Vichy, began his own company in Paris during the 1880s. He is known for his single-figure automata, usually sweet French children, or young ladies with Jumeau heads; heads were also purchased from Gaultier and Simon & Halbig. Bases are usually cube-shaped with rounded corners or rectangular and cloth-draped. Keys are usually marked "LB."

AUTOMATON: 1880s–1920s

Single bisque-head figure, hair wig, paperweight eyes, closed mouth, fabric-covered base housing musical and mechanical works

Heights listed include bases.

- French Lady (Jumeau head): 1880s
    - 17″ (43 cm)   3500–4500
    - 23–25″ (58–64 cm)   6000–8000

- Tête Jumeau–marked head, three movements: ca. 1900
    - 18–21″ (46–53 cm)   3500–4500

- Simon & Halbig–marked head
    - 17″ (43 cm)   3000–4000
    - 20″ (51 cm)   5000–6000

Lambert flower seller automaton, 18½″. Courtesy of Christie's East.

RENOU

Louis Marie Renou was (according to the Colemans) the director, from 1890 to 1928, of the Maison Dehais, a French company that produced mechanical dolls throughout much of the 19th century. Bisque heads for dolls of the Renou period were purchased from Jumeau, Simon & Halbig, and others.

Type I: single-figure, two or three simple movements; Type II: two figures, several complex or amusing movements

Heights include bases.

- Type I, German head
    - 14–17″ (36–43 cm)   2000–2500

- French head
    - 17–19″ (43–48 cm)   3500–4500

• Type II, French head
17–20″ (43–51 cm) 4000–6000

ROULLET & DECAMPS

Founded during the 1860s by Jean Roullet, and later directed by the widow and son of Roullet's partner, Ernst Decamps, this company produced walking dolls and a wide variety of musical automata until 1921. Many can be identified by keys marked "RD" and by their oblong bases with angled corners. Bisque heads were purchased from Kestner, Simon & Halbig, S.F.B.J., and Jumeau among others.

AUTOMATON: LATE 19TH–EARLY 20TH CENTURY

One or more bisque-head figures mounted on a fabric-covered box containing music and mechanical works, or a single figure with key-wound clockwork housed in torso.

Heights listed include bases.

• Single figure, two or three simple movements
  17–19″ (43–48 cm) 3500–5000

• Multiple figures, several complex or amusing movements
  20–24″ (51–61 cm) 6000+

Decamps bicyclist automaton, 13 ½″ high. *Courtesy of Sotheby's, New York.*

WALKING DOLL: CA. 1890+

Bisque head, hair or mohair wig, glass eyes, open mouth, jointed body with straight legs, mechanism housed in torso; some include voice boxes; heads supplied by Simon & Halbig, Jumeau, and others

- French head
  15–17″ (38–43 cm)   1800–2400

- German or late French head
  21–24″ (53–61 cm)   1500–2000

Decamps walking doll with Simon & Halbig 1079 head, 23″. *Courtesy of Christie's East.*

THEROUDE

One of the earliest of the French mechanical-doll makers, Alexandre Theroude was in business by the 1840s, and his company was active until the end of the century. Many of his dolls "walk" or "dance"; the earlier specimens have composition heads with open mouths and bamboo teeth, which many collectors find unattractive.

EARLY WALKING DOLL: 1850s

Composition head, hair wig, glass pupilless eyes, open mouth with two rows of bamboo teeth, composition body, kid arms, three-wheeled base with clockwork mechanism; doll travels forward while turning head and lifting arm

16″ (41 cm) (includes base)
                              2000–2250

LADY WITH GUITAR: CA. 1865

Wax-over-composition head, hair wig, glass eyes, wooden hands; head turns

and nods, eyes sometimes blink, one or
both hands move on guitar

13–15″ (33–38 cm)   3000–3500
Excellent example at auction   6000

BISQUE-HEAD AUTOMATA:
1870s+

Lady or gentleman bisque character or
"Fashion"-type head.

17″ (43 cm)   4500–6000

GERMAN MANIVELLES

The small-scale, hand-cranked cous-
ins to the French key-wound automata
are extremely appealing and affordably
priced. Their movements are simple and
accompanied by music.

SINGLE BISQUE-HEAD FIGURE:
CA. 1890–1910

German bisque head, fixed glass eyes,
open or closed mouth, wooden lower
arms and legs, rectangular wooden base
covered with colorful paper (often
printed with a marbleized design)

13–15″ (33–38 cm) (includes base)
1200–1600

**German Pierotte dancer manivelle
with Simon & Halbig head, 14″.**
Courtesy of Christie's East.

SMALL FIGURE GROUPINGS: 1890–1910

Small bisque-head dancing children or amusing animal groups on paper-covered rectangular bases

14″ sq. (36 cm)   **900–1200**

AMERICAN
——— *WALKING* ———
DOLLS

AUTOPERIPATETIKOS: 1860s+

Shoulderhead of china, molded-hair bisque, painted cloth or composition; heavy metal feet, key wound; feet move slowly forward, one at a time, beneath bell-shaped carton skirt; patented by Enoch Morrison; distributed by various American and European companies

• Bisque or china head
     10–13″ (25–33 cm)   1000–1500

TYPICAL MARKS:

> Patented July 15th, 1862;
> also, in England.

OR

> Patented July 15, 1862;
> also in Europe, 20 Dec. 1862.

• Stiffened cloth or composition head
  10″ (25 cm)   **800–1200**

**China-head autoperipatetikos,
10³/₄″. *Courtesy of Christie's East.***

MAROTTES

Marottes are traditional baby and toddler toys, and one can see why these colorful, twirling, musical harlequins enchant very young children. One can also see how easily little hands could turn these toys into hammers, perhaps one reason why marottes are relatively rare today.

BISQUE-HEAD MAROTTE: LATE 19TH–TO EARLY 20TH CENTURY

Bisque head, mohair wig, fixed glass eyes, open or closed mouth, carton torso often housing a musical mechanism, bright-colored silk costume sometimes hung with bells, turned-wood handle usually ending in a whistle

**German bisque-head marotte,
11¹/₂″. *Private collection.***

• German
  10–14″ (25–35 cm)   **300–500**

• French
  10–14″ (25–35 cm)   **700–900**

386

MULTI-FACE AND TOPSY-TURVY DOLLS

— MULTI-FACE —

Multi-face dolls have two or more faces on a single head, a cap or bonnet keeping all but one from view at a time. The best-known multi-face dolls are the bisque ones produced by Carl Bergner at the beginning of this century; however, the design has remained popular through composition and plastic versions to the present day.

GERMAN MANUFACTURERS
Carl Bergner

MULTI-FACE DOLL: CA. 1900
Bisque head with two or three faces (usually laughing, crying, and sleeping or laughing and crying); knob on top of head turns desired face to front; mohair wig, glass eyes, open/closed or closed mouth, carton body with composition arms and legs

TYPICAL MARK:

C B

STAMPED ON BACK OR NO MARK

11–12″ (28–31 cm)	750–800
14–16″ (36–41 cm)	850–1000

Bergner three-faced doll, black, brown, and white, 14″.
Courtesy of Richard W. Withington, Inc.

Simon & Halbig

MULTI-FACE DOLL: 1887+

Bisque head with two faces (usually smiling and frowning), mohair wig, glass eyes, open/closed or closed mouth; papier-mâché torso, arms, and legs. Mold number: 202 (GM 1887)

12″ (31 cm)	1500–1700
16–17″ (41–43 cm)	2000–2250

TYPICAL MARK:

DEP
202

Jumeau two-faced doll, incised 7,
18″. *Courtesy of Sotheby's, New York*.

388

AMERICAN MANUFACTURERS
Three-in-One Doll Corporation

TRUDY: 1946+
Composition head with cloth body, some with blond mohair wigs, painted faces (smiling, sleeping, and crying), original clothes; designed by Elsie Gilbert

14–16" (36–41 cm)	**200–235**
20" (51 cm)	**250–275**

DOLLS ARE UNMARKED

TOPSY-TURVY

These inexpensive dolls were popular novelty items in the early part of this century. Nearly all were made of cloth, often with a black head at one end and a white head at the other. The doll not being played with was covered by a reversible skirt.

HOMEMADE CLOTH: LATE 19TH–EARLY 20TH CENTURY
All-cloth, embroidered or painted features (usually including hair)

14–16" (36–41 cm)	**125+**

Composition topsy-turvy doll, ca. 1890, 9". *Courtesy of Christie's East*.

PRINTED CLOTH: 1900–1920
All-cloth with printed features (usually including hair), commercial dress, and bonnet

12–15" (31–38 cm)   **100+**

COMPOSITION: 1920s–1940s
All-composition, painted features, jointed at shoulders, black and white heads, mediocre quality

7–10" (18–25 cm)   **40–60**

Composition topsy-turvy doll, ca. 1940, 9". *Private collection*.

MODERN DOLL ARTISTS

EMMA CLEAR

Emma Clear began making reproduction dolls at her Humpty Dumpty doll repair hospital in 1939. The first one was a china shoulderhead called Jenny Lind. By 1949, Mrs. Clear had made many other shoulderheads of both bisque and china, including Princess Maria Augusta, Mona Lisa, Augusta Victoria, Little Kate Greenaway, Claudia, Parthenia, Sir Galahad, Gibson Girl, The Blue Scarf Doll, Barbary Coast Gent, Young Victoria, Elizabeth Parian, Dolley Madison, Spill Curls, and Curly Top. Besides reproductions, Mrs. Clear also made four portrait dolls designed by Martha Oathout Ayers: George and Martha Washington, Danny, and American Madonna.

TYPICAL MARK:

Reproduction shoulderhead
250–350

- Portraits
  George or Martha Washington
  300–400
  Danny   **300–350**

Emma Clear "George and Martha Washington," portrait dolls. *Courtesy of Christie's East.*

DEWEES COCHRAN

Dewees Cochran's career as a doll designer began in 1934 when she interested an exclusive Manhattan toy store in marketing her "Portrait" dolls. Orders from wealthy parents were soon flooding in for one-of-a-kind dolls representing their children. To make her work more manageable, Cochran eventually created six basic facial types, four of which were used by Effanbee in 1936 for its American Children series. After World War II, Cochran teamed with a latex production company to produce her newest doll, "Cindy." Unfortunately, the company did not share Cochran's high standards, and she left the project. She resumed making her dolls from the six basic types in 1948. In 1951, she came up with another original idea, the "Grow-up" series. This was a group of dolls that represented girls at the ages of five, seven, eleven, sixteen, and twenty years and boys at five, fourteen, and twenty-three. The girls were called Susan Stormalong, Angela Appleseed, and Belinda Bunyon; the boys were Peter Ponsett and Jefferson Jones.

DEWEES COCHRAN DOLLS

All-latex, human hair wig, painted eyes (some with inset lashes), open/closed or closed mouths (laughing, smiling, or pensive); jointed at neck, shoulders, and hips

Cindy, 1947–1948	600–700
Grow-up, 1951+	900–1100
Look-a-Like, 1936+	1000–1200
Portrait, 1934+	1200–1350

Dewees Cochran type A "Look-a-Like" portrait girl, 15″. *Courtesy of Christie's East.*

ORIENTAL DOLLS

GERMAN COMPANIES

KESTNER

CHARACTER BABY

Bisque socket head, wig, glass sleep eyes, open mouth, composition bent-limb baby body.
Mold number: 243

12–15″ (31–38 cm)	**3500–3800**
18″ (46 cm)	**4700–5000**

TYPICAL MARK:

243
J.D.K.

Kestner mold 243, Oriental baby, 15½″. *Courtesy of Christie's East*.

ARMAND MARSEILLE

CHARACTER BABY

Bisque solid-dome socket head, glass sleep eyes, closed mouth, composition bent-limb baby body

- Ellar Star
  - 8″ (20 cm) — 550–600
  - 14″ (36 cm) — 1300–1500
- Mold 343: GM 1927
  - 16″ (41 cm) — 1200–1300
- Mold 353
  - 10–12″ (25–31 cm) — 750–900
  - 18″ (46 cm) — 1500–1800

TYPICAL MARK:

A.M.
WITH MOLD NUMBER OR
"ELLAR" ENCLOSED IN A
STAR

Armand Marseille 343 Oriental baby, 10″. *Courtesy of Marvin Cohen Auctions.*

BRUNO SCHMIDT

CHARACTER CHILD

Bisque socket head, wig, glass sleep eyes, pierced ears, open mouth, ball-jointed composition and wood body
Mold number: 500

- 13″ (33 cm) — 1200–1500
- 17″ (43 cm) — 1700–1900

TYPICAL MARK:

SCHOENAU & HOFFMEISTER

CHARACTER CHILD

Bisque socket head, wig, fixed glass eyes, open mouth, ball-jointed or jointed composition body.
Mold number: 4900

12″ (31 cm)	450–550
18–20″ (46–51 cm)	1100–1500

TYPICAL MARK:

Schoenau & Hoffmeister Oriental child, 16″. *Courtesy of Christie's East.*

SIMON & HALBIG

CHARACTER CHILD

Bisque socket head, mohair or human hair wig, sleep or fixed glass eyes, open mouth, ball-jointed composition or wood and composition body

- Mold 164
14″ (36 cm)	1500–1750

- Mold 1129
7–8″ (18–20 cm)	600–750
11″ (28 cm)	1000–1200
15″ (38 cm)	1700–1900

TYPICAL MARKS:

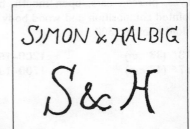

- Mold 1199
  - **11–12″ (28–31 cm)** **1300–1500**
- Mold 1329
  - **13–14″ (33–36 cm)** **1600–1800**
  - **18–19″ (46–48 cm)** **2200–2400**
  - **21″ (53 cm)** **2800–3000**

Simon & Halbig 164 Oriental child, 14″. *Courtesy of Christie's East.*

Simon & Halbig 1329 Oriental child, 18″. *Courtesy of Christie's East.*

JAPANESE

BISQUE

BABY: 1930s+

White bisque socket head, black wig, glass sleep eyes, closed mouth, composition bent-limb baby body, traditional Japanese costume

6″ (15 cm) **35–50**

Japanese bisque-head baby, 6″. *Private collection.*

COMPOSITION

DOLL: CA. 1900+

Composition head and lower arms and
legs, cloth or composition body, cloth
or paper upper arms and legs, black
wig, inset glass eyes, open-closed
mouth, traditional Japanese costume

* Child

8″ (20 cm)	50–75
16″ (41 cm)	125–175

* Adult

12″ (31 cm)	200–250
17″ (43 cm)	400–450

Japanese composition child, 8″.
Private collection.

Japanese adult ceremonial dolls, matte finish composition heads, 12 and 17″.
Courtesy of Marvin Cohen Auctions.

CHINESE

WOOD

DOOR OF HOPE MISSION DOLL: CA. 1900+

Carved wooden head, painted eyes, cloth body, cloth or wood hands and feet; dressed to represent various Chinese classes of the times

- Adult
  11″ (28 cm)   **200–300**
- Child
  6–7″ (15–18 cm)   **300–400**

Carved wood Door of Hope Mission dolls, 8–11 1/2″. *Courtesy of Richard W. Withington, Inc.*

PART 3

APPENDIXES

DOLL BODY TYPES

CLOTH

Gesland stockinette body with composition arms and lower legs.
Courtesy of Christie's East.

Cloth baby body with composition hands.
Courtesy of Christie's East.

Cloth body with china limbs.
Courtesy of Christie's East.

COMPOSITION

From left to right. French ball-jointed composition body. *Courtesy of Christie's East.* German ball-jointed composition body. *Courtesy of Marvin Cohen Auctions.* German ball-jointed composition lady body. *Courtesy of Christie's East.* German bent-limb composition baby body. *Courtesy of Christie's East.* German five-piece composition body. *Courtesy of Christie's East.*

LEATHER

Courtesy of Richard W. Withington, Inc.

Courtesy of Christie's East.

Courtesy of Christie's East.

Julie Collier.

French kid-over-wood lady body.

French stiff-limbed kid lady body.

Bru kid body with bisque shoulderplate and lower arms, composition lower legs.

German gusseted-kid body with bisque arms.

WOOD

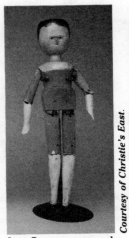

Courtesy of Sotheby's, New York.

Courtesy of Christie's East.

Courtesy of Christie's East.

French articulated wood lady body.

Late German peg-wooden body.

Schoenhut articulated wood body.

MISCELLANEOUS

Taufling-type composition body with cloth joints. *Courtesy of Marvin Cohen Auctions*.

Steiner composition and kid mechanical bébé body. *Courtesy of Sotheby's, New York*.

GLOSSARY

APPLIED EARS: ears molded separately and affixed to a bisque head before firing.

AUTOMATON: a mechanical toy, usually representing a figure or animal, that moves by itself, often accompanied by music.

BALD HEAD: smooth-finished head with no opening cut into the crown.

BALL-JOINTED BODY: elastic-strung composition and wood body employing separate wooden balls at points of articulation for versatile movement.

BÉBÉ: French word for "baby"; term used to describe a French child doll, as in "Jumeau bébé."

BELTON-TYPE: misnomer applied to a category of bisque-head dolls with two or three small holes (probably for stringing or attaching the wig) pierced into an otherwise bald pate. They have no relation to the Belton doll-making firm as far as is known.

BENT-LIMB BODY: a five-piece composition baby body with curved limbs; designed to be displayed in a seated position.

BIEDERMEIER: misnomer applied to china dolls that have bald heads with painted black pates. These dolls date from the 1850s to the 1870s and not from the earlier Biedermeier period.

BISQUE: unglazed porcelain, usually flesh-tinted, used for making doll heads and small all-porcelain dolls.

BONNET DOLLS: see "Hatted dolls."

BOUDOIR DOLLS: long-limbed adult dolls popular in the 1920s and 1930s, usually made of cloth.

BREATHER: doll with holes pierced for nostrils.

BREVÉTÉ: French word for "patented," often found as part of a doll's mark (abbreviated form: Bté)

BRUSH MARKS: individual brush strokes visible along a doll's painted hairline, a desirable feature indicating greater care in the decoration process.

CARACUL: newborn lambskin used to make doll wigs, characterized by short, silky curls.

CELLULOID: a plastic-like material made from cellulose nitrate and camphor, used for making dolls and doll heads from the late 19th century to the mid-20th century.

CHARACTER DOLL: a doll modeled with realistic features and expression. Although the term was first coined by early-20th-century German dollmakers to denote particular types of dolls, it is used in a more general sense by today's collectors.

CHINA: glazed porcelain, usually untinted, used to make doll heads, limbs, and Frozen Charlottes.

CLOCKWORK: key-wound spring mechanism similar to that found in clocks and watches, used to power mechanical dolls and toys.

COMB MARKS: ridges molded into a doll's hair representing the path left by a comb.

COMPOSITION: a pressed wood-pulp mixture used to make doll heads and bodies; a term mainly used in reference to 20th-century dolls, although the material is basically the same as the papier-mâché used in 19th-century doll making.

CRAZING: fine age lines that develop on the surface of painted composition and, less often, on glazed porcelain surfaces; caused by changes in temperature and/or humidity.

CRÈCHE FIGURES: figures used in religious displays, usually with painted terra-cotta heads and of Italian origin.

D.R.G.M.: German mark signifying a registered design or patent.

DEP: mark found on dolls signifying registration; it is the abbreviation for both the German *deponirt* and the French *deposé*.

DOLL ARTIST DOLL: a doll of original design, usually produced by hand and in small quantity.

DOLLHOUSE DOLL: a small doll specifically designed to the scale of a dollhouse, usually with porcelain head and limbs on a cloth body.

DOLLY FACE: term used to describe the idealized but rather vacuous face found on the typical bisque doll of the early 20th century.

EMBOSSED MARK: raised design or lettering found on the back of a doll's head or shoulders.

FEATHERED BROWS: eyebrows painted with short individual strokes to create a more natural look.

FIVE-PIECE BODY: body composed of torso, arms, and legs.

FIXED EYES: eyes set in a stationary position.

FLANGE NECK: a neck molded with a protruding rim, sometimes pierced with sew-holes by which it is attached to the body, often found on baby dolls with cloth bodies.

FLAPPER KNEES: knees modeled well below the joints of composition legs, a design implemented during the 1920s to accommodate the new shorter skirts.

FLIRTING EYES: eyes that move from side to side by means of a weight when the doll's head is tilted.

FLOCKED HAIR: a coating of short fibers glued to a doll's head to represent hair.

FORK HANDS: carved hands with prong-shaped fingers found on early wooden dolls.

FORTUNE-TELLING DOLLS: 19th-century novelty dolls, the skirts of which are fashioned of folded paper fortunes.

FRENCH FASHION DOLLS: term applied to elegantly dressed French lady dolls of the late 19th century when it was thought they were used to advertise the latest couture; French lady doll or Parisienne is now preferred.

FROZEN CHARLOTTE: a doll modeled without movable parts, usually of china.

G.M.:   German design patent; the number assigned to a particular patent can be used to determine the date of the first appearance of that mold.

GEOGRAPHIC DOLLS: dolls from various parts of the world dressed in native costume, usually sold as souvenirs.

GOOGLY EYES: large, round eyes, usually looking sideways, that give the doll an impish, comical appearance, popular during the 1910s and 1920s (also called "roguish" eyes).

GUSSET: insertion sewn at the site of a knee, elbow, or hip joint on a cloth or leather body to provide flexibility.

GUTTA-PERCHA: a rubber-like substance that dries into a brittle state, used as a major ingredient in novelty dolls during the 19th century.

HALF-DOLL: doll modeled with head and torso in one piece, usually of bisque or china with cloth upper limbs; small overall size; not to be confused with pincushion figures.

HARD PLASTIC: inflexible cellulosic thermoplastic used in doll manufacture from the late 1940s to the mid-1950s.

HATTED DOLL: doll with a hat molded in one piece with its head, also called "bonnnet doll."

INCISED MARK: term used to describe the numbers, letters, or symbols impressed into the back of a doll's head or shoulderplate.

INTAGLIO EYES: painted eyes that have concave irises and pupils to give them greater depth and realism.

KID BODY: leather bodies, usually white, used extensively on commercially made dolls during the 19th and early 20th centuries.

LADY DOLL: doll with adult face and body proportions.

LOW-BROW HAIR STYLE: short hair modeled low on the foreheads of late china dolls.

MAROTTE: toy composed of a bisque head and carton torso mounted on a stick, often dressed in harlequin costume; music plays when the stick is twirled.

MASK FACE: a stiff face, usually made of cloth, celluloid, or composition, that covers only the front of the doll's head.

MILLINER'S MODEL: a name erroneously given by early collectors to composition dolls of the first half of the 19th century in the belief that they had been used as props in millinery shops.

MINT CONDITION: pristine, original condition.

MOHAIR: any of several varieties of long goat hair used for making doll wigs.

MOLD: a form into which a liquid is poured or flexible material is pressed in order to make doll parts.

MOLDED HAIR: hair created all in one piece and of the same material as the head.

MOLD NUMBER: the impressed or embossed number (usually found on the back of a doll's head) that indicates its particular design.

MOTSCHMANN-TYPE BODY: body with "floating" cloth joints, probably patterned after the construction of 19th-century Japanese doll bodies. As Motschmann was only one of many doll makers who used this type of body, the term "taufling" is preferred in describing this type of doll.

MULTI-FACE DOLL: doll with two or more faces on the same head, each individually revealed by rotating the head.

MULTI-HEAD DOLL: doll with two or more interchangeable heads.

OPEN-CLOSED MOUTH: mouth molded to appear open but with no actual aperture between the lips.

ORIGINAL CLOTHES: commercial or homemade clothing made for a particular doll during the early years of its original ownership.

PAINTED BISQUE: bisque that was painted after firing was completed. This cheaper method of applying color produced a poor surface that flakes and chips with age.

PAPERWEIGHT EYES: flat-backed blown glass eyes of unusual depth in which the colored element is located at the center of the eye beneath a dome of clear glass, as in a fine paperweight.

PAPIER-MÂCHÉ: a paste and wood-pulp mixture used to fashion doll heads and limbs; a type of composition.

PARIAN-TYPE: a fine untinted bisque meant to resemble Parian marble, used most often for mid- to late-19th-century lady dolls with elaborately molded hair styles. Because the material is not true parian ware, collectors are attempting to phase out this term.

PARISIENNE: name used by Jumeau to describe his high-quality lady dolls and often used today by collectors as a generic term.

PATE: a cardboard, cork, or plaster cap that fits over the opening cut into the crown of a doll's head.

412

PEDDLER DOLL: a novelty doll popular during the 19th century representing a street peddler, its wares displayed on a tray strapped around its neck.

PEG-WOODEN DOLL: an articulated wooden doll fashioned with mortise-and-tenon joints, also called a Dutch doll.

PIERCED EARS: hole for earring passing through both front and back of doll's ear lobe.

PIERCED-IN EARS: hole for earring passing through front of doll's ear-lobe and straight into the head.

PINCUSHION FIGURE: a half figure, usually of painted china, that is affixed to a pincushion, clothes brush, or other boudoir article, popular in the 1920s.

PINK BISQUE: bisque that is colored pink in the slip so that it need not be painted between firings.

PORTRAIT DOLL: a doll that depicts an actual person, often a celebrity or historical figure.

POUPARD: an infant doll with real or molded swaddling clothing.

POURED-WAX DOLL: doll made from wax poured into a mold and built up by layers.

POUTY: name given by collectors to a closed-mouth doll with a solemn or petulant expression.

QUEEN ANNE–TYPE DOLL: early carved wooden doll of the 17th and 18th centuries.

REGIONAL COSTUME: term usually used to describe a traditional costume worn in a certain region or country, found most often on geographic or souvenir dolls.

REPRODUCTION: a doll produced from a mold taken from an existing doll.

RUB: a spot, usually on bisque or china, from which the color has worn away, usually on nose, cheek, or molded hair.

SARAN: polyvinylidene chloride fiber developed by Dow in 1940 and used for making doll wigs that are shiny, soft, and durable.

S.G.D.G.: French abbreviation for *Sans Garantie du Gouvernement* (without government guarantee), found as part of a doll's mark.

SHOULDERHEAD: head and shoulders of one material, usually molded in one piece, mounted on a body of another material. A "turned" shoulderhead is molded in a position permanently turned toward one side, nearly always toward the right.

SHOULDERPLATE: the shoulders and bust of a shoulderhead; it can be molded in one piece with the head or molded separately and attached to the head by a swivel joint.

SLEEP EYES: eyes that automatically close when the doll is laid on its back; the weight-operated mechanism is by far the most common eye assembly used in the 20th century.

SLIT HEAD: doll's head with narrow slit down the center for the insertion of hair.

SOCKET HEAD: a head with rounded neck bottom that fits into an opening between the doll's shoulders.

SPOON HANDS: hands molded or carved in a cupped shape without separated fingers.

SPRING-JOINTED: assembled with metal springs instead of elastic; springs were used most frequently during World War I when rubber was not available.

STARFISH HANDS: small outstretched hands with pointed fingers, such as those found on Kewpie dolls.

STATIONARY EYES: see "Fixed eyes."

STOCKINETTE: a soft jersey fabric used as a covering for doll bodies or heads.

STONE BISQUE: coarse-grade, grainy bisque found on poor-quality dolls, usually untinted.

SWIVEL HEAD: a head that is mounted into a socket between the doll's shoulders and can be turned in various directions.

TAUFLING: mid-19th-century German infant dolls with floating cloth joints.

TODDLER BODY: a short, chubby body representing that of a two or three-year-old child, ball-jointed or five-piece.

TOPSY-TURVY DOLL: doll with a head at each end, one usually covered by a reversible skirt while the other is displayed, often black and white.

TRADE NAME: a name such as "Alma" or "Rosebud" used by a maker or distributor to help promote a doll by giving it a special identity.

TREMBLING TONGUE: tongue mounted on a light spring mechanism so that it vibrates when touched, usually found on bisque-head character babies; also referred to as "quivering" or "movable" tongue.

TUCK COMB: carved wooden comb, often painted yellow, fashioned as a hair ornament and found on early 19th-century wooden dolls.

TURNED SHOULDER-HEAD: a shoulderhead molded in one piece in which the head is permanently turned in one direction, usually toward the right.

VINYL: a soft plastic derived from ethylene and used to make dolls from the 1950s on.

WATERMELON MOUTH: a closed, smiling mouth, usually painted with a single line.

WAX-OVER-COMPOSITION: composition head or limbs coated with wax.

WIRE EYES: eyes that open and close by means of a hand-operated lever projecting from the doll's head.

INITIALS FOUND
IN DOLL MARKS

ABG	Alt, Beck & Gottschalck
AB&G	Alt, Beck & Gottschalck
AC	American Character Doll Co.
AHW	Adolf Hülss
AL	A. Lanternier
AL&CIE	A. Lanternier
AM	Armand Marseille
AR	Theodor Recknagel
AS	Arthur Schoenau
AT	probably A. Thullier
AW	Adolf Wislizenus
B&P	Baehr & Proeschild
BF	(Bébé Français) Danel & Cie.
BJ&CO	B. Illfelder & Co.
BP	Swaine & Co.
BP	Baehr & Proeschild
BS	Bruno Schmidt
BSW	Bruno Schmidt
CH	Carl Hartmann
CMB	C. M. Bergmann
COD	Cuno & Otto Dressel
CP	Catterfelder Puppenfabrik
CP	Charles Pierotte
C&S	Curnen & Steiner
D	Cuno & Otto Dressel
DI	Swaine & Co.
DIP	Swaine & Co.
DV	Swaine & Co.
EB	E. Barrois
ED	unknown French bébé, probably Etienne Denamur
EH	Ernst Heubach
EHK	Ernst Heubach
EIH	E. I. Horsman Co.

EIH CO	E. I. Horsman Co.
EJ	Emile Jumeau
E.U.ST.	Edmund Ulrich Steiner
F&B	Fleischmann & Bloedel
F&BF	Fleischmann & Bloedel
FG	François Gaultier
FP	Swaine & Co.
FS	Franz Schmidt
FS&CO	Franz Schmidt
G	Giebeler-Falk Doll Corp.
GB	George Borgfeldt
GH	Gebruder Heubach
GK	Gebruder Kuhnlenz
GBR K	Gebruder Kuhnlenz
GKN	Gebruder Knoch
GS	Gans & Seyfarth
G&S	Gans & Seyfarth
H	Heinrich Handwerck
HCH H	Heinrich Handwerck
H&CO	Hamburger & Co.
HH	Heinrich Handwerck
HHW	Heinrich Handwerck
HS	Hermann Steiner
HSN	Hermann Steiner
HST	Hermann Steiner
HW	Heinrich Handwerck
JDK	Kestner
JV	J. Verlingue
K	Kling
KH	Karl Hartmann
KH	Kley & Hahn
K&H	Kley & Hahn
K&K	K&K Toy Co.
KPM	Königliche Porzellanmanufaktur
KR	Kämmer & Reinhardt
K&R	Kämmer & Reinhardt
K&W	Koenig & Wernicke
KWW	Koenig & Wernicke
LA&S	Louis Amberg & Son
LL&S	Louis Lindner & Söhne
LW&C	Louis Wolf & Co.

M.B.	Morimura Brothers
MOA	Max Oscar Arnold
OG	Otto Gans
PD	Petit & Dumontier
PG	Pintel & Godchaux
PM	Porzellanfabrik Mengersgereuth
PSCH	Peter Scherf
RA	Theodor Recknagel
R&B	Arranbee Doll Co.
RD	Rabery & Delphieu
RD	Roullet & Decamps
S&C	Swaine & Co.
S&C	Franz Schmidt
S&H	Simon & Halbig
SFBJ	Société Française de Fabrication de Bébés & Jouets
SH	Simon & Halbig
SPBH	Schoenau & Hoffmeister
S&Q	Schutzmeister & Quendt
SQ	Schutzmeister & Quendt
STE	Jules Steiner
SUR	Seyfarth & Reinhardt
SW	Strobel & Wilken
S&W	Strobel & Wilken
WG	Goebel
WSK	Wiesenthan, Schindel & Kallenberg
WUZI	Wagner & Zetsche
WZ	Wagner & Zetsche
WZI	Wagner & Zetsche

TRADEMARK NAMES

(WITH DATE OF REGISTRATION OR FIRST USE)

ALICE IN WONDERLAND:	Alexander Doll Co., 1933
ALICE SWEET ALICE:	Nancy Ann, 1943
ALICE THRU THE LOOKING GLASS:	Nancy Ann, 1944
ALMA:	George Borgfeldt & Co., 1901
AMERICAN BEAUTY:	Ströbel & Wilken, 1905
ANNIE AT THE GARDEN GATE:	Nancy Ann, 1943
ANNIE LAURIE:	Alexander Doll Co., 1937
APRIL GIRL:	Nancy Ann, 1943
AUGUST GIRL:	Nancy Ann, 1943
BABY BETTY:	Butler Brothers, 1912
BABY BO-KAYE:	George Borgfeldt, 1926
BABY BUD:	Butler Brothers, 1915
BABY BUMPS:	E. I. Horsman, 1911
BABY COOS:	Ideal Novelty & Toy Co., 1948
BABY SISTER:	Alexander Doll Co., 1979
BABY SNOOKS:	Ideal Novelty & Toy Co., 1938
BAMBINA:	Cuno & Otto Dressel, 1909
BARBIE:	Mattel, Inc., 1959
BÉBÉ BRU:	Paul Girard, 1981
BÉBÉ CARMENCITA:	Arthur Schoenau, 1913
BÉBÉ COSMOPOLITE:	Heinrich Handwerck, 1898
BÉBÉ ÉLITE:	Max Handwerck, 1901
BÉBÉ FRANÇAIS:	Danel et Cie, 1891
BÉBÉ FRANÇAIS:	Emile Jumeau, 1896
BÉBÉ JUMEAU:	Emile Jumeau, 1886
BÉBÉ MASCOTTE:	May Brothers, 1890
BÉBÉ PHENIX:	Mme La Fosse, 1895
BÉBÉ PRODIGE:	Emile Jumeau, 1896
BÉBÉ SOLEIL:	Jean-Marie Guepratte, 1891
BÉBÉ SUPERIOR:	Heinrich Handwerck, 1913
BÉBÉ TRIOMPHE:	Fleischmann & Bloedel, 1898

BETSY:	George Borgfeldt, 1923
BILLY DOLL:	Margarete Steiff, 1909
BINNIE WALKER:	Alexander Doll Co., 1954
BISCULOID:	Hertwig & Co., 1929
BONNIE BABE:	George Borgfeldt & Co., 1926
BOTTLETOT, A PETITE BABY:	American Character Doll Co., 1926
BUBBLES:	Fleischaker & Baum, 1926
BUPORIT:	Baehr & Proeschild, 1910
BYE-LO:	George Borgfeldt & Co., 1925
CELLOBRIN:	Franz Schmidt & Co., 1909
CELLUNOVA:	Kley & Hahn, 1913
CHARAKTERPUPPE	
(CHARACTER DOLL):	Kämmer & Reinhardt, 1909
CINDERELLA:	Nancy Ann, by 1948
CINDERELLA-BABY:	C. M. Bergmann, 1897
CINDERELLA BABY:	Louis Wolf, 1897
CISSY:	Alexander Doll Co., 1955
CISSETTE:	Alexander Doll Co., 1957
COLUMBIA:	C. M. Bergmann, 1904
CURLY LOCKS:	Nancy Ann, 1943
DAFFY-DOWN-DILLY:	Nancy Ann, by 1948
DAINTY DOLLY PINK AND	
BLUE:	Nancy Ann, by 1948
DAISY:	Edmund Ulrich Steiner, 1903
DAISY BELLE:	Nancy Ann, by 1948
DEBU TEEN:	Arranbee Doll Co., 1938
DECEMBER GIRL:	Nancy Ann, 1941
DEGAS GIRL:	Alexander Doll Co., 1967
DER SCHELM (THE ROGUE):	Kämmer & Reinhardt, 1908
DER UNART (THE NAUGHTY	
ONE):	Kämmer & Reinhardt, 1915
DIE KOKETTE:	Kämmer & Reinhardt, 1907
DIONNE QUINTS:	Alexander Doll Co., 1936
DOLLY DIMPLE:	Hamburger & Co., 1907
DOLLY DIMPLE:	Butler Brothers, 1913
DOLLY MINE:	Gans & Seyfarth, 1911
DORA PETZOLD:	Dora Petzold, 1920
DOTTY:	George Borgfeldt, 1913
EDEN-BÉBÉ:	Fleischmann & Bloedel, 1890
EDEN-PUPPE:	Fleischmann & Bloedel, 1891
ELFE:	Seyfarth & Reinhardt, 1922

ELISE:	Alexander Doll Co., 1957
ELSIE:	George Borgfeldt & Company, 1898
ELSIE MARLEY:	Nancy Ann, 1943
THE FAIRY KID:	Peter Scherf, 1916
FEBRUARY GIRL:	Nancy Ann, 1943
FIFTH AVE DOLLS:	Cuno & Otto Dressel, 1903
FINE JOINTED DOLL:	Gans & Seyfarth, 1910
FIVE LITTLE PEPPERS:	Alexander Doll Co., 1936
THE FLIRT:	Kämmer & Reinhardt, 1908
FLORODORA:	George Borgfeldt & Co., 1901
FLOSSIE FLIRT:	Ideal Novelty & Toy Corp., 1924
FRIDAY'S CHILD:	Nancy Ann, 1943
FULPER:	Fulper Pottery Co., 1918
G. I. JOE:	Hasbro, Inc., 1964
GEE GEE DOLLY:	E. I. Horsman Co., 1913
GLADDIE:	George Borgfeldt & Co., 1928
GLOBE BABY:	Carl Hartmann, 1899
GOLDILOCKS:	Nancy Ann, 1941
GRANDMA JANE:	Alexander Doll Co., 1970
GUMMOID:	Nöckler & Tittel, 1901
HANDWERCK'S BÉBÉ	
COSMOPOLITE:	Heinrich Handwerck, 1895
HANDWERCK'S BÉBÉ	
DE RECLAME:	Heinrich Handwerck, 1898
HAPPIFAT:	George Borgfeldt & Co., 1914
HARALD:	Wagner & Zetsche, 1915
HE LOVES ME:	Nancy Ann, 1943
HEBEE-SHEBEES:	E. I. Horsman Co., 1925
HEINRICH HANDWERCK:	Heinrich Handwerck, 1898
HERZ (HEART):	Bruno Schmidt, 1910
IDEALTOY:	Ideal Novelty & Toy Co., 1945
IMPERIAL H&CO:	Hamburger & Co., 1901
INTERNATIONAL DOLLS:	Alexander Doll Co., 1965
JANUARY GIRL:	Nancy Ann, 1943
JENNIE:	Nancy Ann, 1943
JOINTED DOLL:	C. M. Bergmann, 1910
JULY GIRL:	Nancy Ann, 1943
JUNE GIRL:	Nancy Ann, 1943
JUST ME:	George Borgfeldt, 1929
JUTTA:	Cuno & Otto Dressel, 1907

KAMKINS—A DOLLY TO LOVE:	Louise R. Kampes, 1928
KÄTHE KRUSE:	Käthe Kruse, 1912
KATHLEEN:	Alexander Doll Co., 1959
KELLY:	Alexander Doll Co., 1957
KEN:	Mattel, Inc., 1960
KEWPIE:	Rose O'Neill Wilson, 1913
KIDDIEJOY:	Jacobs & Kassler, 1926
KITTEN:	Alexander Doll Co., 1961
KLEINER SONNENSCHEIN (LITTLE SUNSHINE):	Catterfelder Puppenfabrik, 1922
KNOPF IM OHR (BUTTON IN EAR):	Margarete Steiff, 1905
LADY IN WAITING:	Nancy Ann, 1943
LASSIE FAIR:	Nancy Ann, by 1948
LITTLE ANNIE ROONEY:	Goerge Borgfeldt, 1926
LITTLE BO PEEP:	Nancy Ann, 1941
LITTLE BRIGHT EYES:	George Borgfeldt, 1912
LITTLE COLONEL:	Alexander Doll Co., 1935
LITTLE HUGGUMS:	Alexander Doll Co., 1963
LITTLE LORD FAUNTLEROY:	Alexander Doll Co., 1936
LITTLE MISS DONNET:	Nancy Ann, 1943
LITTLE MISS MUFFET:	Nancy Ann, 1944
LITTLE MISS, SWEET MISS:	Nancy Ann, 1944
LITTLE SUNSHINE:	Catterfelder Puppenfabrik, 1922
LITTLE SWEETHEART:	Max Illfelder, 1902
LITTLE WOMEN:	Alexander Doll Co., 1933
LOVUMS:	Fleischaker & Baum, 1928
LUCINDA:	Alexander Doll Co., 1969
LUCY LOCKET:	Nancy Ann, 1943
McGUFFEY-ANA:	Alexander Doll Co., 1937
MADELINE:	Alexander Doll Co., 1940
MAIDEN GAY:	Nancy Ann, by 1948
MAJESTIC DOLL:	Kämmer & Reinhardt, 1902
MARCH GIRL:	Nancy Ann, 1943
MARGOT:	Alexander Doll Co., 1961
MARJORIE DAW:	Nancy Ann, 1947
MARY ELLEN:	Alexander Doll Co., 1954
MARY HAD A LITTLE LAMB:	Nancy Ann, 1944
MARY MINE:	Alexander Doll Co., 1977
MAUSI:	Robert Carl, 1908

MAY GIRL:	Nancy Ann, 1943
MEIN GLUCKSKIND (MY LUCKY CHILD):	Adolph Wislizenus, 1919
MEIN LIEBLING:	Kämmer & Reinhardt, 1902
MEIN SONNENSCHEIN (MY SUNSHINE):	Catterfelder Puppenfabrik, 1910
MEIN STOLZ (MY PRIDE):	Koenig & Warnicke, 1914
MEINE EINZIGE (MY ONLY ONE):	Kley & Hahn, 1911
MERRIE LITTLE MAID:	Nancy Ann, 1943
MERRY WIDOW:	Max Illfelder, 1908
MICHU:	Fleischmann & Bloedel, 1914
MIDGE:	Mattel, Inc., 1963
MIMI:	George Borgfeldt, 1923
MIMI:	Alexander Doll Co., 1961
MISS MILLIONARE:	Butler Brothers, 1913
MISTRESS MARY:	Nancy Ann, 1943
MOLLEYES:	Meyer Goldman, 1931
MOMMIES PET:	Alexander Doll Co., 1976
MON TRESOR:	Henri Rostal, 1914
MONDAY'S CHILD:	Nancy Ann, 1943
MOTHER GOOSE:	Nancy Ann, 1942
MY DARLING:	Kämmer & Reinhardt, 1906
MY DREAM BABY:	Arranbee Doll Co., 1925
MY FAIRY:	Seyfarth & Reinhardt, 1922
MY GIRLIE:	George Borgfeldt & Co., 1921
MY PLAYMATE:	George Borgfeldt & Co., 1903
NANNETTE:	Arranbee Doll Co., 1934
NAUGHTY:	Kämmer & Reinhardt, 1920
NELLIE BIRD:	Nancy Ann, 1947
NOBBIKID:	George Borgfeldt, 1915
NOVEMBER GIRL:	Nancy Ann, 1943
OCTOBER GIRL:	Nancy Ann, 1943
OLD GLORY JOINTED DOLL:	Adolph Wislizenus, 1902
ONE-TWO:	Nancy Ann, by 1948
ORPHANT ANNIE:	Alexander Doll Co., 1965
OVER THE HILLS:	Nancy Ann, 1943
PANSY:	George Borgfeldt, 1921
PARIS-BÉBÉ:	Emile Jumeau, 1886
PATSY:	Fleischaker & Baum, 1927
PETITE:	American Character Doll Co., 1923

PHENIX BÉBÉ:	Jules Mettais, 1899
PLASSIE:	Ideal Novelty & Toy Co., 1942
POLLY PUT THE KETTLE ON:	Nancy Ann, 1941
POPPY DOLLS:	Cuno & Otto Dressel, 1912
PORTRAIT DOLLS:	Alexander Doll Co., 1966
PORTRAITS OF HISTORY:	Alexander Doll Co., 1980
PORTRETTES:	Alexander Doll Co., 1968
PRETTY MAID:	Nancy Ann, 1943
PRINCE SOUCI:	Nancy Ann, 1943
PRINCESS:	George Borgfeldt & Co., 1898
PRINCESS ALEXANDRIA:	Alexander Doll Co., 1937
PRINCESS MINON MINETTE:	Nancy Ann, 1943
PRINCESS ROSANIE:	Nancy Ann, 1943
PRIZE BABY:	George Borgfeldt, 1914
PUDDIN:	Alexander Doll Co., 1966
PUSSYCAT:	Alexander Doll Co., 1965
QUEEN LOUISE:	Louis Wolf & Co., 1910
QUEEN OF HEARTS:	Nancy Ann, 1943
RACKER:	Gans & Seyfarth, 1919
RAIN, RAIN:	Nancy Ann, by 1948
REBECCA:	Alexander Doll Co., 1967
RED RIDING HOOD:	Nancy Ann, by 1948
RENOIR GIRL:	Alexander Doll Co., 1967
RING AROUND A ROSY:	Nancy Ann, 1943
ROSEBUD:	Max Illfelder, 1902
ROSEBUD:	Alexander Doll Co., 1952
ROSES ARE RED:	Nancy Ann, 1943
SANTA:	Hamburger & Co., 1900
SATURDAY'S CHILD:	Nancy Ann, 1943
SAYCO:	Sayco Doll Corp., 1947
SCARLET O'HARA:	Alexander Doll Co., 1937
SCHALK (ROGUE):	Gans & Seyfarth, 1919
SCHLENKERCHEN:	Käthe Kruse, 1922
SCHNEEWITTCHEN (SNOW WHITE):	Kley & Hahn, 1910
SCHOOL DAYS:	Nancy Ann, 1943
SCOOTLES:	George Borgfeldt, 1935
SEPTEMBER GIRL:	Nancy Ann, 1943
SILKS AND SATINS:	Nancy Ann, by 1948
SMARTY:	Alexander Doll Co., 1962
SNOOZIE:	Ideal Novelty & Toy Co., 1933

SNOW QUEEN:	Nancy Ann, by 1948
SNOW WHITE:	Alexander Doll Co., 1937
STEIFF:	Margarete Steiff, 1907
STEIFF ORIGINAL:	Margarete Steiff, 1908
STEIFF'S CHEMISCH REINE SPIELWÄREN (CHEMICALLY PURE PLAYTHINGS):	Margarete Steiff, 1908
STEIFF'S PRIMA SPIELWÄREN (FIRST-CLASS PLAYTHINGS):	Margarete Steiff, 1908
STEINERS MAJESTIC DOLL:	Edmund Ulrich Steiner, 1902
SUNDAY'S CHILD:	Nancy Ann, 1941
SUZY:	Alexander Doll Co., 1970
SWEET TEARS:	Alexander Doll Co., 1965
SWEET VIOLET:	Alexander Doll Co., 1954
THURSDAY'S CHILD:	Nancy Ann, 1943
TICKLETOES:	Ideal Novelty & Toy Co., 1929
TINTAIR:	Effanbee Doll Co., 1951
TINY TEARS:	American Character Doll Co., 1950
TO MARKET:	Nancy Ann, 1943
TOOTSIE:	George Borgfeldt, 1906
TUESDAY'S CHILD:	Nancy Ann, 1943
UN POULBOT:	Francisque Poulbot, 1913
UNE POULBOT:	Francisque Poulbot, 1913
UWANTA:	George Borgfeldt & Co., 1899
VANTA:	Louis Amberg & Sons, 1927
VIOLA:	Hamburger & Co., 1903
WEDNESDAY'S CHILD:	Nancy Ann, 1943
WHEN SHE WAS GOOD:	Nancy Ann, 1943

ABBREVIATIONS USED IN DOLL ADVERTISEMENTS

Doll advertisers have developed a strange "language" of their own. If you think you may be in the market for a MA SSOM MIBNRFB, the following will be helpful.

a/o:	all original
bj:	ball-jointed
bjb:	ball-jointed body
bjcb:	ball-jointed composition body
bk:	bendable knees
bkw:	bendable knees, walks
bl.:	blue
blk.:	black
br.:	brown
brn.:	brown
cl.m.:	closed mouth
cl.mo.:	closed mouth
clo.:	clothes
cm:	closed mouth
comp.:	composition
compo.:	composition
disc.:	discontinued
e.c.:	excellent condition
f.c.:	fair condition
Fcb:	French composition body
Fr.:	French
g.c.:	good condition
gl.:	glass
GWTW:	Gone with the Wind
h.c.:	head circumference
hd.:	head
h.h.:	human hair
hp:	hard plastic
jb:	jointed body
jcb:	jointed composition body

jtd.	jointed
LSOM:	Sound of Music (Large set)
Ltd. Ed.:	Limited Edition
MA:	Mme Alexander
MIB:	mint in box
MIP:	mint in package
mkd:	marked
ml:	molded lashes
mld:	molded
MNB:	mint, no box
MWT:	mint, wrist tag
NASB:	Nancy Ann Storybook
NB:	no box
NBNWT:	no box, no wrist tag
NM:	near mint
n/o:	not original
NRFB:	never removed from box
o/c:	original cothes
o/cm:	open/closed mouth
oft.:	outfit
olao:	only looked at once
o.m.:	open mouth
p.e.:	pierced ears
pl:	painted lashes
pt:	paint
ptd:	painted
pw:	paperweight
pw.e.:	paperweight eyes
ptd.:	painted
redr.:	redressed
repl.:	replaced
reptd.:	repainted
sh.:	shoulder
shd.hd.:	shoulderhead
sl.:	sleep
sl:	straight legs
slw:	straight legs, walks
SSOM:	Sound of Music (Small set)
S.T.:	Shirley Temple
st.:	stationary

sta.:	stationary
v.g.c .:	very good condition
w/:	with
wt:	wrist tag

DOLL MUSEUMS

A number of the museums below are open seasonally or have unusual hours, so a call in advance of your visit would be advisable.

UNITED STATES

EAST

AUNT LEN'S DOLL HOUSE, INC.
6 Hamilton Terrace
New York, NY 10031
(212) 926-4172, 281-4143

FAIRFIELD HISTORICAL SOCIETY
636 Old Post Road
Fairfield, CT 06430
(203) 259-1598

THE MARY MERRIT DOLL MUSEUM
Route 422
Douglasville, PA 20015
(215) 385-3809

THE MUSEUM OF THE CITY OF NEW YORK
1220 Fifth Avenue
New York, NY 10029
(212) 534-1673

THE MARGARET WOODBURY STRONG MUSEUM
1 Manhattan Square
Rochester, NY 14607
(716) 263-2700

NATIONAL MUSEUM OF AMERICAN HISTORY
14th Street and Constitution Avenue, NW
Washington, DC 20567
(202) 357-2308

WASHINGTON DOLLS HOUSE AND TOY MUSEUM
5236 44th Street, NW, Chevy Chase
Washington, DC 20015
(202) 244-0024

WENHEM HISTORICAL ASSOCIATION AND MUSEUM, INC.
132 Main Street
Wenhem, MA 01984
(617) 888-2377

YESTERYEARS MUSEUM
Main and River Streets
Sandwich, MA 02563
(617) 888-1711

TOWN OF YORKTOWN MUSEUM
1974 Commerce Street
Yorktown Heights, NY 10598
(914) 962-2811

VICTORIAN DOLL MUSEUM
4332 Buffalo Road
West Chili, NY 14514
(716) 247-0130

CENTRAL
ELIZA CRUCE HALL DOLL MUSEUM
Grand at E. Northwest
Ardmore, OK 73401
(405) 223-8290

ENCHANTED WORLD DOLL MUSEUM
615 North Main
Mitchell, SD 57301
(605) 996-9896

EUGENE FIELD HOUSE AND TOY MUSEUM
634 Broadway St.
St. Louis, MO 63102
(314) 499-2968

LOLLY'S DOLL AND TOY MUSEUM
225 Magazine Street
Galena, IL 61036

McCURDY'S HISTORICAL DOLL MUSEUM
246 North 100th Street East
Provo, UT
84601

MILAN HISTORICAL MUSEUM, INC.
10 Edison Drive
Mailing address: P.O. Box 308
Milan, OH 44846
(419) 499-2968

THOMAS COUNTY HISTORICAL SOCIETY AND MUSEUM
1525 West 4th Street
Colby, KS 67701
(913) 462-6972

TOY AND MINIATURE MUSEUM OF KANSAS CITY
5235 Oak Street
Kansas City, MO 64112
(816) 333-2055

WEST
HOUSE OF A THOUSAND DOLLS
P.O. Box 136
Loma, MT 59301
(406) 232-0635

MUSEUM OF MODERN MYTHOLOGY
693 Mission Street, Suite 900
San Francisco, CA 94105
(415) 546-0202

HOBBY CITY DOLL AND TOY MUSEUM
1238 South Beach Boulevard
Anaheim, CA 92804
(714) 527-2323

SOUTH
FRANK'S ANTIQUE DOLL MUSEUM
211 West Grand Avenue (U.S. 80)
Marshall, TX 75670
(214) 935-3065

MUSEUM OF ANTIQUE DOLLS
5050 President Street East
Savannah, GA 31401

SOUTH CAROLINA ANTIQUE TOY MUSEUM
Pendleton, SC

EUROPE

UNITED KINGDOM
BETHNEL GREEN MUSEUM OF CHILDHOOD
Cambridge Heath Road
London E2 9PA, U.K.

VICTORIA AND ALBERT MUSEUM
Cromwell Road
London SW7, U.K.

MONACO
NATIONAL MUSEUM OF MONACO
Collection de Galia

WEST GERMANY
CITY OF NÜRNBERG TOY MUSEUM
Karlstrasse 13
8500 Nürnberg, FRG
(0911) 16-31 64

AUCTION GALLERIES

The following auction galleries in the United States and the United Kingdom sell dolls on a more or less regular basis.

RICHARD A. BOURNE
P.O. Box 141
Hyannisport, MA 02647

BUTTERFIELD AND BUTTERFIELD
220 San Bruno Avenue
San Francisco, CA 94103

CHRISTIE'S EAST
219 East 67th Street
New York, NY 10021

CHRISTIE'S SOUTH KENSINGTON
85 Old Brompton Road
London SW7 3LD, U.K.

MARVIN COHEN AUCTIONS
Box 425, Rt. 20 & 22
New Lebanon, NY 12125

FRASHER'S
Rt. 1, Box 142
Oak Grove, MO 64075

ROBERT W. SKINNER GALLERIES, INC.
Route 117
Bolton, MA 01740

SOTHEBY PARKE BERNET, INC.
1334 York Avenue
New York, NY 10021

SOTHEBY PARKE BERNET, INC.
34-35 New Bond Street
London W1A 2AA, U.K.

THERIAULT'S
P.O. Box 151
Annapolis, MD 21404

RICHARD W. WITHINGTON, INC.
RD 2, Box 440
Hillsboro, NH 03244

BIBLIOGRAPHY

Adams, Margaret, Ed. *Collectible Dolls and Accessories of the Twenties and Thirties from Sears, Roebuck and Co. Catalogs.* New York: Dover Publications, Inc., 1986.

Alexander Doll Co., Inc. Catalogs and reprints. New York: 1952–1987.

American Association of Museums. *The Official Museum Directory.* Washington, D.C.: American Association of Museums, 1986.

Anderton, Johana. *Twentieth Century Dolls.* North Kansas City, MO: Trojan Press, 1971.

——. *More Twentieth Century Dolls.* North Kansas City, MO: Athena Publishing Co., 1974.

Angione, Geneviene. *All-bisque & Half-bisque Dolls.* Exton, PA: Schiffer Publishing, 1981.

Angione, Geneviene, and Judith Wharton. *All Dolls Are Collectible.* Hanover, PA: Everybody's Press Inc., 1977.

Axe, John. *Effanbee: A Collector's Encyclopedia, 1949–1983,* 1983.

——. *The Encyclopedia of Celebrity Dolls.* Cumberland, MD: Hobby House Press, 1983.

Bachmann, Manfred, and Claus Hansmann. *Dolls the Wide World Over,* New York: Crown Publishers, 1973.

Benezit, E. *Dictionnaire Critique et Documentaire des Peintres, Sculpteurs, Dessinateurs et Graveurs.* Libraire Grund, 1976.

Biggs, Marge. *Madame Alexander "Little People,"* 1979.

Borgfeldt, Geo. & Co. *The Twenty-Fifth Anniversary of the House of Geo. Borgfeldt & Company New York.* New York: 1905.

Burke, W.J., and Will D. Howe. *American Authors and Books.* New York: Crown Publishers, 1962.

Business Week. New York: 1950, 1984, 1985.

Cameron, Elisabeth. *Encyclopedia of Pottery and Porcelain 1800–1960.* London: Cameron Books.

Celebrity Doll Journal. Puyallup, WA: Loraine Burdick, 1973, 1976, 1979.

Chain Store Age, 1984, 1985.

Christian Science Monitor, weekly magazine section, 1938.

Cieslick, Jurgen, and Marianne Cieslik. *German Doll Encyclopedia 1800–1939.* Cumberland, MD: Hobby House Press, 1985.

——. *German Doll Marks and Identification Book.* Cumberland, MD: Hobby House Press, 1986.

Coleman, Dorothy S., Ed. *My Darling Dolls,* 1972.

Coleman, Dorothy S., Elizabeth Ann Coleman, and Evelyn Jane Coleman.

The Collector's Book of Doll Clothes, Costumes in Miniature. New York: Crown Publishers, 1975.

——. *The Collector's Encyclopedia of Dolls.* New York: Crown Publishers, 1968.

——. *The Collector's Encyclopedia of Dolls,* Vol. 2. New York: Crown Publishers, 1986.

Collier's, 1949.

Consumer's Report. Mount Vernon, NY: 1949.

Coronet, 1948.

Cox, Warren E. *The Book of Pottery and Porcelain,* Vol. 1, 2. New York: Crown Publishers, 1944.

Currey, J. Seymour. *Chicago: Its History and Its Builders.* Chicago, IL: S. J. Clarke Publishing Company, 1912.

Dewein, Sibyl, and Joan Ashabraner. *Collector's Encyclopedia of Barbie Dolls & Collectibles.*

Directory of Corporate Affiliations. Wilmette, IL: National Publishing Company, 1988.

Doll Museum. Barengasse Zurich, Sasha Morgenthaler.

Dubois, J. H. *Plastics,* 1943.

Ellenburg, M. Kelly. *Effanbee: The Dolls with the Golden Hearts.* North Kansas City, MO: Trojan Press, 1973.

Esquire. New York: 1984.

Fawcett, Clara Hallard. *Dolls, A New Guide for Collectors.* Boston, MA: Charles T. Branford Co., 1964.

——. *On Making, Mending and Dressing Dolls.* New York: H. L. Lindquist Publications, 1949.

Forbes Magazine. New York: 1983, 1984.

Fortune. New York: 1936, 1957, 1984.

Foulke, Jan. *Kestner, King of Dollmakers.* Cumberland, MD: Hobby House Press, 1982.

Fraser, Antonia. *Dolls.* New York: G. P. Putnam's Sons, 1963.

Freeman, Ruth. *Encyclopedia of American Dolls.* Watkins Glen, NY: Century House, 1952.

Gilbert, Paul, and Charles Lee Bryson. *Chicago and Its Makers.* Chicago, IL: Felix Mendelsohn, 1929.

Good Housekeeping. New York: 1955.

Harper's. New York: 1983.

Hart, Luella. *Directory of German Dolls Trademarks 1875–1960.* Luella Hart, 1964.

Hasbro, Inc. *Annual Report,* 1986.

——. *Annual Report to Securities and Exchange Commission,* 1986.

Herzberg, Max J. *Reader's Encyclopedia of American Literature.* New York: Crowell, 1962.

Heyerdahl, Virginia Ann. *The Best of the Doll Reader,* Vol. 2. Cumberland, MD: Hobby House Press, 1986.

Hillier, Mary. *Dolls and Doll Makers*. New York: G. P. Putnam's Sons, 1968.

——. *Pollock's Dictionary of English Dolls*. New York: Crown Publishers, 1983.

Hobbies Magazine. Chicago, IL: 1950, 1951, 1985.

Honey, W. B. *Dresden China*. New York: Tudor Publishing Company, 1946.

Hubbard, C. Horace, and Justus Dartt. *History of the Town of Springfield, Vermont 1752–1895*. Boston, MA: Geo. Walker & Company, 1895.

Jacobs, Flora Gill, and Estrid Faurholt. *Dolls & Doll Houses*. Rutland, VT: Charles E. Tuttle Co., 1967.

Johl, Janet Pagter. *The Fascinating Story of Dolls*. New York: H. L. Lindquist, 1941.

——. *Your Dolls and Mine*. New York: H. L. Lindquist, 1952.

Judd, Polly, and Pam Judd. *Hard Plastic Dolls*. Cumberland, MD: Hobby House Press, 1985.

Kenner Parker Toys. Annual reports, 1985, 1986.

King, Constance Eileen. *The Collector's History of Dolls*. New York: St. Martin's Press, 1978.

——. *Dolls and Dolls' Houses*. London: Hamlyn, 1977.

Kunitz, Stanley J., and Howard Haycroft. *American Authors 1600–1900*. New York: H. W. Wilson Company, 1938.

Lavitt, Wendy. *Dolls*. New York: Alfred A. Knopf, 1983.

Literary Digest, 1915, 1926.

Look. Des Moines, IA: 1957.

MacDowell, Robert, and Karin MacDowell. *The Collector's Digest on German Character Dolls*. Cumberland, MD: Hobby House Press, 1981.

Manos, Susan, and Paris Manos. *The World of Barbie Dolls*. Paducah, KY: Collector Books, 1983.

Marketing and Media Decisions, 1986.

Marquis, Albert Nelson, Ed. *The Book of Chicagoans*. Chicago, IL: A. N. Marquis and Company, 1911.

Merchandise Manual for Toys and Playthings. Toy Manufacturers of the U.S.A., Inc., 1936.

Million Dollar Directory Series. Parsippany, NJ: Dun's Marketing Services, Inc., 1987.

Money. New York: 1984.

National Review. New York: 1972.

Newsweek. New York: 1982, 1983.

New York Times, The. New York: 1903, 1909, 1918, 1937, 1938, 1944, 1949, 1950, 1957, 1960.

New Yorker, The. New York: 1950, 1984.

Niswonger, Jeanne Duchateau. *That Doll Ginny*. Kissimmee, FL: Cody Publications, 1983.

Noble, John. *A Treasury of Beautiful Dolls.* New York: Hawthorn Books, 1971.

———. *Dolls.* New York: Walker and Company, 1967.

Parents Magazine. New York: 1951, 1956, 1985, 1986.

Popular Science Monthly. New York: 1938.

Redfarn, C. A. *A Guide to Plastics,* 1951.

Revi, Albert Christian, Ed. *The Spinning Wheel's Complete Book of Antiques,* 1972.

———. *The Spinning Wheel's Complete Book of Dolls.* New York: Galahad Books, 1975.

Richter, Lydia. *The Beloved Kathe Kruse Dolls, Yesterday and Today.* Cumberland, MD: Hobby House Press, 1983.

———. *Treasury of French Dolls, Album 2.* Cumberland, MD: Hobby House Press, 1984.

———. *Treasury of German Dolls, Album 1.* Cumberland, MD: Hobby House Press, 1984.

Sasha Dolls Limited. Catalog. Stockport, Cheshire, England: 1985.

Schmidt, Hubert G. *Rural Hunterdon: An Agricultural History.* New Brunswick, NJ: Rutgers University Press, 1946.

Schroeder, Joseph J., Jr., Ed. *The Wonderful World of Toys, Games & Dolls,* 1971.

Scientific American. New York: 1900, 1902.

Sears, Roebuck & Co. Catalog. Chicago, IL: 1902.

Shoemaker, Rhoda. *Compo Dolls, Cute and Collectible.* Menlo Park, CA: 1971.

———. *Compo Dolls, Cute and Collectible,* Vol. 2. Menlo Park, CA: 1973.

Simonds, Herbert R., and James M. Church. *A Concise Guide to Plastics,* 1957.

———. *A Concise Guide to Plastics,* 2nd ed., 1963.

Smith, Patricia R. *Antique Collector's Dolls.* Paducah, KY: Collector Books, 1968.

———. *Antique Collector's Dolls* (2nd series). Paducah, KY: Collector Books, 1976.

———. *Effanbee Dolls That Touch Your Heart.* Paducah, KY: Collector Books, 1983.

———. *Madame Alexander Collector's Dolls.* Paducah, KY: Collector Books, 1978.

———. *Madame Alexander Collector's Dolls* (2nd series). Paducah, KY: Collector Books, 1981.

———. *Modern Collector's Dolls.* Paducah, KY: Collector Books, 1973.

———. *Modern Collector's Dolls* (2nd series). Paducah, KY: Collector Books, 1975.

———. *Modern Collector's Dolls* (3rd series). Paducah, KY: Collector Books, 1976.

———. *Modern Collector's Dolls* (4th series). Paducah, KY: Collector Books, 1979.

———. *Modern Collector's Dolls* (5th series). Paducah, KY: Collector Books, 1984.

———. *Vogue Ginny Dolls*. Paducah, KY: Collector Books, 1985.

———. *The World of Alexander-kins*. Paducah, KY: Collector Books, 1985.

St. George, Eleanor. *The Dolls of Yesterday*. New York: Charles Scribner's Sons, 1948.

Standard and Poor Corp. *Standard and Poor's Register of Corporations, Directors and Executives*, Vols. 1–3. New York: Standard and Poor Corp., 1987.

Tarnowska, Maree. *Rare Character Dolls*. Cumberland, MD: Hobby House Press, 1987.

Time. New York: 1944, 1966, 1983.

Toy and Hobby World, Trow's Business Directory of the Boroughs of Brooklyn and Queens. New York: Trow Directory Printing and Book-binding Co., 1920–1940.

Uhl, Marjorie Victoria Sturges. *Madame Alexander Dolls Are Made with Love*. Dallas, TX: Taylor Publishing Co., 1983.

———. *Madame Alexander's Ladies of Fashion*. Dallas, TX: Taylor Publishing Co., 1979.

———. *Madame Alexander Dolls on Review*. Dallas, TX: Taylor Publishing Co., 1981.

United Federation of Doll Clubs, Inc. *Glossary*, 1978.

Vogue Dolls, Inc. Catalog. Medford, MA: 1958.

Von Armin, Tenner. *Cincinnati Sonst*, 1878.

Whitton, Margaret. *The Jumeau Doll*. New York: Dover Publications, 1980.

Who's Who in America. Vols. 5, 9. Chicago, IL: A. N. Marquis Company.

Who's Who in Chicago. Chicago, IL: A. N. Marquis Company, 1931.

Winnetka Talk. Wilmette, IL: Pioneer Press, 1917–1958.

Woman Citizen, 1925.

World's Work, New York: 1916.

PICTORIAL TRADEMARK INDEX

― ROUNDELS ―

Theodor Recknagel. Alexandrinenthal,
Thüringia, Germany.

Seyfarth & Reinhardt. Waltershausen,
Thüringia, Germany.

439

Franz Schmidt & Co. Georgenthal, Thüringia, Germany.

George Borgfeldt & Co. New York, USA, and Sonneberg, Germany.

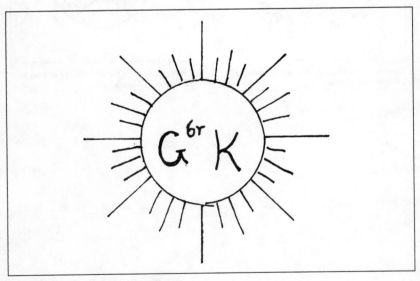

Gebrüder Kühnlenz. Kronach, Bavaria.

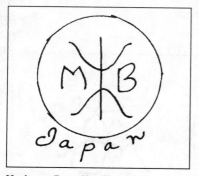

Morimura Bros. New York City importers of Japanese dolls.

Adolf Hülss. Waltershausen, Thüringia, Germany.

Bru Jne. & Cie. Paris, France.

— MONOGRAMS —

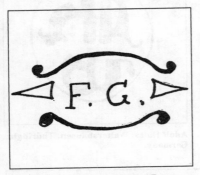

François Gaultier. Near Paris, France.

Alt, Beck & Gottschalck. Ohrdruf,
Thüringia, Germany.

Wagner & Zetzsche. Ilmenau,
Thüringia, Germany.

J. D. Kestner. Waltershausen,
Thüringia, Germany.

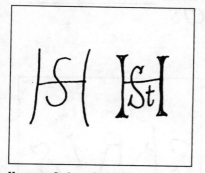

Hermann Steiner. Sonneberg and Neustadt, Thüringia, Germany.

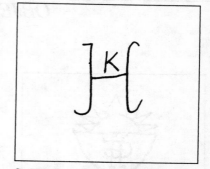

Carl Hartmann. Neustadt, Thüringia, Germany.

PICTORIAL OBJECTS

Gebrüder Heubach. Sonneberg, Thüringia, Germany.

C. F. Kling & Co. Ohrdruf, Thüringia, Germany.

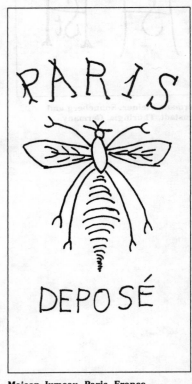

Maison Jumeau. Paris, France.

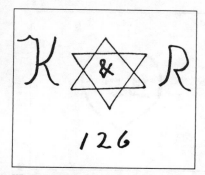

Kämmer & Reinhardt. Waltershausen,
Thüringia, Germany.

Bruno Schmidt. Waltershausen,
Thüringia, Germany.

Dressel, Kister & Co. Schwarzburg,
Germany.

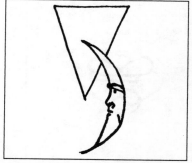

William Goebel. Oeslau, near Coburg,
Thüringia, Germany.

Schmitt & Fils. Paris, France.

Bähr & Pröschild. Ohrdruf, Thüringia, Germany.

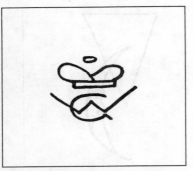

William Goebel. Coburg, Thüringia, Germany.

Cuno & Otto Dressel. Sonneberg, Thüringia, Germany.

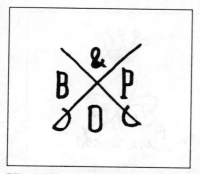

Bähr & Pröschild. Ohrdruf, Thüringia,
Germany.

Rheinische Gummi und Celluloid Fabrik
Co. Mannheim–Neckarau, Bavaria.

Max Oscar Arnold. Neustadt,
Thüringia, Germany.

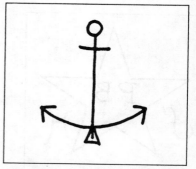

Armand Marseille. Sonneberg and
Koppelsdorf, Thüringia, Germany.

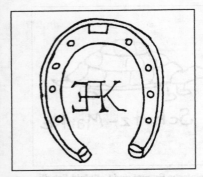

Köppelsdorfer Porzellanfabrik (Ernst Heubach). Köppelsdorf, Thüringia, Germany.

Limbach Porzellanfabrik. Limbach, Thüringia, Germany.

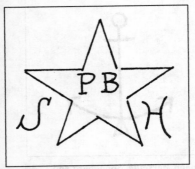

Schoenau & Hoffmeister (Porzellanfabrik Burggrub). Sonneberg and Burggrub, Thüringia, Germany.

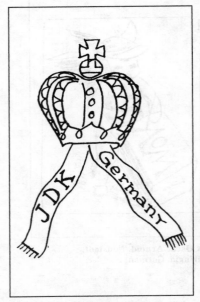

J. D. Kestner. Waltershausen, Thüringia, Germany.

448

Martha Jenks Chase. Pawtucket, Rhode Island.

Buschow and Beck. Germany.

INDEX BY MOLD NUMBER

Mold 22, *154*
Mold 29, *141*
Mold 32, *141*
Mold 34, *353*
Mold 44, *141*
Mold 60, *86*
Mold 76, *141*
Mold 98, *140*
Mold 99, *111, 140*
Mold 100, *125, 351*
Mold 101, *127, 161*
Mold 102, *33*
Mold 107, *127*
Mold 109, *111,127*
Mold 110, *176*
Mold 112, *127*
Mold 114, *127*
Mold 114X, *128*
Mold 115, *128*
Mold 115A, *126, 128*
Mold 116, *126*
Mold 116A, *126, 129*
Mold 117, *128*
Mold 117A, *128*
Mold 117N, *128–129*
Mold 117X, *129*
Mold 118A, *129*
Mold 119, *111, 351*
Mold 120, *128*
Mold 121, *126, 129*
Mold 122, *126*
Mold 126, *126, 129, 154, 351*
Mold 127, *116, 129*
Mold 128, *127*
Mold 129, *132*
Mold 130, *32–33*

Mold 131, *370*
Mold 133, *33*
Mold 136, *132*
Mold 141, *116*
Mold 142, *115*
Mold 143, *132*
Mold 148, *131*
Mold 149, *116*
Mold 150, *32–33, 115*
Mold 151, *115, 167*
Mold 152, *115, 132*
Mold 154, *131*
Mold 155, *132*
Mold 156, *124, 131–132*
Mold 157, *116*
Mold 160, *33*
Mold 162, *135*
Mold 163, *368*
Mold 164, *132, 396*
Mold 165, *141, 369*
Mold 166, *131, 138*
Mold 167, *132, 137*
Mold 168, *132*
Mold 169, *131, 139*
Mold 171, *132*
Mold 172, *136, 369*
Mold 174, *132*
Mold 178, *33, 133*
Mold 180, *33, 371*
Mold 183, *133*
Mold 184, *33*
Mold 185, *133*
Mold 189, *370*
Mold 192, *125*
Mold 196, *132*
Mold 200, *371*

Mold 201, *161*
Mold 202, *388*
Mold 208, *34, 104*
Mold 210, *371*
Mold 211, *134–135*
Mold 214, *132*
Mold 220, *133, 135*
Mold 221, *370*
Mold 224, *99*
Mold 226, *87–88, 134*
Mold 227, *87*
Mold 230, *86*
Mold 231, *147*
Mold 233, *148*
Mold 235, *87, 135*
Mold 236, *87–89*
Mold 237, *87, 134*
Mold 238, *87*
Mold 239, *87*
Mold 243, *394*
Mold 244, *100*
Mold 245, *134, 351*
Mold 247, *88, 99, 134–135*
Mold 249, *133*
Mold 250, *117*
Mold 251, *89, 117, 147–148, 180–181*
Mold 252, *88–89, 371*
Mold 253, *371*
Mold 254, *372*
Mold 257, *34, 134–135*
Mold 260, *133, 135*
Mold 263, *104*
Mold 264, *104*
Mold 267, *118*
Mold 269, *99*
Mold 272, *89*
Mold 275, *117*
Mold 281, *99*
Mold 289, *99*
Mold 297, *99*

Mold 300, *118, 151*
Mold 301, *86*
Mold 302, *117*
Mold 310, *147*
Mold 312, *117*
Mold 320, *99, 118, 372*
Mold 321, *118*
Mold 322, *372*
Mold 323, *372*
Mold 325, *99, 372*
Mold 327, *181*
Mold 329, *149, 181*
Mold 341, *150*
Mold 342, *117–118*
Mold 343, *149, 395*
Mold 351, *150, 352*
Mold 352, *150*
Mold 353, *395*
Mold 362, *352*
Mold 370, *143*
Mold 390, *144, 352*
Mold 399, *350*
Mold 400, *151*
Mold 403, *125*
Mold 418, *350*
Mold 500, *149, 395*
Mold 508, *34*
Mold 518, *149*
Mold 520, *138*
Mold 525, *137*
Mold 526, *138*
Mold 530, *165*
Mold 536, *101*
Mold 540, *165*
Mold 550, *147, 165*
Mold 560, *148*
Mold 560a, *147–148*
Mold 570, *165*
Mold 585, *101*
Mold 590, *147–149*
Mold 612, *103*

Mold 619, *101*
Mold 624, *101*
Mold 678, *101*
Mold 686, *367*
Mold 719, *162, 165, 354*
Mold 739, *354*
Mold 886, *34*
Mold 905, *162, 164*
Mold 908, *165*
Mold 914, *152*
Mold 919, *164*
Mold 924, *152*
Mold 929, *164*
Mold 939, *162, 164*
Mold 940, *162*
Mold 949, *162–165, 354*
Mold 971, *148–149*
Mold 979, *165*
Mold 980, *148–149*
Mold 985, *149*
Mold 989, *164*
Mold 990, *148–149*
Mold 1000, *196*
Mold 1008, *196*
Mold 1009, *163, 165, 354*
Mold 1028, *196*
Mold 1030, *196*
Mold 1039, *154*
Mold 1078, *165, 354*
Mold 1079, *165, 354*
Mold 1080, *163*
Mold 1129, *396*
Mold 1159, *166*
Mold 1160, *163*
Mold 1199, *397*
Mold 1248, *165*
Mold 1249, *165, 354*
Mold 1250, *163*
Mold 1255, *158*
Mold 1260, *163*
Mold 1269, *165*

Mold 1271, *158*
Mold 1272, *158*
Mold 1279, *167*
Mold 1294, *166–167, 355*
Mold 1295, *158*
Mold 1297, *353*
Mold 1299, *166–167*
Mold 1329, *397*
Mold 1339, *142*
Mold 1348, *105*
Mold 1349, *105*
Mold 1358, *355*
Mold 1469, *107*
Mold 1488, *167*
Mold 1489, *166, 355*
Mold 1894, *143, 145*
Mold 1906, *159*
Mold 1907, *153*
Mold 1909, *159*
Mold 2048, *157*
Mold 2068, *157*
Mold 2085, *157*
Mold 2087, *157*
Mold 2096, *156*
Mold 2097, *156*
Mold 3200, *143*
Mold 3500, *143*
Mold 4900, *396*
Mold 5000, *354*
Mold 5730, *119*
Mold 6894, *119*
Mold 6969, *119*
Mold 6970, *119*
Mold 6971, *119*
Mold 7072, *119*
Mold 7109, *120*
Mold 7246, *120*
Mold 7247, *120*
Mold 7407, *120*
Mold 7602, *120*
Mold 7603, *120*

Mold 7604, *120*

Mold 7605, *121*

Mold 7622, *121*

Mold 7631, *121*

Mold 7644, *121*

Mold 7711, *121*

Mold 7759, *121*

Mold 7852, *121*

Mold 7911, *121*

Mold 7975, *122*

Mold 7977, *122*

Mold 8035, *122*

Mold 8191, *122*

Mold 8192, *122*

Mold 8306, *122*

Mold 8420, *123*

Mold 8724, *123*

Mold 8774, *123*

Mold 9457, *123*

Mold 10633, *123*

INDEX OF LETTERS FOUND
IN DOLL MARKS

Note: A comprehensive listing of marks can be found on page 417.

AB&G, Alt, Beck & Gottschalck, 96–98, 196

ABG, Alt, Beck & Gottschalck, 96–98, 196

AC, American Character Doll Co., 298–300

AHW, Adolf Hülss, 123–124

AL&CIE, A. Lanternier, 76–78

AL, A. Lanternier, 76–78

AM, Armand Marseille, 142–151, 352, 371–372, 395

AR, Theodor Recknagel, 153–154, 353

AW, Adolf Wislizenus, 175–176

B&P, Baehr & Proeschild, 98–101, 367

BS, Bruno Schmidt, 155–157, 395

BSW, Bruno Schmidt, 155–157, 395

CMB, C. M. Bergmann, 102–103

COD, Cuno & Otto Dressel, 104–108

CP, Catterfelder Puppenfabrik, 103–104

D, Cuno & Otto Dressel, 104–108

DI, Swaine & Co., 169–172

DIP, Swaine & Co., 169–172

DV, Swaine & Co., 169–172

EH, Ernst Heubach, 116–118, 350

EHK, Ernst Heubach, 116–118, 350

EIH, E. I. Horsman Co., 41, 212–213, 261–265

EIH CO, E. I. Horsman Co., 41, 212–213, 261–265

EJ, Emile Jumeau, 69–75, 348

E.U.ST., Edmund Ulrich Steiner, 168

F&B, Fleischmann & Bloedel, 62–63

F&BF, Fleischmann & Bloedel, 62–63

FG, François Gaultier, 63–65, 349

FP, Swaine & Co., 169–172

FS&CO, Franz Schmidt, 157–158, 353

FS, Franz Schmidt, 157–158, 353

G&S, Gans & Seyfarth, 109–110

GB, George Borgfeldt, 40–41, 178–181

GBR K, Gebrüder Kuhnlenz, 140–141

GH, Gebrüder Heubach, 30–31,
118–123, 369
GK, Gebrüder Kuhnlenz, 140–141
GS, Gans & Seyfarth, 109–110

H&CO, Hamburger & Co., 183–185
H, Heinrich Handwerck, 111–112
HCH H, Heinrich Handwerck,
111–112
HH, Heinrich Handwerck, 111–112
HHW, Heinrich Handwerck, 111–
112
HS, Hermann Steiner, 168–169
HSN, Hermann Steiner, 168–169
HST, Hermann Steiner, 168–169
HW, Heinrich Handwerck, 111–112

JDK, Kestner, 129–136, 351, 370,
394
JV, J. Verlingue, 94

K&H, Kley & Hahn, 136–139, 371
K&R, Kämmer & Reinhardt, 124–
129, 350–351, 370
K&W, Koenig & Wernicke, 139–
140
KH, Kley & Hahn, 136–139, 371
KR, Kämmer & Reinhardt, 124–
129, 350–351, 370
KWW, Koenig & Wernicke, 139–
140

LA&S, Louis Amberg & Son,
177–178, 239–242, 356–
357
LL&S, Louis Lindner & Söhne,
141–142

M.B., Morimura Brothers, 47–49

PD, Petit & Dumontier, 79–80
PM, Porzellanfabrik Mengersger-
euth, 151–152
PSCH, Peter Scherf, 155

R&B, Arranbee Doll Co., 242–
244, 301
RA, Theodor Recknagel, 153–
154, 353
RD, Rabery & Delphieu, 81–82

S&C
Franz Schmidt, 157–158, 353
Swaine & Co., 169–172
S&H, Simon & Halbig, 161–167,
354–355, 388, 396–397
S&Q, Schutzmeister & Quendt,
160–161
SFBJ, Société Française de Fabri-
cation de Bébés & Jouets,
85–89
SH, Simon & Halbig, 161–167,
354–355, 388, 396–397
SPBH, Schoenau & Hoffmeister,
159–160, 353–354, 396
SQ, Schutzmeister & Quendt,
160–161
STE, Jules Steiner, 349

WG, Goebel, 110–111
WUZI, Wagner & Zetsche, 173–
174
WZ, Wagner & Zetsche, 173–174
WZI, Wagner & Zetsche, 173–174

GENERAL INDEX

Abbreviations, used in doll advertisements, 426–428
Alabama Indestructible Doll, cloth dolls, 205
Alexander Doll Co., Inc.
  black dolls, 358–360
  cloth dolls, 206
  composition/papier-mâché dolls, 233–239
  plastic dolls, 280–298
Alice in Wonderland, 206
All-bisque dolls
  American, Nancy Ann Dressed Dolls, 39
  American distributors
    E. I. Horsman Co., 41
    George Borgfeldt & Co., 40–41
  bye-lo babies, 364
  French type, 28
  general information, 27
  German
    Gebrüder Heubach, 30–31
    Hertel & Schwab, 29
    Hertwig & Co., 29
    miscellaneous manufacturers, 31–38
  Japanese, 42–43
  kewpies, 376–377
  price adjustments for condition, 27
Alt, Beck & Gottschalck
  china dolls, 196
  German bisque dolls, 96–98
Louis Amberg & Son
  American dolls/German bisque heads, 177–178

black dolls, 356–357
composition/papier-mâché dolls, 239–242
American Character Doll Co., Inc., plastic dolls, 298–300
American Fulper, bisque dolls, 45–46
Anne Shirley, 252
Arranbee Doll Company
  composition/papier-mâché dolls, 242–244
  plastic dolls, 301
Art Fabric Mills, cloth dolls, 207
A. T., French bisque dolls, 52
Auctions
  auction galleries, listing of, 432
  buying at, 19–21
  selling at, 24
Averill Manufacturing Company, composition/papier-mâché dolls, 244–245

Baby Bo Kaye, 245
Baby Dainty, 252
Baby Dimples, 262
Baby Genius, 233
Baby Gloria, 150
Baby Grumpy, 253
Baby Sandy, 260
Baehr & Proeschild
  German bisque dolls, 98–101
  googly-eyed dolls, 367
Barbie, 321

Belton-type dolls, 347
C. M. Bergmann, German bisque
 dolls, 102–103
Carl Bergner, 387–388
Betsy McCall, 299, 311
Betty Boop, 43, 247
Billiken, 262
Bisque dolls
 American dolls/German bisque
  heads
  Louis Amberg & Son, 177–
   178
  Geo. Borgfeldt & Co., 178–
   181
  Century Doll Co., 182
  Hamburger & Co., 183–185
 American Fulper, 45–46
 black dolls
  Bru Jeune & Cie, 348
  Gaultier, 349
  Ernst Heubach, 350
  Jumeau, 348
  Kämmer & Reinhardt, 350–
   351
  Kestner, 351
  Armand Marseille, 352
  Theodor Recknagel, 353
  Franz Schmidt, 353
  Schoenau & Hoffmeister,
   353–354
  S.F.B.J., 349
  Simon & Halbig, 354–355
  Jules Steiner, 349
 English, Goss, 46–47
 googly-eyed dolls
  Baehr & Proeschild, 367
  Demalcol, 367
  Gebrüder Heubach, 369
  Max Handwerck, 368
  Hertel & Schwab, 368–369
  Kämmer & Reinhardt, 370

Kestner, 370
 Kley & Hahn, 371
 Armand Marseille, 371–372
 Japanese, 397–398
 Morimura Brothers, 47–49
 molded-hair bisque, lady dolls,
  188–189
 price adjustments for condition,
  44
 See also All-bisque dolls;
  French bisque dolls; Ger-
  man bisque dolls.
Bisque heads
 American dolls/German heads,
  177–185
 bye-lo babies, 363–364
 kewpies, 378
Black dolls
 bisque dolls
  Bru Jeune & Cie, 348
  Gaultier, 349
  Ernst Heubach, 350
  Jumeau, 348
  Kämmer & Reinhardt, 350–
   351
  Kestner, 351
  Armand Marseille, 352
  Theodor Recknagel, 353
  Franz Schmidt, 353
  Schoenau & Hoffmeister,
   353–354
  S.F.B.J., 349
  Simon & Halbig, 354–355
  Jules Steiner, 349
 cloth dolls, 356
 composition dolls
  Cameo, 357
  Effanbee, 357–358
  Louis Amberg & Son, 356—
   357
 general information, 348

plastic dolls, Alexander Doll
Co., Inc. 358–360
wood dolls, Schoenhut, 360
Bobby Q, 206
Bonnie Babe, 40, 179
George Borgfeldt & Co.
all-bisque dolls, 40–41
American dolls/German bisque
heads, 178–181
composition/papier-mâché
dolls, 245–246
Boudoir dolls, 361–362
Brownies, cloth dolls, 208
Bruckner, cloth dolls, 208–209
Bru Jeune & Cie
black dolls, 348
French bisque dolls, 53–59
Bubbles, 253
A. Bucherer, metal dolls, 276
Buschow & Beck, metal dolls,
277
Bye-lo babies
all-bisque, 364
bisque head, 363–364
celluloid, 365
composition, 365
general information, 363
vinyl, 365
wax, 366

Cabbage Patch Kid, 302
Cameo Doll Company
black dolls, 357
composition/papier-mâché
dolls, 246–250
Campbell Kids, 241, 263
Candy Kid, 254
Caroline, 282
Catterfelder Puppenfabrik, Ger-
man bisque dolls, 103–104

Celluloid dolls
all-celluloid dolls, 191–192
bye-lo babies, 365
celluloid head dolls, 192–193
kewpies, 378
Century Doll Co., American
dolls/German bisque
heads, 182
Chad Valley, cloth dolls, 209–210
Charlie Chaplin, 240
Chase, cloth dolls, 210–211
China dolls
Alt, Beck & Gottschalck, 196
general inormation, 194
German manufacturers, un-
known origin, 197–203
Hertwig & Co., 196
price adjustments for condition,
195
Chin-chin Baby, 30
Cissette Face, 282–283
Cissy Face, 282–283
Cleaning, of dolls, 16
Clear, Emma, 391
Cloth dolls
Alabama Indestructible Doll,
205
Alexander Doll Co., 206
Art Fabric Mills, 207
black dolls, 356
Brownies, 208
Bruckner, 208–209
Chad Valley, 209–210
Chase, 210–211
Columbian, 211–212
general information, 204
E. I. Horsman Co., 212–213
Izannah Walker, 225
Kamkins, 213
Käthe Kruse, 214–217
kewpies, 378

Cloth dolls (*cont.*)
Lenci, 218–220
Missionary Ragbabies, 221
Norah Wellings, 226
Philadelphia Baby, 221
price adjustments for condition, 204
Raggedy Ann, 222
Rollinson, 223
Steiff, 223–224
Cochran, Dewees, 392–393
Coco, 284
Coleco Industries, Inc., plastic dolls, 302–303
Columbian, cloth dolls, 211–212
Composition/papier-mâché dolls
Alexander Doll Company, Inc., 233–239
Louis Amberg and Son, 239–242
American manufacturers, unknown origin, 273–274
Arranbee Doll Co., 242–244
Averill Manufacturing Company, 244–245
black dolls
Louis Amberg & Son, 356–357
Cameo, 357
Effanbee, 357–358
Geo. Borgfeldt and Company, 245–246
bye-lo babies, 365
Cameo Doll Company, 246–250
Dora Petzold Art Dolls, 272
Effanbee Doll Corporation, 250–259
French type dolls, 230
Freundlich Novelty Corporation, 259–260
general information, 227
German dolls, 229–230, 232

googly-eyed dolls, 373
Greiner, 230–231
E. I. Horsman Company, 261–265
Mary Hoyer Doll Mfg. Co., 260–261
Ideal Novelty and Toy Company, 266–271
kewpies, 379
Monica Studios, 271
price adjustments for condition, 228
Raleigh Dolls, 272–273
Vogue Dolls, Inc., 273
Condition, general information on, 5–6
Connie Lynn, 329
Coos Family, 311
Cosmopolitan Doll & Toy Corp., plastic dolls, 304
Crazing, 6, 15
Crissy, 312
Cuddly Kissy, 313
Cuno & Otto Dressel, German bisque dolls, 104–108
Cynthia, 358

Danel & Cie, French bisque dolls, 59–60
Dating of dolls, 13–15
Deanna Durbin, 266
Debu Teen, 243
Demalcol, googly-eyed dolls, 367
Dionne Quints, 234
Display, of dolls, 15
Dollikin, 331
Dolls
abbreviations, used in doll advertisements, 426–428
auction galleries, listing of, 432

buying tips
   condition, 5–6
   investment tips, 4–5
   marks, 10–12
   originality, 8–9
   quality, 7–8
   rarity, 9–10
   restoration, 6–7
   size, 8
care of, 15–17
   cleaning, 16
   display, 15
   redressing, 17
   repairing, 16–17
   storage, 16
dating of, 13–15
doll museums, listing of, 429–431
fakes, 13
insect infestations, 15
market trends, 2–3
places for buying
   auctions, 19–21
   flea markets, 22
   house sales, 22
   mail, buying by, 21
   shops, 17–18
   shows, 18–19
reproductions, 12–13
selling tips, 23–24
terms related to (glossary), 405–415
trademark names, listing of, 419–425
Dolly Dimple, 183
Door of Hope Mission doll, 399
Dora Petzold Art Dolls, composition/papier-mâché dolls, 272
Douglas MacArthur, 260

Dressel & Kister, pincushion figures, 375
Dy-Dee Baby, 305

E. D., French bisque dolls, 61
Edwina, 240
Effanbee Doll Corporation
   black dolls, 357–358
   composition/papier-mâché dolls, 250–259
   plastic dolls, 305–307
E. I. Horsman Co., all-bisque dolls, 41
Eisenmann & Co., German bisque dolls, 108–109
Elise, 285
Elizabeth, Princess, 160
English manufacturers, wax dolls, 337

Fakes, 13
First Ladies, 286
Flea markets, buying dolls, 22
Fleischmann & Bloedel, French bisque dolls, 62–63
Florodora, 145
François Gaultier, French bisque dolls, 63–65
French bisque dolls
   A. T., 52
   Bru Jeune & Cie, 53–59
   Danel & Cie, 59–60
   E. D., 61
   Fleischmann & Bloedel, 62–63
   François Gaultier, 63–65
   general information, 50
   Gesland, 65–66
   Huret, 66–67
   Jullien, 67–68

French bisque dolls (*cont.*)
Jumeau, 69–75
lady dolls, 75–76
Lanternier, 76–78
A. Marque, 78–79
Mothereau, 78
Petit & Dumontier, 79–80
Phenix, 80
Pintel & Godchaux, 81
price adjustments for condition, 51
Rabery & Delphieu, 81–82
Rohmer, 82–83
Rostal, 83–84
Schmitt & Fils, 84–85
Société Française de Fabrication de Bébé & Jouets (S.F.B.J.), 85–89
Steiner, 89–93
J. Verlingue, 94
French type dolls
all-bisque dolls, 28
composition/papier-mâché dolls, 230
Freundlich Novelty Corporation, composition/papier-mâché dolls, 259–260

Gans & Seyfarth, German bisque dolls, 109–110
Gaultier, black dolls, 349
Gebrüder Heubach
all-bisque dolls, 30–31
German bisque dolls, 118–123
googly-eyed dolls, 369
German bisque dolls
Alt, Beck & Gottschalck, 96–98
Baehr & Proeschild, 98–101
C. M. Bergmann, 102–103

Catterfelder Puppenfabrik, 103–104
Cuno & Otto Dressel, 104–108
Eisenmann & Co., 108–109
Gans & Seyfarth, 109–110
Gebrüder Heubach, 118–123
Gebrüder Kuhnlenz, 140–141
general information, 95
Goebel, 110–111
Heinrich Handwerck, 111–112
Max Hartmann, 113–114
Hertel, Schwab & Co., 114–116
Ernst Heubach, 116–118
Adolf Hülss, 123–124
Kämmer & Reinhardt, 124–129
Kestner, 129–136
Kley & Hahn, 136–139
Koenig & Wernicke, 139–140
Louis Lindner & Söhne, 141–142
Armand Marseille, 142–151
Gebrüder Ohlhauer, 152–153
Porzellanfabrik Mengersgereuth, 151–152
price adjustments for condition, 95
Theodor Recknagel, 153–154
Peter Scherf, 155
Bruno Schmidt, 155–157
Franz Schmidt, 157–158
Schoenau & Hoffmeister, 159–160
Schutzmeister & Quendt, 160–161
Simon & Halbig, 161–167
E. U. Steiner, 168
Hermann Steiner, 168–169
Swaine & Company, 169–172
Hermann von Berg, 172–173
Wagner & Zetsche, 173–174
Welsch & Company, 174–175
Adolf Wislizenus, 175–176

German Manivelles, mechanical dolls, 384–385
Gesland, French bisque dolls, 65–66
Giggles, 247
G. I. Joe, 308–309
Ginger, 304
Ginny, 332–333
Gladdie, 246
Goebel, German bisque dolls, 110–111
Googly-eyed dolls
  bisque
    Baehr & Proeschild, 367
    Demalcol, 367
    Gebrüder Heubach, 369
    Max Handwerck, 368
    Hertel & Schwab, 368–369
    Kämmer & Reinhardt, 370
    Kestner, 370
    Kley & Hahn, 371
    Armand Marseille, 371–372
  composition dolls, 373
  general information, 367
Goss, bisque dolls, 46–47
Gregor, 328
Greiner, composition/papier-mâché dolls, 230–231

Hamburger & Co., American dolls/German bisque heads, 183–185
Heinrich Handwerck, German bisque dolls, 111–112
Max Handwerck, googly-eyed dolls, 368
Happifats, 40
Harriet Hubbard Ayer, 313
Max Hartmann, German bisque dolls, 113–114

Hasbro, Inc., plastic dolls, 307–309
HEbee-SHEbee, 41, 263
Hertel & Schwab
  all-bisque dolls, 29
  German bisque dolls, 114–116
  googly-eyed dolls, 368
Hertwig & Co.
  all-bisque dolls, 29
  china dolls, 196
Ernst Heubach
  black dolls, 350
  German bisque dolls, 116–118
Honey, 305
E. I. Horsman Co.
  cloth dolls, 212–213
  composition/papier-mâché dolls, 261–265
House sales, buying dolls, 22
Mary Hoyer Doll Mfg. Co.
  composition/papier-mâché dolls, 260–261
  plastic dolls, 309–310
Adolf Hülss, German bisque dolls, 123–124
Huret, French bisque dolls, 66–67

Ideal Novelty and Toy Company, composition/papier-mâché dolls, 266–271
Ideal Toy Corporation, plastic dolls, 310–318
Insect infestations, of dolls, 15
Izannah Walker, cloth dolls, 225

Jacqueline Face, 286–287
Jane Withers, 235
Janie Face, 287
Jeanne, 264

Jeannie Walker, 235
Jeff, 334
Jerri Lee, 330
Jill, 334
Jo-Jo, 264
Joy, 248
Judy Garland, 268
Jullien, French bisque dolls, 67–68
Jumeau
  black dolls, 348
  French bisque dolls, 69–75
Just Me, 181

Kamkins, cloth dolls, 213
Kämmer & Reinhardt
  black dolls, 350–351
  German bisque dolls, 124–129
  googly-eyed dolls, 370
Käthe Kruse
  child doll, 193
  cloth dolls, 214–217
Kelly Face, 288
Kenn, 322
Kenner Parker Toys, Inc., plastic dolls, 319–320
Kestner
  black dolls, 351
  German bisque dolls, 129–136
  googly-eyed dolls, 370
  oriental dolls, 394
Kewpies
  all-bisque, 376–377
  bisque head, 378
  celluloid, 378
  cloth, 378
  composition, 379
  general information, 376
  vinyl, 379

Kley & Hahn
  German bisque dolls, 136–139
  googly-eyed dolls, 371
Koenig & Wernicke, German bisque dolls, 139–140
Gebrüder Kuhnlenz, German bisque dolls, 140–141

Lady dolls, 188–189
Leopold Lambert, mechanical dolls, 380–381
Lanternier, French bisque dolls, 76–78
Lenci
  boudoir dolls, 361
  cloth dolls, 218–220
Leslie, 359
Linda Baby, 330
Lissy Face, 288–289
Little Betty, 236
Little Brother or Sister, 244
Little Genius, 289
Little Lady, 255
Little Shaver, 206
Little Women, 290
Lori Baby, 170
Louise Lindner & Söhne, German bisque dolls, 141–142
Louise, Queen, 146
Lovums, 255

Madame Hendren Dolls, 245
Madeline, 290
Mae Starr, 255
Maggie Face, 291
Maggie Mixup, 292
Mail, buying dolls by, 21
Mammy doll, 356
Margaret Face, 236, 292

Margie, 249
Marilee, 256
Marion, 325
Marks, general information on, 10–12
Marottes, 386
A. Marque, French bisque dolls, 78–79
Armand Marseille
  black dolls, 352
  German bisque dolls, 142–151
  googly-eyed dolls, 371–372
  oriental dolls, 395
Mary Ann Face, 293
Mary Ellen, 295
Mary Hoyer Doll, 261
Mattel, Inc., plastic dolls, 320–324
Mechanical dolls
  general information, 380
  German Manivelles, 384–385
  Leopold Lambert, 380–381
  marottes, 386
  Renou, 381
  Roulett & DeCamps, 382–383
  Theroude, 383–384
  walking dolls, American, 385–386
Metal dolls
  A. Bucherer, 276
  Buschow & Beck, 277
  general information, 275
  price adjustments for condition, 275
Midge, 323
Mimi, 40
Minerva, 277
Miss Ideal, 314
Missionary Ragbabies, cloth dolls, 221
Miss Revlon, 314

Modern doll artists
  Clear, Emma, 391
  Cochran, Dewees, 392–393
Molded-hair bisque, lady dolls, 188–189
Monica Studios
  composition/papier-mâché dolls, 271
  plastic dolls, 325
Morimura Brothers, bisque dolls, 47–49
Mothereau, French bisque dolls, 78
Muffie, 325
Multi-face dolls
  Carl Bergner, 387–388
  general information, 387
  Simon & Halbig, 388
  Three-in-One Doll Corporation, 389
Museums, doll, listing of, 429–431

Nancy, 243
Nancy Ann Dressed Dolls, plastic dolls, 325–327
Nancy Drew Face, 295
Nancy Lee, 244
Nanette, 301
Nodders, 35
Norah Wellings, cloth dolls, 226

Gebrüder Ohlhauer, German bisque dolls, 152–153
Oriental dolls
  Chinese, wood, 399
  Japanese bisque, 397–398
  Kestner, 394
  Armand Marseille, 395
  Bruno Schmidt, 395

Oriental dolls (*cont.*)
Schoenau & Hoffmeister, 396
Simon & Halbig, 396–397
Originality, general information on, 8–9

Papier-mâché dolls. *See* Composition/papier-mâché dolls
Parsons-Jackson Baby, 192
Patsy Series, 256–258, 357
Peggy Baby, 177
Peter Pan Set, 296
Petit & Dumontier, French bisque dolls, 79–80
Phenix, French bisque dolls, 80
Philadelphia Baby, cloth dolls, 221
Piano Babies, 31, 37
Pincushion figures
Dressel & Kister, 375
general information, 374
Pinkie, 249
Pintel & Godchaux, French bisque dolls, 81
Plastic dolls
Alexander Doll Company, Inc., 280–298
black dolls, 358–360
American Character Doll Co., Inc., 298–300
Arranbee Doll Company, 301
Coleco Industries, Inc., 302–303
Cosmopolitan Doll & Toy Corp., 304
Effanbee Doll Corp., 305–307
general information, 278
Hasbro, Inc., 307–309
Mary Hoyer Doll Mfg. Co., 309–310
Ideal Toy Corporation, 310–318

Kenner Parker Toys, Inc., 319–320
Mattel, Inc., 320–324
Monica Studios, 325
Nancy Ann Dressed Dolls, 325–327
price adjustments for condition, 279
Sasha Dolls Limited, 327–328
Terri Lee, 329–331
Uneeda Doll Co., Inc., 331–332
Vogue Dolls, Inc., 332–334
Playpal Family, 315
Polly, 296
Porzellanfabrik Mengersgereuth, German bisque dolls, 151–152
Princess Elizabeth Face, 237

Quality, general information on, 7–8
Queue San Baby, 42

Rabery & Delphieu, French bisque dolls, 81–82
Raggedy Ann, cloth dolls, 222
Raleigh Dolls, composition/papier-mâché dolls, 272–273
Rarity, general information on, 9–10
Theodor Recknagel
black dolls, 353
German bisque dolls, 153–154
Redressing, of dolls, 17
Renou, mechanical dolls, 381
Repairing, of dolls, 16–17
Reproductions, dolls, 12–13
Restoration, general information on, 6–7

Rohmer, French bisque dolls, 82–83

Rollinson, cloth dolls, 223

Rosebud, 265

Rosemary, 258

Rostal, French bisque dolls, 83–84

Roulett & DeCamps, mechanical dolls, 382–383

Sally, 242

Santa, 184

Sasha Dolls Limited, plastic dolls, 327–328

Saucy Walker, 315

Peter Scherf, German bisque dolls, 155

Bruno Schmidt
German bisque dolls, 155–157
oriental dolls, 395

Franz Schmidt
black dolls, 353
German bisque dolls, 157–158

Schmitt & Fils, French bisque dolls, 84–85

Schoenau & Hoffmeister
black dolls, 353–354
German bisque dolls, 159–160
oriental dolls, 396

Schoenhut
black dolls, 360
wooden dolls, 342–343

Schutzmeister & Quendt, German bisque dolls, 160–161

Scootles, 250, 357

Shari Lewis, 297

Shirley Temple, 269, 316

Shops, buying dolls, 17–18

Shows, buying dolls, 18–19

Simon & Halbig, 388
black dolls, 354–355
German bisque dolls, 161–167
oriental dolls, 396–397

Size, general information on, 8

Skipper, 324

Skippy, 258

Skooter, 324

Sleeping Beauty, 297

Smarty, 297

Snow White, 269

Société Française de Fabrication de Bébé & Jouets (S.F.B.J.)
black dolls, 349
French bisque dolls, 85–89

Sonja Henie, 238

Sound of Music Sets, 298

Springfield Vermont dolls, wooden dolls, 341–342

Star Wars Set, 320

Steiff, cloth dolls, 223–224

Steiner, French bisque dolls, 89–93

E. U. Steiner, German bisque dolls, 168

Hermann Steiner, German bisque dolls, 168–169

Jules Steiner, black dolls, 349

Storage, of dolls, 16

Susie Q, 206

Suzanne, 259

Suzie Sunshine, 307

Swaine & Company, German bisque dolls, 169–172

Sweet Sue, 299

Tammy, 318

Terri Lee, 330
plastic dolls, 329–331

Theroude, mechanical dolls, 383–384

Three-in-One Doll Corporation, 389
Tiny Jerri Lee, 331
Tiny Tears, 300
Tiny Terri Lee, 331
Toni, 318–319
Toodles, 273
Topsy-turvy dolls, 389–390
Trademark names, listing of, 419–425
Trudy, 389
Tynie Baby, 41, 265

Uneeda Doll Co., Inc., plastic dolls, 331–332
Uneeda Kid, 271

Vanta Baby, 241
J. Verlingue, French bisque dolls, 94
Vinyl dolls
  bye-lo babies, 365
  kewpies, 379
Viola, 185
Vivi, 41
Vogue Dolls, Inc.
  composition/papier-mâché dolls, 273
  plastic dolls, 332–334

Hermann von Berg, German bisque dolls, 172–173

Wagner & Zetsche, German bisque dolls, 173–174
Walking dolls, American, 385–386
Wax dolls
  bye-lo babies, 366
  English manufacturers, 337
  general information, 335
  German manufacturers, 338
  price adjustments for condition, 336
Welsch & Company, German bisque dolls, 174–175
Wendy-Ann Face, 238
Adolf Wislizenus, German bisque dolls, 175–176
Wooden dolls
  Chinese, 39
  general information, 339
  price adjustments for condition, 340
  Schoenhut, 342–343
    black dolls, 360
  Springfield Vermont dolls, 341–342
  unknown makers, 341

ABOUT THE AUTHOR

Julie E. Collier, former assistant vice president and head of the Collectibles Department of Christie, Manson and Woods International, Inc., was a leading specialist in the field of collectibles and an authority on dolls. Joining Christie's Fine Art Auctioneers, New York, in 1978, she organized sales of dolls, toys, and film memorabilia. Earlier she had worked for Christie's in London, England. She started her business career as an appraiser at Butterfield & Butterfield, San Francisco.

Ms. Collier was born in Colorado Springs. She graduated from California State University with a Bachelor of Arts degree in Art History. Later, she earned a Master of Arts degree from the University of California at Berkeley.

As a professional appraiser and collector of antique dolls for twenty-five years, dolls were prominent in both her professional and private collecting life.

The HOUSE OF COLLECTIBLES Series

☐ Please send me the following price guides—
☐ I would like the most current edition of the books listed below.

THE OFFICIAL PRICE GUIDES TO:

☐ 753-3	**American Folk Art** (ID) 1st Ed.	$14.95
☐ 199-3	**American Silver & Silver Plate** 5th Ed.	11.95
☐ 513-1	**Antique Clocks** 3rd Ed.	10.95
☐ 283-3	**Antique & Modern Dolls** 3rd Ed.	10.95
☐ 287-6	**Antique & Modern Firearms** 6th Ed.	11.95
☐ 755-X	**Antiques & Collectibles** 9th Ed.	11.95
☐ 289-2	**Antique Jewelry** 5th Ed.	11.95
☐ 362-7	**Art Deco** (ID) 1st Ed.	14.95
☐ 447-X	**Arts and Crafts: American Decorative Arts, 1894–1923** (ID) 1st Ed.	12.95
☐ 539-5	**Beer Cans & Collectibles** 4th Ed.	7.95
☐ 521-2	**Bottles Old & New** 10th Ed.	10.95
☐ 532-8	**Carnival Glass** 2nd Ed.	10.95
☐ 295-7	**Collectible Cameras** 2nd Ed.	10.95
☐ 548-4	**Collectibles of the '50s & '60s** 1st Ed.	9.95
☐ 740-1	**Collectible Toys** 4th Ed.	10.95
☐ 531-X	**Collector Cars** 7th Ed.	12.95
☐ 538-7	**Collector Handguns** 4th Ed.	14.95
☐ 748-7	**Collector Knives** 9th Ed.	12.95
☐ 361-9	**Collector Plates** 5th Ed.	11.95
☐ 296-5	**Collector Prints** 7th Ed.	12.95
☐ 001-6	**Depression Glass** 2nd Ed.	9.95
☐ 589-1	**Fine Art** 1st Ed.	19.95
☐ 311-2	**Glassware** 3rd Ed.	10.95
☐ 243-4	**Hummel Figurines & Plates** 6th Ed.	10.95
☐ 523-9	**Kitchen Collectibles** 2nd Ed.	10.95
☐ 080-6	**Memorabilia of Elvis Presley and The Beatles** 1st Ed.	10.95
☐ 291-4	**Military Collectibles** 5th Ed.	11.95
☐ 525-5	**Music Collectibles** 6th Ed.	11.95
☐ 313-9	**Old Books & Autographs** 7th Ed.	11.95
☐ 298-1	**Oriental Collectibles** 3rd Ed.	11.95
☐ 761-4	**Overstreet Comic Book** 18th Ed.	12.95
☐ 522-0	**Paperbacks & Magazines** 1st Ed.	10.95
☐ 297-3	**Paper Collectibles** 5th Ed.	10.95
☐ 744-4	**Political Memorabilia** 1st Ed.	10.95
☐ 529-8	**Pottery & Porcelain** 6th Ed.	11.95
☐ 524-7	**Radio, TV & Movie Memorabilia** 3rd Ed.	11.95
☐ 081-4	**Records** 8th Ed.	16.95
☐ 763-0	**Royal Doulton** 6th Ed.	12.95
☐ 280-9	**Science Fiction & Fantasy Collectibles** 2nd Ed.	10.95
☐ 747-9	**Sewing Collectibles** 1st Ed.	8.95
☐ 358-9	**Star Trek/Star Wars Collectibles** 2nd Ed.	8.95
☐ 086-5	**Watches** 8th Ed.	12.95
☐ 248-5	**Wicker** 3rd Ed.	10.95

THE OFFICIAL:

☐ 760-6	**Directory to U.S. Flea Markets** 2nd Ed.	5.95
☐ 365-1	**Encyclopedia of Antiques** 1st Ed.	9.95
☐ 369-4	**Guide to Buying and Selling Antiques** 1st Ed.	9.95
☐ 414-3	**Identification Guide to Early American Furniture** 1st Ed.	9.95
☐ 413-5	**Identification Guide to Glassware** 1st Ed.	9.95
☐ 412-7	**Identification Guide to Pottery & Porcelain** 1st Ed.	$9.95
☐ 415-1	**Identification Guide to Victorian Furniture** 1st Ed.	9.95

THE OFFICIAL (SMALL SIZE) PRICE GUIDES TO:

☐ 309-0	**Antiques & Flea Markets** 4th Ed.	4.95
☐ 269-8	**Antique Jewelry** 3rd Ed.	4.95
☐ 085-7	**Baseball Cards** 8th Ed.	4.95
☐ 647-2	**Bottles** 3rd Ed.	4.95
☐ 544-1	**Cars & Trucks** 3rd Ed.	5.95
☐ 519-0	**Collectible Americana** 2nd Ed.	4.95
☐ 294-9	**Collectible Records** 3rd Ed.	4.95
☐ 306-6	**Dolls** 4th Ed.	4.95
☐ 762-2	**Football Cards** 8th Ed.	4.95
☐ 540-9	**Glassware** 3rd Ed.	4.95
☐ 526-3	**Hummels** 4th Ed.	4.95
☐ 279-5	**Military Collectibles** 3rd Ed.	4.95
☐ 764-9	**Overstreet Comic Book Companion** 2nd Ed.	4.95
☐ 278-7	**Pocket Knives** 3rd Ed.	4.95
☐ 527-1	**Scouting Collectibles** 4th Ed.	4.95
☐ 494-1	**Star Trek/Star Wars Collectibles** 3rd Ed.	3.95
☐ 088-1	**Toys** 5th Ed.	4.95

THE OFFICIAL BLACKBOOK PRICE GUIDES OF:

☐ 092-X	**U.S. Coins** 27th Ed.	4.95
☐ 095-4	**U.S. Paper Money** 21st Ed.	4.95
☐ 098-9	**U.S. Postage Stamps** 11th Ed.	4.95

THE OFFICIAL INVESTORS GUIDE TO BUYING & SELLING:

☐ 534-4	**Gold, Silver & Diamonds** 2nd Ed.	12.95
☐ 535-2	**Gold Coins** 2nd Ed.	12.95
☐ 536-0	**Silver Coins** 2nd Ed.	12.95
☐ 537-9	**Silver Dollars** 2nd Ed.	12.95

THE OFFICIAL NUMISMATIC GUIDE SERIES:

☐ 254-X	**The Official Guide to Detecting Counterfeit Money** 2nd Ed.	7.95
☐ 257-4	**The Official Guide to Mint Errors** 4th Ed.	7.95

SPECIAL INTEREST SERIES:

☐ 506-9	**From Hearth to Cookstove** 3rd Ed.	17.95
☐ 504-2	**On Method Acting** 8th Printing	6.95

TOTAL	

SEE REVERSE SIDE FOR ORDERING INSTRUCTIONS

FOR IMMEDIATE DELIVERY

VISA & MASTER CARD CUSTOMERS
ORDER TOLL FREE!
1-800-638-6460

This number is for orders only; it is not tied into the customer service or business office. Customers not using charge cards must use mail for ordering since payment is required with the order—sorry, no C.O.D.'s.

OR SEND ORDERS TO

THE HOUSE OF COLLECTIBLES
201 East 50th Street
New York, New York 10022

___ POSTAGE & HANDLING RATES ___

First Book $1.00
Each Additional Copy or Title $0.50

Total from columns on order form. Quantity_____ $_____

☐ Check or money order enclosed $_____ (include postage and handling)

☐ Please charge $_____to my: ☐ MASTERCARD ☐ VISA

Charge Card Customers Not Using Our Toll Free Number Please Fill Out The Information Below

Account No. _____Expiration Date_____
(all digits)
Signature_____

NAME (please print)_____PHONE_____

ADDRESS_____APT. #_____

CITY_____STATE_____ZIP_____